Imperialism

Part Two of *The Origins of Totalitarianism*

Hannah Arendt

Imperialism

A Harvest/HBJ Book

HARCOURT BRACE JOVANOVICH
New York and London

Library of Congress Catalog Card Number: 66-22273

Printed in the United States of America

DE

Preface

R ARELY could the beginnings of a historical period be dated with such precision and seldom were the chances for contemporary observers to witness its definite end so good as in the case of the imperialist era. For imperialism, which grew out of colonialism and was caused by the incongruity of the nation-state system with the economic and industrial developments in the last third of the nineteenth century, started its politics of expansion for expansion's sake no sooner than around 1884, and this new version of power politics was as different from national conquests in border-wars as it was from true empire-building Roman style. Its end seemed unavoidable after "the liquidation of His Majesty's Empire," over which Churchill had refused "to preside," had become an accomplished fact with the declaration of Indian independence. That the British liquidated their colonial rule voluntarily is still one of the most momentous events of twentieth-century history, and after this had happened no European nation could hold on to its overseas possessions. The only exception is Portugal, and her strange ability to continue a fight that all other European colonial powers had to give up may be due to her national backwardness even more than to Salazar's dictatorship; for it was not mere weakness or the exhaustion due to two murderous wars in one generation but also the moral scruples and political apprehensions of the fully developed nation states that advised against extreme measures, the introduction of "administrative massacres" (A. Carthill) that might well have broken the non-violent rebellion in India, and against a continuation of the "government of subject races" (Lord Cromer) because of the much-feared boomerang effect upon the mother countries. When finally France, thanks to the then still intact authority of De Gaulle, dared to give up Algeria, which she had always considered as much a part of France as the *département de la Seine,* a point of no return seemed to have been reached.

Whatever the merits of this hope might have been if the hot war against Nazi Germany had not been followed by the cold war between Soviet Russia and the United States, in retrospect one is tempted to look upon the last two decades as the time-span during which the two most powerful countries of the earth jockeyed for position in a competitive struggle for predominance in more or less the same regions in which European nations had ruled before. In the same vein one is tempted to look upon the new uneasy détente between

Russia and America as the result of the emergence of a third potential world power, China, rather than as the healthy and natural consequence of Russia's detotalitarization after Stalin's death. And if further developments should validate such tentative interpretations, it would mean in historical terms that we are back, on an enormously enlarged scale, where we started from, that is, in the imperialist era and on the collision course that led to World War I.

It has often been said that the British acquired their empire in a fit of absent-mindedness, as consequence of automatic trends, yielding to what seemed possible and what was tempting, rather than as a result of deliberate policy. If this is true, then the road to hell may just as well be paved with no intentions as with the proverbial good ones. And the objective facts that invite a return to imperialist policies are indeed so strong today that one is inclined to believe at least in the half-truth of the statement, the hollow assurances of good intentions on both sides—American "commitments" to the nonviable status quo of corruption and incompetence on one side, Russian pseudo-revolutionary talk about wars of national liberation on the other—notwithstanding. The processes of nation-building in backward areas where lack of all prerequisites for national independence is in exact proportion to a rampant, sterile chauvinism have resulted in enormous power vacuums, for which the competition between the superpowers is all the fiercer, as with the development of nuclear weapons a direct confrontation of their means of violence as a last resort to "solve" all conflicts seems to be definitely ruled out. Not only does every conflict between the small, undeveloped countries in these vast areas, be it a civil war in Vietnam or a national conflict in the Middle East, immediately attract the potential or actual intervention of the superpowers, but their very conflicts, or at least the timing of their outbreaks, are suspect of having been manipulated or directly caused by interests and maneuvers that have nothing whatsoever to do with the conflicts and interests at stake in the region itself. Nothing was so characteristic of power politics in the imperialist era than this shift from localized, limited and therefore predictable goals of national interest to the limitless pursuit of power after power that could roam and lay waste the whole globe with no certain nationally and territorially prescribed purpose and hence with no predictable direction. This backsliding has become apparent also on the ideological level, for the famous domino-theory, according to which American foreign policy feels committed to wage war in one country for the sake of the integrity of others that are not even its neighbors, is clearly but a new version of the old "Great Game" whose rules permitted and even dictated the consideration of whole nations as stepping-stones, or as pawns, in today's terminology, for the riches and the rule over a third country, which in turn became a mere stepping-stone in the unending process of power expansion and accumulation. It was this chain reaction, inherent in imperialist power politics and best represented on the human level by the figure of the secret agent, of which Kipling said (in *Kim*), "When every one is dead the Great Game is finished. Not before"; and the only reason his prophecy did not come true was the constitutional restraint of the nation-state, while today our only hope that it will not come true in the future is based on the constitutional restraints of the American republic plus the technological restraints of the nuclear age.

This is not to deny that the unexpected revival of imperialist policies and methods takes place under vastly changed conditions and circumstances. The initiative for overseas expansion has shifted westward from England and Western Europe to America, and the initiative for continental expansion in close geographic continuity no longer comes from Central and Eastern Europe but is exclusively located in Russia. Imperialist policies, more than any other single factor, have brought about the decline of Europe, and the prophecies of statesmen and historians that the two giants flanking the European nations on the east and on the west would ultimately emerge as the heirs of her power seem to have come true. No one justifies expansion any longer by "the white man's burden" on one side and an "enlarged tribal consciousness" to unite people of similar ethnic origin on the other; instead we hear of "commitments" to client states, of the responsibilities of power, and of solidarity with revolutionary national liberation movements. The very word "expansion" has disappeared from our political vocabulary, which now uses the words "extension" or, critically, "overextension" to cover a very similar meaning. Politically more important, private investments in distant lands, originally the prime mover of imperialist developments, are today surpassed by foreign aid, economic and military, provided directly by governments. (In 1966 alone, the American government spent $4.6 billion in economic aid and foreign credits plus $1.3 billion a year in military aid in the decade 1956-1965, while the outflow of private capital in 1965 was $3.69 billion and in 1966 $3.91 billion.).[1] This means that the era of the so-called dollar imperialism, the specifically American version of pre-World War II imperialism that was politically the least dangerous, is definitely over. Private investments—"the activities of a thousand U.S. companies operating in a hundred foreign countries" and "concentrated in the most modern, the most strategic, the most rapidly growing sectors of the foreign economy"—create many political problems even if they are not protected by the power of the nation,[2] but foreign aid, even if given for purely humanitarian reasons, is political by nature precisely because it is not motivated by the search for profit. Billions of dollars have been spent in political and economic wastelands where corruption and incompetence have caused them to disappear before anything productive could be started, and this money is no longer the "superfluous" capital that could not be invested productively and profitably in the home country but the weird outgrowth of sheer abundance that the rich countries, the haves as against the have-nots, can afford to lose. In other words, the profit motive,

[1] The figures are quoted from Leo Model, "The Politics of Private Foreign Investment and Kenneth M. Kauffman and Helena Stalson, "U.S. Assistance to less developed Countries, 1956-65" respectively, both in *Foreign Affairs,* July, 1967.

[2] L. Model's article quoted above (p. 641) gives a very valuable and pertinent analysis of these problems.

whose importance for imperialist policies was frequently overrated even in the past, has now completely disappeared; only very rich and very powerful countries can afford to take the huge losses involved in imperialism.

It probably is too early, and certainly beyond the scope of my considerations, to analyze and ascertain with any degree of confidence these recent trends. What seems uncomfortably clear even now is the strength of certain, seemingly uncontrollable processes that tend to shatter all hopes for constitutional development in the new nations and to undermine the republican institutions in the old. Examples are too many to permit even cursory enumeration, but the rise of an "invisible government" by secret services, whose reach into domestic affairs, the cultural, educational, and economic sectors of our life, has only recently been revealed, is too ominous a sign to be passed under silence. There is no reason to doubt Mr. Allan W. Dulles' statement that Intelligence in this country has enjoyed since 1947 "a more influential position in our government than Intelligence enjoys in any other government of the world,"[3] nor is there any reason to believe that this influence has decreased since he made this statement in 1958. The deadly danger of "invisible government" to the institutions of the "visible government" has often been pointed out; what is perhaps less well known is the intimate traditional connection between imperialist politics and rule by "invisible government" and secret agents. It is an error to believe that the creation of a net of secret services in this country after World War II was the answer to a direct threat to its national survival by the espionage network of Soviet Russia; the war had propelled the United States to the position of the greatest world power and it was this world power, rather than national existence, that was challenged by the revolutionary power of Moscow-directed communism.[4]

Whatever the causes for American ascendancy to world power, the deliberate pursuit of a foreign policy leading to it or any claim to global rule are not among them. And the same is probably true for the country's recent and still tentative steps in the direction of imperialist power politics for which its form of government is less fitted than that of any other country. The enormous gap between the Western countries and the rest of the world, not only and not primarily in riches but in education, technical know-how, and general competence, has plagued international relations ever since the beginnings of genuine world politics. And this gulf, far from decreasing in recent decades under the pressure of the rapidly developing communication systems and the resulting

[3] This is what Mr. Dulles said in a speech at Yale University in 1957, according to David Wise and Thomas B. Ross, *The Invisible Government,* New York, 1964, p. 2.

[4] According to Mr. Dulles, the government had to "fight fire with fire," and then with a disarming frankness by which the former head of the CIA distinguished himself from his colleagues in other countries, he went on to explain what this meant. The CIA, by implication, had to model itself upon the Soviet State Security Service, which "is more than a secret police organization, more than an intelligence and counter-intelligence organization. It is an instrument for *subversion, manipulation and violence, for secret intervention in the affairs of other countries.*" (Italics added.) See Allen W. Dulles, *The Craft of Intelligence,* New York, 1963, p. 155.

shrinkage of distance on the earth, has constantly grown and is now assuming truly alarming proportions. "Population growth rates in less developed countries were double those in the more advanced countries,"[5] and while this factor alone would make it imperative for them to turn to those with surplus food and surplus technological and political knowledge, it is also this same factor which defeats all help. Obviously, the larger the population the less help per capita it will receive, and the truth of the matter is that after two decades of massive help programs all the countries that had not been able to help themselves to begin with—like Japan—are poorer, further away from either economic or political stability than ever. As for the chances of imperialism, this situation improves them frightfully for the simple reason that sheer numbers have never mattered less; white rule in South Africa where the tyrannical minority is outnumbered almost ten to one probably was never more secure than today. It is this objective situation that turns all foreign aid into an instrument of foreign domination and puts all countries that needs this help for their decreasing chances of physical survival before the alternative of accepting some form of "government of subject races" or sinking rapidly into anarchic decay.

This book deals only with the strictly European colonial imperialism whose end came with the liquidation of British rule in India. It tells the story of the disintegration of the nation state that proved to contain nearly all the elements necessary for the subsequent rise of totalitarian movements and governments. Before the imperialist era, there was no such thing as world politics, and without it, the totalitarian claim to global rule would not have made sense. During this period, the nation-state system proved incapable of either devising new rules for the handling of foreign affairs that had become global affairs or enforcing a Pax Romana on the rest of the world. Its political narrowness and shortsightedness ended in the disaster of totalitarianism, whose unprecedented horrors have overshadowed the ominous events and the even more ominous mentality of the preceding period. Scholarly inquiry has almost exclusively concentrated on Hitler's Germany and Stalin's Russia at the expense of their less harmful predecessors. Imperialist rule, except for the purpose of name-calling, seems half-forgotten, and the chief reason why this is deplorable is that its relevance for contemporary events has become rather obvious in recent years. Thus, the controversy about the United States' undeclared war in Vietnam has been conducted from both sides in terms of analogies with Munich or other examples drawn from the thirties when indeed totalitarian rule was the only clear and present, all-too present, danger, but the threats of today's policies in deeds and words bear a much more portentous resemblance to the deeds and verbal justifications that preceded the outbreak of World War I, when a spark in a peripheral region of minor interest to all concerned could start a world-wide conflagration.

To stress the unhappy relevance of this half-forgotten period for contempo-

[5] See the very instructive article by Orville L. Freeman, "Malthus, Marx and the North American Breadbasket," in *Foreign Affairs,* July, 1967.

rary events does not mean, of course, either that the die is cast and we are entering a new period of imperialist policies or that imperialism under all circumstances must end in the disasters of totalitarianism. No matter how much we may be capable of learning from the past, it will not enable us to know the future.

Hannah Arendt

July 1967

Contents

Imperialism

I would annex the planets if I could.

CECIL RHODES

CHAPTER ONE: The Political Emancipation of the Bourgeoisie

T HE THREE DECADES from 1884 to 1914 separate the nineteenth century, which ended with the scramble for Africa and the birth of the pan-movements, from the twentieth, which began with the first World War. This is the period of Imperialism, with its stagnant quiet in Europe and breath-taking developments in Asia and Africa.[1] Some of the fundamental aspects of this time appear so close to totalitarian phenomena of the twentieth century that it may be justifiable to consider the whole period a preparatory stage for coming catastrophes. Its quiet, on the other hand, makes it appear still very much a part of the nineteenth century. We can hardly avoid looking at this close and yet distant past with the too-wise eyes of those who know the end of the story in advance, who know it led to an almost complete break in the continuous flow of Western history as we had known it for more than two thousand years. But we must also admit a certain nostalgia for what can still be called a "golden age of security," for an age, that is, when even horrors were still marked by a certain moderation and controlled by re-spectability, and therefore could be related to the general appearance of sanity. In other words, no matter how close to us this past is, we are perfectly aware that our experience of concentration camps and death factories is as remote from its general atmosphere as it is from any other period in Western history.

The central inner-European event of the imperialist period was the po-litical emancipation of the bourgeoisie, which up to then had been the first class in history to achieve economic pre-eminence without aspiring to politi-cal rule. The bourgeoisie had developed within, and together with, the nation-state, which almost by definition ruled over and beyond a class-divided so-ciety. Even when the bourgeoisie had already established itself as the ruling class, it had left all political decisions to the state. Only when the nation-state proved unfit to be the framework for the further growth of capitalist economy did the latent fight between state and society become openly a struggle for power. During the imperialist period neither the state nor the

[1] J. A. Hobson, *Imperialism*, London, 1905, 1938, p. 19: "Though, for convenience, the year 1870 has been taken as indicative of the beginning of a conscious policy of Imperialism, it will be evident that the movement did not attain its full impetus until the middle of the eighties . . . from about 1884."

bourgeoisie won a decisive victory. National institutions resisted throughout the brutality and megalomania of imperialist aspirations, and bourgeois attempts to use the state and its instruments of violence for its own economic purposes were always only half successful. This changed when the German bourgeoisie staked everything on the Hitler movement and aspired to rule with the help of the mob, but then it turned out to be too late. The bourgeoisie succeeded in destroying the nation-state but won a Pyrrhic victory; the mob proved quite capable of taking care of politics by itself and liquidated the bourgeoisie along with all other classes and institutions.

I: *Expansion and the Nation-State*

"EXPANSION IS everything," said Cecil Rhodes, and fell into despair, for every night he saw overhead "these stars . . . these vast worlds which we can never reach. I would annex the planets if I could." [2] He had discovered the moving principle of the new, the imperialist era (within less than two decades, British colonial possessions increased by 4½ million square miles and 66 million inhabitants, the French nation gained 3½ million square miles and 26 million people, the Germans won a new empire of a million square miles and 13 million natives, and Belgium through her king acquired 900,000 square miles with 8½ million population [3]); and yet in a flash of wisdom Rhodes recognized at the same moment its inherent insanity and its contradiction to the human condition. Naturally, neither insight nor sadness changed his policies. He had no use for the flashes of wisdom that led him so far beyond the normal capacities of an ambitious businessman with a marked tendency toward megalomania.

"World politics is for a nation what megalomania is for an individual," [4] said Eugen Richter (leader of the German progressive party) at about the same historical moment. But his opposition in the Reichstag to Bismarck's proposal to support private companies in the foundation of trading and maritime stations, showed clearly that he understood the economic needs of a nation in his time even less than Bismarck himself. It looked as though those who opposed or ignored imperialism—like Eugen Richter in Germany, or Gladstone in England, or Clemenceau in France—had lost touch with reality and did not realize that trade and economics had already involved every nation in world politics. The national principle was leading into provincial ignorance and the battle fought by sanity was lost.

[2] S. Gertrude Millin, *Rhodes*, London, 1933, p. 138.

[3] These figures are quoted by Carlton J. H. Hayes, *A Generation of Materialism*, New York, 1941, p. 237, and cover the period from 1871-1900.—See also Hobson, *op. cit.*, p. 19: "Within 15 years some 3¾ millions of square miles were added to the British Empire, 1 million square miles with 14 millions inhabitants to the German, 3½ millions square miles with 37 millions inhabitants to the French."

[4] See Ernst Hasse, *Deutsche Weltpolitik*, Flugschriften des Alldeutschen Verbandes, No. 5, 1897, p. 1.

Moderation and confusion were the only rewards of any statesman's consistent opposition to imperialist expansion. Thus Bismarck, in 1871, rejected the offer of French possessions in Africa in exchange for Alsace-Lorraine, and twenty years later acquired Heligoland from Great Britain in return for Uganda, Zanzibar, and Vitu—two kingdoms for a bathtub, as the German imperialists told him, not without justice. Thus in the eighties Clemenceau opposed the imperialist party in France when they wanted to send an expeditionary force to Egypt against the British, and thirty years later he surrendered the Mosul oil fields to England for the sake of a French-British alliance. Thus Gladstone was being denounced by Cromer in Egypt as "not a man to whom the destinies of the British Empire could safely be entrusted."

That statesmen, who thought primarily in terms of the established national territory, were suspicious of imperialism was justified enough, except that more was involved than what they called "overseas adventures." They knew by instinct rather than by insight that this new expansion movement, in which "patriotism . . . is best expressed in money-making" (Huebbe-Schleiden) and the national flag is a "commercial asset" (Rhodes), could only destroy the political body of the nation-state. Conquest as well as empire building had fallen into disrepute for very good reasons. They had been carried out successfully only by governments which, like the Roman Republic, were based primarily on law, so that conquest could be followed by integration of the most heterogeneous peoples by imposing upon them a common law. The nation-state, however, based upon a homogeneous population's active consent to its government (*"le plébiscite de tous les jours"* [5]), lacked such a unifying principle and would, in the case of conquest, have to assimilate rather than to integrate, to enforce consent rather than justice, that is, to degenerate into tyranny. Robespierre was already well aware of this when he exclaimed: *"Périssent les colonies si elles nous en coûtent l'honneur, la liberté."*

Expansion as a permanent and supreme aim of politics is the central political idea of imperialism. Since it implies neither temporary looting nor the more lasting assimilation of conquest, it is an entirely new concept in the long history of political thought and action. The reason for this surprising originality—surprising because entirely new concepts are very rare in politics—is simply that this concept is not really political at all, but has its origin in the realm of business speculation, where expansion meant the permanent broadening of industrial production and economic transactions characteristic of the nineteenth century.

In the economic sphere, expansion was an adequate concept because industrial growth was a working reality. Expansion meant increase in actual

[5] Ernest Renan in his classical essay *Qu'est-ce qu'une nation?*, Paris, 1882, stressed "the actual consent, the desire to live together, the will to preserve worthily the undivided inheritance which has been handed down" as the chief elements which keep the members of a people together in such a way that they form a nation. Translation quoted from *The Poetry of the Celtic Races, and other Studies*, London, 1896.

production of goods to be used and consumed. The processes of production are as unlimited as the capacity of man to produce for, establish, furnish, and improve on the human world. When production and economic growth slowed down, their limits were not so much economic as political, insofar as production depended on, and products were shared by, many different peoples who were organized in widely differing political bodies.

Imperialism was born when the ruling class in capitalist production came up against national limitations to its economic expansion. The bourgeoisie turned to politics out of economic necessity; for if it did not want to give up the capitalist system whose inherent law is constant economic growth, it had to impose this law upon its home governments and to proclaim expansion to be an ultimate political goal of foreign policy.

With the slogan "expansion for expansion's sake," the bourgeoisie tried and partly succeeded in persuading their national governments to enter upon the path of world politics. The new policy they proposed seemed for a moment to find its natural limitations and balances in the very fact that several nations started their expansions simultaneously and competitively. Imperialism in its initial stages could indeed still be described as a struggle of "competing empires" and distinguished from the "idea of empire in the ancient and medieval world (which) was that of a federation of States, under a hegemony, covering . . . the entire recognized world." [6] Yet such a competition was only one of the many remnants of a past era, a concession to that still prevailing national principle according to which mankind is a family of nations vying for excellence, or to the liberal belief that competition will automatically set up its own stabilizing predetermined limits before one competitor has liquidated all the others. This happy balance, however, had hardly been the inevitable outcome of mysterious economic laws, but had relied heavily on political, and even more on police institutions that prevented competitors from using revolvers. How a competition between fully armed business concerns—"empires"—could end in anything but victory for one and death for the others is difficult to understand. In other words, competition is no more a principle of politics than expansion, and needs political power just as badly for control and restraint.

In contrast to the economic structure, the political structure cannot be expanded indefinitely, because it is not based upon the productivity of man, which is, indeed, unlimited. Of all forms of government and organizations of people, the nation-state is least suited for unlimited growth because the genuine consent at its base cannot be stretched indefinitely, and is only rarely, and with difficulty, won from conquered peoples. No nation-state could with a clear conscience ever try to conquer foreign peoples, since such a conscience comes only from the conviction of the conquering nation that it is imposing a superior law upon barbarians.[7] The nation, however,

[6] Hobson, *op. cit.*

[7] This bad conscience springing from the belief in consent as the basis of all political organization is very well described by Harold Nicolson, *Curzon: The Last Phase 1919-1925,* Boston-New York, 1934, in the discussion of British policy in Egypt: "The

conceived of its law as an outgrowth of a unique national substance which was not valid beyond its own people and the boundaries of its own territory.

Wherever the nation-state appeared as conqueror, it aroused national consciousness and desire for sovereignty among the conquered people, thereby defeating all genuine attempts at empire building. Thus the French incorporated Algeria as a province of the mother country, but could not bring themselves to impose their own laws upon an Arab people. They continued rather to respect Islamic law and granted their Arab citizens "personal status," producing the nonsensical hybrid of a nominally French territory, legally as much a part of France as the Département de la Seine, whose inhabitants are not French citizens.

The early British "empire builders," putting their trust in conquest as a permanent method of rule, were never able to incorporate their nearest neighbors, the Irish, into the far-flung structure either of the British Empire or the British Commonwealth of Nations; but when, after the last war, Ireland was granted dominion status and welcomed as a full-fledged member of the British Commonwealth, the failure was just as real, if less palpable. The oldest "possession" and newest dominion unilaterally denounced its dominion status (in 1937) and severed all ties with the English nation when it refused to participate in the war. England's rule by permanent conquest, since it "simply failed to destroy" Ireland (Chesterton), had not so much aroused her own "slumbering genius of imperialism" [8] as it had awakened the spirit of national resistance in the Irish.

The national structure of the United Kingdom had made quick assimilation and incorporation of the conquered peoples impossible; the British Commonwealth was never a "Commonwealth of Nations" but the heir of the United Kingdom, *one* nation dispersed throughout the world. Dispersion and colonization did not expand, but transplanted, the political structure, with the result that the members of the new federated body remained closely tied to their common mother country for sound reasons of common past and common law. The Irish example proves how ill fitted the United Kingdom was to build an imperial structure in which many different peoples could live contentedly together.[9] The British nation proved to be adept not at the

---

justification of our presence in Egypt remains based, not upon the defensible right of conquest, or on force, but upon our own belief in the element of consent. That element, in 1919, did not in any articulate form exist. It was dramatically challenged by the Egyptian outburst of March 1919."

[8] As Lord Salisbury put it, rejoicing over the defeat of Gladstone's first Home Rule Bill. During the following twenty years of Conservative—and that was at that time imperialist—rule (1885-1905), the English-Irish conflict was not only not solved but became much more acute. See also Gilbert K. Chesterton, *The Crimes of England,* 1915, pp. 57 ff.

[9] Why in the initial stages of national development the Tudors did not succeed in incorporating Ireland into Great Britain as the Valois had succeeded in incorporating Brittany and Burgundy into France, is still a riddle. It may be, however, that a similar process was brutally interrupted by the Cromwell regime, which treated Ireland as one great piece of booty to be divided among its servants. After the Cromwell revolution, at any rate, which was as crucial for the formation of the British

Roman art of empire building but at following the Greek model of colonization. Instead of conquering and imposing their own law upon foreign peoples, the English colonists settled on newly won territory in the four corners
of the world and remained members of the same British nation.[10] Whether
the federated structure of the Commonwealth, admirably built on the reality
of one nation dispersed over the earth, will be sufficiently elastic to balance
the nation's inherent difficulties in empire building and to admit permanently non-British peoples as full-fledged "partners in the concern" of the
Commonwealth, remains to be seen. The present dominion status of India—
a status, by the way, flatly refused by Indian nationalists during the war—has
frequently been considered to be a temporary and transitory solution.[11]

The inner contradiction between the nation's body politic and conquest as
a political device has been obvious since the failure of the Napoleonic dream.
It is due to this experience and not to humanitarian considerations that conquest has since been officially condemned and has played a minor role in
the adjustment of borderline conflicts. The Napoleonic failure to unite
Europe under the French flag was a clear indication that conquest by a
nation led either to the full awakening of the conquered people's national
consciousness and to consequent rebellion against the conqueror, or to
tyranny. And though tyranny, because it needs no consent, may successfully
rule over foreign peoples, it can stay in power only if it destroys first of all
the national institutions of its own people.

The French, in contrast to the British and all other nations in Europe,

nation as the French Revolution became for the French, the United Kingdom had
already reached that stage of maturity that is always accompanied by a loss of the
power of assimilation and integration which the body politic of the nation possesses
only in its initial stages. What then followed was, indeed, one long sad story of
"coercion [that] was not imposed that the people might live quietly but that people
might die quietly" (Chesterton, op. cit., p. 60).

For a historical survey of the Irish question that includes the latest developments,
compare the excellent unbiased study of Nicholas Mansergh, Britain and Ireland (in
Longman's Pamphlets on the British Commonwealth, London, 1942).

[10] Very characteristic is the following statement of J. A. Froude made shortly before
the beginning of the imperialist era: "Let it be once established that an Englishman
emigrating to Canada or the Cape, or Australia, or New Zealand did not forfeit his
nationality, that he was still on English soil as much as if he was in Devonshire or
Yorkshire, and would remain an Englishman while the English Empire lasted; and
if we spent a quarter of the sums which were sunk in the morasses at Balaclava in
sending out and establishing two millions of our people in those colonies, it would
contribute more to the essential strength of the country than all the wars in which
we have been entangled from Agincourt to Waterloo." Quoted from Robert Livingston
Schuyler, The Fall of the Old Colonial System, New York, 1945, pp. 280-81.

[11] The eminent South African writer, Jan Disselboom, expressed very bluntly the
attitude of the Commonwealth peoples on this question: "Great Britain is merely a
partner in the concern . . . all descended from the same closely allied stock. . . .
Those parts of the Empire which are not inhabited by races of which this is true,
were never partners in the concern. They were the private property of the predominant partner. . . . You can have the white dominion, or you can have the
Dominion of India, but you cannot have both." (Quoted from A. Carthill, The Lost
Dominion, 1924.)

actually tried in recent times to combine *ius* with *imperium* and to build an empire in the old Roman sense. They alone at least attempted to develop the body politic of the nation into an imperial political structure, believed that "the French nation (was) marching . . . to spread the benefits of French civilization"; they wanted to incorporate overseas possessions into the national body by treating the conquered peoples as "both . . . brothers and . . . subjects—brothers in the fraternity of a common French civilization, and subjects in that they are disciples of French light and followers of French leading." [12] This was partly carried out when colored delegates took their seats in the French Parliament and when Algeria was declared to be a department of France.

The result of this daring enterprise was a particularly brutal exploitation of overseas possessions for the sake of the nation. All theories to the contrary, the French Empire actually was evaluated from the point of view of national defense,[13] and the colonies were considered lands of soldiers which could produce a *force noire* to protect the inhabitants of France against their national enemies. Poincaré's famous phrase in 1923, "France is not a country of forty millions; she is a country of one hundred millions," pointed simply to the discovery of an "economical form of gunfodder, turned out by mass-production methods." [14] When Clemenceau insisted at the peace table in 1918 that he cared about nothing but "an unlimited right of levying black troops to assist in the defense of French territory in Europe if France were attacked in the future by Germany," [15] he did not save the French nation from German aggression, as we are now unfortunately in a position to know, although his plan was carried out by the General Staff; but he dealt a deathblow to the still dubious possibility of a French Empire.[16] Compared with

[12] Ernest Barker, *Ideas and Ideals of the British Empire*, Cambridge, 1941, p. 4.

See also the very good introductory remarks on the foundations of the French Empire in *The French Colonial Empire* (in *Information Department Papers* No. 25, published by The Royal Institute of International Affairs, London, 1941), pp. 9 ff. "The aim is to assimilate colonial peoples to the French people, or, where this is not possible in more primitive communities, to 'associate' them, so that more and more the difference between *la France métropole* and *la France d'outremer* shall be a geographical difference and not a fundamental one."

[13] See Gabriel Hanotaux, "Le Général Mangin" in *Revue des Deux Mondes* (1925), Tome 27.

[14] W. P. Crozier, "France and her 'Black Empire'" in *New Republic*, January 23, 1924.

[15] David Lloyd George, *Memoirs of the Peace Conference*, New Haven, 1939, I, 362 ff.

[16] A similar attempt at brutal exploitation of overseas possessions for the sake of the nation was made by the Netherlands in the Dutch East Indies after the defeat of Napoleon had restored the Dutch colonies to the much impoverished mother country. By means of compulsory cultivation the natives were reduced to slavery for the benefit of the government in Holland. Multatuli's *Max Havelaar*, first published in the sixties of the last century, was aimed at the government at home and not at the services abroad. (See de Kat Angelino, *Colonial Policy*, Vol. II, *The Dutch East Indies*, Chicago, 1931, p. 45.)

This system was quickly abandoned and the Netherlands Indies, for a while, be-this blind desperate nationalism, British imperialists compromising on the mandate system looked like guardians of the self-determination of peoples. And this despite the fact that they started at once to misuse the mandate system by "indirect rule," a method which permits the administrator to govern a people "not directly but through the medium of their own tribal and local authorities." [17]

The British tried to escape the dangerous inconsistency inherent in the nation's attempt at empire building by leaving the conquered peoples to their own devices as far as culture, religion, and law were concerned, by staying aloof and refraining from spreading British law and culture. This did not prevent the natives from developing national consciousness and from clamoring for sovereignty and independence—though it may have retarded the process somewhat. But it has strengthened tremendously the new imperialist consciousness of a fundamental, and not just a temporary, superiority of man over man, of the "higher" over the "lower breeds." This in turn exacerbated the subject peoples' fight for freedom and blinded them to the unquestionable benefits of British rule. From the very aloofness of their administrators who, "despite their genuine respect for the natives as a people, and in some cases even their love for them . . . almost to a man, do not believe that they are or ever will be capable of governing themselves without supervision," [18] the "natives" could not but conclude that they were being excluded and separated from the rest of mankind forever.

Imperialism is not empire building and expansion is not conquest. The British conquerors, the old "breakers of law in India" (Burke), had little in common with the exporters of British money or the administrators of the Indian peoples. If the latter had changed from applying decrees to the making of laws, they might have become empire builders. The point, however, is that the English nation was not interested in this and would hardly have supported them. As it was, the imperialist-minded businessmen were followed by civil servants who wanted "the African to be left an African," while quite a few, who had not yet outgrown what Harold Nicolson once called

---

came "the admiration of all colonizing nations." (Sir Hesketh Bell, former Governor of Uganda, Northern Nigeria, etc., *Foreign Colonial Administration in the Far East,* 1928, Part I). The Dutch methods have many similarities with the French: the granting of European status to deserving natives, introduction of a European school system, and other devices of gradual assimilation. The Dutch thereby achieved the same result: a strong national independence movement among the subject people.

In the present study Dutch and Belgian imperialism are being neglected. The first is a curious and changing mixture of French and English methods; the second is the story not of the expansion of the Belgian nation or even the Belgian bourgeoisie, but of the expansion of the Belgian king personally, unchecked by any government, unconnected with any other institution. Both the Dutch and the Belgian forms of imperialism are atypical. The Netherlands did not expand during the eighties, but only consolidated and modernized their old possessions. The unequalled atrocities committed in the Belgian Congo, on the other hand, would offer too unfair an example for what was generally happening in overseas possessions.

[17] Ernest Barker, *op. cit.,* p. 69.
[18] Selwyn James, *South of the Congo,* New York, 1943, p. 326.

their "boyhood-ideals," [19] wanted to help them to "become a better African" [20]—whatever that may mean. In no case were they "disposed to apply the administrative and political system of their own country to the government of backward populations," [21] and to tie the far-flung possessions of the British Crown to the English nation.

In contrast to true imperial structures, where the institutions of the mother country are in various ways integrated into the empire, it is characteristic of imperialism that national institutions remain separate from the colonial administration although they are allowed to exercise control. The actual motivation for this separation was a curious mixture of arrogance and respect: the new arrogance of the administrators abroad who faced "backward populations" or "lower breeds" found its correlative in the respect of old-fashioned statesmen at home who felt that no nation had the right to impose its law upon a foreign people. It was in the very nature of things that the arrogance turned out to be a device for rule, while the respect, which remained entirely negative, did not produce a new way for peoples to live together, but managed only to keep the ruthless imperialist rule by decree within bounds. To the salutary restraint of national institutions and politicians we owe whatever benefits the non-European peoples have been able, after all and despite everything, to derive from Western domination. But the colonial services never ceased to protest against the interference of the "inexperienced majority"—the nation—that tried to press the "experienced minority"—the imperialist administrators—"in the direction of imitation," [22] namely, of government in accordance with the general standards of justice and liberty at home.

That a movement of expansion for expansion's sake grew up in nation-states which more than any other political bodies were defined by boundaries and the limitations of possible conquest, is one example of the seemingly absurd disparities between cause and effect which have become the hallmark of modern history. The wild confusion of modern historical terminology is only a by-product of these disparities. By comparisons with ancient Empires, by mistaking expansion for conquest, by neglecting the difference between Commonwealth and Empire (which pre-imperialist historians called the difference between plantations and possessions, or colonies and dependencies, or, somewhat later, colonialism and imperialism [23]), by neglecting, in other

[19] About these boyhood ideals and their role in British imperialism, see chapter vii. How they were developed and cultivated is described in Rudyard Kipling's *Stalky and Company*.

[20] Ernest Barker, *op. cit.*, p. 150.

[21] Lord Cromer, "The Government of Subject Races," in *Edinburgh Review*, January, 1908.

[22] *Ibid.*

[23] The first scholar to use the term imperialism to differentiate clearly between the "Empire" and the "Commonwealth" was J. A. Hobson. But the essential difference was always well known. The principle of "colonial freedom" for instance, cherished by all liberal British statesmen after the American Revolution, was held valid only

words, the difference between export of (British) people and export of (British) money,[24] historians tried to dismiss the disturbing fact that so many of the important events in modern history look as though molehills had labored and had brought forth mountains.

Contemporary historians, confronted with the spectacle of a few capitalists conducting their predatory searches round the globe for new investment possibilities and appealing to the profit motives of the much-too-rich and the gambling instincts of the much-too-poor, want to clothe imperialism with the old grandeur of Rome and Alexander the Great, a grandeur which would make all following events more humanly tolerable. The disparity between cause and effect was betrayed in the famous, and unfortunately true, remark that the British Empire was acquired in a fit of absent-mindedness; it became cruelly obvious in our own time when a World War was needed to get rid of Hitler, which was shameful precisely because it was also comic. Something similar was already apparent during the Dreyfus Affair when the best elements in the nation were needed to conclude a struggle which had started as a grotesque conspiracy and ended as a farce.

The only grandeur of imperialism lies in the nation's losing battle against it. The tragedy of this half-hearted opposition was not that many national representatives could be bought by the new imperialist businessmen; worse than corruption was the fact that the incorruptible were convinced that imperialism was the only way to conduct world politics. Since maritime stations and access to raw materials were really necessary for all nations, they came to believe that annexation and expansion worked for the salvation of the nation. They were the first to fail to understand the fundamental difference between the old foundation of trade and maritime stations for the sake of trade and the new policy of expansion. They believed Cecil Rhodes when he told them to "wake up to the fact that you cannot live unless you have the trade of the world," "that your trade is the world, and your life is the world, and not England," and that therefore they "must deal with these questions of expansion and retention of the world." [25] Without wanting to, sometimes even without knowing it, they not only became accomplices in imperialist politics, but were the first to be blamed and exposed for their "imperialism." Such was the case of Clemenceau who, because he was so desperately worried about the future of the French nation, turned "im-

---

insofar as the colony was "formed of the British people or . . . such admixture of the British population as to make it safe to introduce representative institutions." See Robert Livingston Schuyler, *op. cit.,* pp. 236 ff.

In the nineteenth century, we must distinguish three types of overseas possessions within the British Empire: the settlements or plantations or colonies, like Australia and other dominions; the trade stations and possessions like India; and the maritime and military stations like the Cape of Good Hope, which were held for the sake of the former. All these possessions underwent a change in government and political significance in the era of imperialism.

[24] Ernest Barker, *op. cit.*
[25] Millin, *op. cit.,* p. 175.

perialist" in the hope that colonial manpower would protect French citizens against aggressors.

The conscience of the nation, represented by Parliament and a free press, functioned, and was resented by colonial administrators, in all European countries with colonial possessions—whether England, France, Belgium, Germany, or Holland. In England, in order to distinguish between the imperial government seated in London and controlled by Parliament and colonial administrators, this influence was called the "imperial factor," thereby crediting imperialism with the merits and remnants of justice it so eagerly tried to eliminate.[26] The "imperial factor" was expressed politically in the concept that the natives were not only protected but in a way represented by the British, the "Imperial Parliament." [27] Here the English came very close to the French experiment in empire building, although they never went so far as to give actual representation to subject peoples. Nevertheless, they obviously hoped that the nation as a whole could act as a kind of trustee for its conquered peoples, and it is true that it invariably tried its best to prevent the worst.

The conflict between the representatives of the "imperial factor" (which should rather be called the national factor) and the colonial administrators runs like a red thread through the history of British imperialism. The "prayer" which Cromer addressed to Lord Salisbury during his administration of Egypt in 1896, "save me from the English Departments," [28] was repeated over and over again, until in the twenties of this century the nation and everything it stood for were openly blamed by the extreme imperialist party for the threatened loss of India. The imperialists had always been deeply resentful that the government of India should have "to justify its existence and its policy before public opinion in England"; this control now made it impossible to proceed to those measures of "administrative mas-

[26] The origin of this misnomer probably lies in the history of British rule in South Africa, and goes back to the times when the local governors, Cecil Rhodes and Jameson, involved the "Imperial Government" in London, much against its intentions, in the war against the Boers. "In fact Rhodes, or rather Jameson, was absolute ruler of a territory three times the size of England, which could be administered 'without waiting for the grudging assent or polite censure of the High Commissioner' " who was the representative of an Imperial Government that retained only "nominal control." (Reginal Ivan Lovell, *The Struggle for South Africa, 1875-1899*, New York, 1934, p. 194.) And what happens in territories in which the British government has resigned its jurisdiction to the local European population that lacks all traditional and constitutional restraint of nation-states, can best be seen in the tragic story of the South African Union since its independence, that is, since the time when the "Imperial Government" no longer had any right to interfere.

[27] The discussion in the House of Commons in May, 1908, between Charles Dilke and the Colonial Secretary is interesting in this respect. Dilke warned against giving self-government to the Crown colonies because this would result in rule of the white planters over their colored workers. He was told that the natives too had a representation in the English House of Commons. See G. Zoepfl, "Kolonien und Kolonialpolitik" in *Handwörterbuch der Staatswissenschaften*.

[28] Lawrence J. Zetland, *Lord Cromer*, 1923, p. 224.

sacres" [29] which, immediately after the close of the first World War, had been tried occasionally elsewhere as a radical means of pacification,[30] and which indeed might have prevented India's independence.

A similar hostility prevailed in Germany between national representatives and colonial administrators in Africa. In 1897, Carl Peters was removed from his post in German Southeast Africa and had to resign from the government service because of atrocities against the natives. The same thing happened to Governor Zimmerer. And in 1905, the tribal chiefs for the first time addressed their complaints to the Reichstag, with the result that when the colonial administrators threw them into jail, the German Government intervened.[31]

The same was true of French rule. The governors general appointed by the government in Paris were either subject to powerful pressure from French colonials as in Algeria, or simply refused to carry out reforms in the treatment of natives, which were allegedly inspired by "the weak democratic principles of (their) government." [32] Everywhere imperialist administrators felt that the control of the nation was an unbearable burden and threat to domination.

And the imperialists were perfectly right. They knew the conditions of modern rule over subject peoples better than those who on the one hand protested against government by decree and arbitrary bureaucracy and on the other hoped to retain their possessions forever for the greater glory of the nation. The imperialists knew better than nationalists that the body politic of the nation is not capable of empire building. They were perfectly aware that the march of the nation and its conquest of peoples, if allowed to follow its own inherent law, ends with the peoples' rise to nationhood and the defeat of the conqueror. French methods, therefore, which always tried to combine national aspirations with empire building, were much less successful than British methods, which, after the eighties of the last century, were openly imperialistic, although restrained by a mother country that retained its national democratic institutions.

[29] A. Carthill, *The Lost Dominion,* 1924, pp. 41-42, 93.

[30] An instance of "pacification" in the Near East was described at great length by T. E. Lawrence in an article "France, Britain and the Arabs" written for *The Observer* (1920): "There is a preliminary Arab success, the British reinforcements go out as a punitive force. They fight their way . . . to their objective, which is meanwhile bombarded by artillery, aeroplanes, or gunboats. Finally perhaps a village is burnt and the district pacified. It is odd that we don't use poison gas on these occasions. Bombing the houses is a patchy way of getting the women and children. . . . By gas attacks the whole population of offending districts could be wiped out neatly; and as a method of government it would be no more immoral than the present system." See his *Letters,* edited by David Garnett, New York, 1939, pp. 311 ff.

[31] In 1910, on the other hand, the Colonial Secretary B. Dernburg had to resign because he had antagonized the colonial planters by protecting the natives. See Mary E. Townsend, *Rise and Fall of Germany's Colonial Empire,* New York, 1930, and P. Leutwein, *Kämpfe um Afrika,* Luebeck, 1936.

[32] In the words of Léon Cayla, former Governor General of Madagascar and friend of Pétain.

II: *Power and the Bourgeoisie*

WHAT IMPERIALISTS actually wanted was expansion of political power without the foundation of a body politic. Imperialist expansion had been touched off by a curious kind of economic crisis, the overproduction of capital and the emergence of "superfluous" money, the result of oversaving, which could no longer find productive investment within the national borders. For the first time, investment of power did not pave the way for investment of money, but export of power followed meekly in the train of exported money, since uncontrollable investments in distant countries threatened to transform large strata of society into gamblers, to change the whole capitalist economy from a system of production into a system of financial speculation, and to replace the profits of production with profits in commissions. The decade immediately before the imperialist era, the seventies of the last century, witnessed an unparalleled increase in swindles, financial scandals, and gambling in the stock market.

The pioneers in this pre-imperialist development were those Jewish financiers who had earned their wealth outside the capitalist system and had been needed by the growing nation-states for internationally guaranteed loans.[33] With the firm establishment of the tax system that provided for sounder government finances, this group had every reason to fear complete extinction. Having earned their money for centuries through commissions, they were naturally the first to be tempted and invited to serve in the placement of capital which could no longer be invested profitably in the domestic market. The Jewish international financiers seemed indeed especially suited for such essentially international business operations.[34] What is more, the governments themselves, whose assistance in some form was needed for investments in faraway countries, tended in the beginning to prefer the well-known

[33] For this and the following compare chapter ii.

[34] It is interesting that all early observers of imperialist developments stress this Jewish element very strongly while it hardly plays any role in more recent literature. Especially noteworthy, because very reliable in observation and very honest in analysis, is J. A. Hobson's development in this respect. In the first essay which he wrote on the subject, "Capitalism and Imperialism in South Africa" (in *Contemporary Review,* 1900), he said: "Most of (the financiers) were Jews, for the Jews are par excellence the international financiers, and, though English-speaking, most of them are of continental origin. . . . They went there (Transvaal) for money, and those who came early and made most have commonly withdrawn their persons, leaving their economic fangs in the carcass of their prey. They fastened on the Rand . . . as they are prepared to fasten upon any other spot upon the globe. . . . Primarily, they are financial speculators taking their gains not out of the genuine fruits of industry, even the industry of others, but out of construction, promotion and financial manipulation of companies." In Hobson's later study *Imperialism,* however, the Jews are not even mentioned; it had become obvious in the meantime that their influence and role had been temporary and somewhat superficial.
For the role of Jewish financiers in South Africa, see chapter vii.

Jewish financiers to newcomers in international finance, many of whom were adventurers.

After the financiers had opened the channels of capital export to the superfluous wealth, which had been condemned to idleness within the narrow framework of national production, it quickly became apparent that the absentee shareholders did not care to take the tremendous risks which corresponded to their tremendously enlarged profits. Against these risks, the commission-earning financiers, even with the benevolent assistance of the state, did not have enough power to insure them: only the material power of a state could do that.

As soon as it became clear that export of money would have to be followed by export of government power, the position of financiers in general, and Jewish financiers in particular, was considerably weakened, and the leadership of imperialist business transactions and enterprise was gradually taken over by members of the native bourgeoisie. Very instructive in this respect is the career of Cecil Rhodes in South Africa, who, an absolute newcomer, in a few years could supplant the all-powerful Jewish financiers in first place. In Germany, Bleichroeder, who in 1885 had still been a co-partner in the founding of the *Ostafrikanische Gesellschaft,* was superseded along with Baron Hirsch when Germany began the construction of the Bagdad railroad, fourteen years later, by the coming giants of imperialist enterprise, Siemens and the Deutsche Bank. Somehow the government's reluctance to yield real power to Jews and the Jews' reluctance to engage in business with political implication coincided so well that, despite the great wealth of the Jewish group, no actual struggle for power ever developed after the initial stage of gambling and commission-earning had come to an end.

The various national governments looked with misgiving upon the growing tendency to transform business into a political issue and to identify the economic interests of a relatively small group with national interests as such. But it seemed that the only alternative to export of power was the deliberate sacrifice of a great part of the national wealth. Only through the expansion of the national instruments of violence could the foreign-investment movement be rationalized, and the wild speculations with superfluous capital, which had provoked gambling of all savings, be reintegrated into the economic system of the nation. The state expanded its power because, given the choice between greater losses than the economic body of any country could sustain and greater gains than any people left to its own devices would have dreamed of, it could only choose the latter.

The first consequence of power export was that the state's instruments of violence, the police and the army, which in the framework of the nation existed beside, and were controlled by, other national institutions, were separated from this body and promoted to the position of national representatives in uncivilized or weak countries. Here, in backward regions without industries and political organization, where violence was given more latitude than in any Western country, the so-called laws of capitalism were actually allowed to create realities. The bourgeoisie's empty desire to have money beget money as men beget men had remained an ugly dream so long as money had to go the long way of investment in production; not money had begotten money, but men had made things and money. The secret of the new happy fulfillment was precisely that economic laws no longer stood in the way of the greed of the owning classes. Money could finally beget money because power, with complete disregard for all laws—economic as well as ethical—could appropriate wealth. Only when exported money succeeded in stimulating the export of power could it accomplish its owners' designs. Only the unlimited accumulation of power could bring about the unlimited accumulation of capital.

Foreign investments, capital export which had started as an emergency measure, became a permanent feature of all economic systems as soon as it was protected by export of power. The imperialist concept of expansion, according to which expansion is an end in itself and not a temporary means, made its appearance in political thought when it had become obvious that one of the most important permanent functions of the nation-state would be expansion of power. The state-employed administrators of violence soon formed a new class within the nations and, although their field of activity was far away from the mother country, wielded an important influence on the body politic at home. Since they were actually nothing but functionaries of violence they could only think in terms of power politics. They were the first who, as a class and supported by their everyday experience, would claim that power is the essence of every political structure.

The new feature of this imperialist political philosophy is not the predominant place it gave violence, nor the discovery that power is one of the basic political realities. Violence has always been the *ultima ratio* in political action and power has always been the visible expression of rule and government. But neither had ever before been the conscious aim of the body politic or the ultimate goal of any definite policy. For power left to itself can achieve nothing but more power, and violence administered for power's (and not for law's) sake turns into a destructive principle that will not stop until there is nothing left to violate.

This contradiction, inherent in all ensuing power politics, however, takes on an appearance of sense if one understands it in the context of a supposedly permanent process which has no end or aim but itself. Then the test of achievement can indeed become meaningless and power can be thought of as the never-ending, self-feeding motor of all political action that corresponds to the legendary unending accumulation of money that begets money. The concept of unlimited expansion that alone can fulfill the hope for unlimited accumulation of capital, and brings about the aimless accumulation of power, makes the foundation of new political bodies— which up to the era of imperialism always had been the upshot of conquest— well-nigh impossible. In fact, its logical consequence is the destruction of all living communities, those of the conquered peoples as well as of the people at home. For every political structure, new or old, left to itself develops

stabilizing forces which stand in the way of constant transformation and expansion. Therefore all political bodies appear to be temporary obstacles
when they are seen as part of an eternal stream of growing power.

While the administrators of permanently increasing power in the past era
of moderate imperialism did not even try to incorporate conquered territories, and preserved existing backward political communities like empty
ruins of bygone life, their totalitarian successors dissolved and destroyed all
politically stabilized structures, their own as well as those of other peoples.
The mere export of violence made the servants into masters without giving
them the master's prerogative: the possible creation of something new.
Monopolistic concentration and tremendous accumulation of violence at
home made the servants active agents in the destruction, until finally totalitarian expansion became a nation- and a people-destroying force.

Power became the essence of political action and the center of political
thought when it was separated from the political community which it should
serve. This, it is true, was brought about by an economic factor. But the resulting introduction of power as the only content of politics, and of expansion
as its only aim, would hardly have met with such universal applause, nor
would the resulting dissolution of the nation's body politic have met with
so little opposition, had it not so perfectly answered the hidden desires and
secret convictions of the economically and socially dominant classes. The
bourgeoisie, so long excluded from government by the nation-state and by
their own lack of interest in public affairs, was politically emancipated by
imperialism.

Imperialism must be considered the first stage in political rule of the
bourgeoisie rather than the last stage of capitalism. It is well known how
little the owning classes had aspired to government, how well contented they
had been with every type of state that could be trusted with protection of
property rights. For them, indeed, the state had always been only a well-
organized police force. This false modesty, however, had the curious consequence of keeping the whole bourgeois class out of the body politic; before
they were subjects in a monarchy or citizens in a republic, they were
essentially private persons. This privateness and primary concern with
money-making had developed a set of behavior patterns which are expressed
in all those proverbs—"nothing succeeds like success," "might is right,"
"right is expediency," etc.—that necessarily spring from the experience of a
society of competitors.

When, in the era of imperialism, businessmen became politicians and were
acclaimed as statesmen, while statesmen were taken seriously only if they
talked the language of successful businessmen and "thought in continents,"
these private practices and devices were gradually transformed into rules
and principles for the conduct of public affairs. The significant fact about
this process of revaluation, which began at the end of the last century and is
still in effect, is that it began with the application of bourgeois convictions
to foreign affairs and only slowly was extended to domestic politics. Therefore, the nations concerned were hardly aware that the recklessness that had

prevailed in private life, and against which the public body always had to defend itself and its individual citizens, was about to be elevated to the one publicly honored political principle.

It is significant that modern believers in power are in complete accord with the philosophy of the only great thinker who ever attempted to derive public good from private interest and who, for the sake of private good, conceived and outlined a Commonwealth whose basis and ultimate end is accumulation of power. Hobbes, indeed, is the only great philosopher to whom the bourgeoisie can rightly and exclusively lay claim, even if his principles were not recognized by the bourgeois class for a long time. Hobbes's *Leviathan* [35] exposed the only political theory according to which the state is based not on some kind of constituting law—whether divine law, the law of nature, or the law of social contract—which determines the rights and wrongs of the individual's interest with respect to public affairs, but on the individual interests themselves, so that "the private interest is the same with the publique." [36]

There is hardly a single bourgeois moral standard which has not been anticipated by the unequaled magnificence of Hobbes's logic. He gives an almost complete picture, not of Man but of the bourgeois man, an analysis which in three hundred years has neither been outdated nor excelled. "Reason . . . is nothing but Reckoning"; "a free Subject, a free Will . . . [are] words . . . without meaning; that is to say, Absurd." A being without reason, without the capacity for truth, and without free will—that is, without the capacity for responsibility—man is essentially a function of society and judged therefore according to his "value or worth . . . his price; that is to say so much as would be given for the use of his power." This price is constantly evaluated and re-evaluated by society, the "esteem of others," depending upon the law of supply and demand.

Power, according to Hobbes, is the accumulated control that permits the individual to fix prices and regulate supply and demand in such a way that they contribute to his own advantage. The individual will consider his advantage in complete isolation, from the point of view of an absolute minority, so to speak; he will then realize that he can pursue and achieve his interest only with the help of some kind of majority. Therefore, if man is actually driven by nothing but his individual interests, desire for power must be the fundamental passion of man. It regulates the relations between individual and society, and all other ambitions as well, for riches, knowledge, and honor follow from it.

[35] All quotes in the following if not annotated are from the *Leviathan*.
[36] The coincidence of this identification with the totalitarian pretense of having abolished the contradictions between individual and public interests is significant enough (see chapter xii). However, one should not overlook the fact that Hobbes wanted most of all to protect private interests by pretending that, rightly understood, they were the interests of the body politic as well, while on the contrary totalitarian regimes proclaim the nonexistence of privacy.

Hobbes points out that in the struggle for power, as in their native capacities for power, all men are equal; for the equality of men is based on the fact that each has by nature enough power to kill another. Weakness can be compensated for by guile. Their equality as potential murderers places all men in the same insecurity, from which arises the need for a state. The *raison d'être* of the state is the need for some security of the individual, who feels himself menaced by all his fellow-men.

The crucial feature in Hobbes's picture of man is not at all the realistic pessimism for which it has been praised in recent times. For if it were true that man is a being such as Hobbes would have him, he would be unable to found any body politic at all. Hobbes, indeed, does not succeed, and does not even want to succeed, in incorporating this being definitely into a political community. Hobbes's Man owes no loyalty to his country if it has been defeated and he is excused for every treachery if he happens to be taken prisoner. Those who live outside the Commonwealth (for instance, slaves) have no further obligation toward their fellow-men but are permitted to kill as many as they can; while, on the contrary, "to resist the Sword of the Commonwealth in defence of another man, guilty or innocent, no man hath Liberty," which means that there is neither fellowship nor responsibility between man and man. What holds them together is a common interest which may be "some Capitall crime, for which every one of them expecteth death"; in this case they have the right to "resist the Sword of the Commonwealth," to "joyn together, and assist, and defend one another. . . . For they but defend their lives."

Thus membership in any form of community is for Hobbes a temporary and limited affair which essentially does not change the solitary and private character of the individual (who has "no pleasure, but on the contrary a great deale of griefe in keeping company, where there is no power to over-awe them all") or create permanent bonds between him and his fellow-men. It seems as though Hobbes's picture of man defeats his purpose of providing the basis for a Commonwealth and gives instead a consistent pattern of attitudes through which every genuine community can easily be destroyed. This results in the inherent and admitted instability of Hobbes's Commonwealth, whose very conception includes its own dissolution—"when in a warre (forraign, or intestine,) the enemies get a final Victory . . . then is the Commonwealth dissolved, and every man at liberty to protect himselfe"—an instability that is all the more striking as Hobbes's primary and frequently repeated aim was to secure a maximum of safety and stability.

It would be a grave injustice to Hobbes and his dignity as a philosopher to consider this picture of man an attempt at psychological realism or philosophical truth. The fact is that Hobbes is interested in neither, but concerned exclusively with the political structure itself, and he depicts the features of man according to the needs of the Leviathan. For argument's and conviction's sake, he presents his political outline as though he started from a realistic insight into man, a being that "desires power after power," and as though he proceeded from this insight to a plan for a body politic best fitted for this power-thirsty animal. The actual process, *i.e.,* the only process in which his concept of man makes sense and goes beyond the obvious banality of an assumed human wickedness, is precisely the opposite.

This new body politic was conceived for the benefit of the new bourgeois society as it emerged in the seventeenth century and this picture of man is a sketch for the new type of Man who would fit into it. The Commonwealth is based on the delegation of power, and not of rights. It acquires a monopoly on killing and provides in exchange a conditional guarantee against being killed. Security is provided by the law, which is a direct emanation from the power monopoly of the state (and is not established by man according to human standards of right and wrong). And as this law flows directly from absolute power, it represents absolute necessity in the eyes of the individual who lives under it. In regard to the law of the state—that is, the accumulated power of society as monopolized by the state—there is no question of right or wrong, but only absolute obedience, the blind conformism of bourgeois society.

Deprived of political rights, the individual, to whom public and official life manifests itself in the guise of necessity, acquires a new and increased interest in his private life and his personal fate. Excluded from participation in the management of public affairs that involve all citizens, the individual loses his rightful place in society and his natural connection with his fellow-men. He can now judge his individual private life only by comparing it with that of others, and his relations with his fellow-men inside society take the form of competition. Once public affairs are regulated by the state under the guise of necessity, the social or public careers of the competitors come under the sway of chance. In a society of individuals, all equipped by nature with equal capacity for power and equally protected from one another by the state, only chance can decide who will succeed.[37]

According to bourgeois standards, those who are completely unlucky and unsuccessful are automatically barred from competition, which is the life of society. Good fortune is identified with honor, and bad luck with shame. By assigning his political rights to the state the individual also delegates his social responsibilities to it: he asks the state to relieve him of the burden of

[37] The elevation of chance to the position of final arbiter over the whole of life was to reach its full development in the nineteenth century. With it came a new genre of literature, the novel, and the decline of the drama. For the drama became meaningless in a world without action, while the novel could deal adequately with the destinies of human beings who were either the victims of necessity or the favorites of luck. Balzac showed the full range of the new genre and even presented human passions as man's fate, containing neither virtue nor vice, neither reason nor free will. Only the novel in its full maturity, having interpreted and re-interpreted the entire scale of human matters, could preach the new gospel of infatuation with one's own fate that has played such a great role among nineteenth-century intellectuals. By means of such infatuation the artist and intellectual tried to draw a line between themselves and the philistines, to protect themselves against the inhumanity of good or bad luck, and they developed all the gifts of modern sensitivity—for suffering, for understanding, for playing a prescribed role—which are so desperately needed by human dignity, which demands of a man that he at least be a willing victim if nothing else.

caring for the poor precisely as he asks for protection against criminals. The difference between pauper and criminal disappears—both stand outside society. The unsuccessful are robbed of the virtue that classical civilization left them; the unfortunate can no longer appeal to Christian charity.

Hobbes liberates those who are excluded from society—the unsuccessful, the unfortunate, the criminal—from every obligation toward society and state if the state does not take care of them. They may give free rein to their desire for power and are told to take advantage of their elemental ability to kill, thus restoring that natural equality which society conceals only for the sake of expediency. Hobbes foresees and justifies the social outcasts' organization into a gang of murderers as a logical outcome of the bourgeoisie's moral philosophy.

Since power is essentially only a means to an end a community based solely on power must decay in the calm of order and stability; its complete security reveals that it is built on sand. Only by acquiring more power can it guarantee the status quo; only by constantly extending its authority and only through the process of power accumulation can it remain stable. Hobbes's Commonwealth is a vacillating structure and must always provide itself with new props from the outside; otherwise it would collapse overnight into the aimless, senseless chaos of the private interests from which it sprang. Hobbes embodies the necessity of power accumulation in the theory of the state of nature, the "condition of perpetual war" of all against all, in which the various single states still remain vis-à-vis each other like their individual subjects before they submitted to the authority of a Commonwealth.[38] This ever-present possibility of war guarantees the Commonwealth a prospect of permanence because it makes it possible for the state to increase its power at the expense of other states.

It would be erroneous to take at its face value the obvious inconsistency between Hobbes's plea for security of the individual and the inherent instability of his Commonwealth. Here again he tries to persuade, to appeal to certain basic instincts for security which he knew well enough could survive in the subjects of the *Leviathan* only in the form of absolute submission to the power which "over-awes them all," that is, in an all-pervading, overwhelming fear—not exactly the basic sentiment of a safe man. What Hobbes actually starts from is an unmatched insight into the political needs of the new social body of the rising bourgeoisie, whose fundamental belief in an unending process of property accumulation was about to eliminate all individual safety. Hobbes drew the necessary conclusions from social and economic behavior patterns when he proposed his revolutionary changes in political constitution. He outlined the only new body politic which could

---

[38] The presently popular liberal notion of a World Government is based, like all liberal notions of political power, on the same concept of individuals submitting to a central authority which "overawes them all," except that nations are now taking the place of individuals. The World Government is to overcome and eliminate authentic politics, that is, different peoples getting along with each other in the full force of their power.

correspond to the new needs and interests of a new class. What he actually achieved was a picture of man as he ought to become and ought to behave if he wanted to fit into the coming bourgeois society.

Hobbes's insistence on power as the motor of all things human and divine (even God's reign over men is "derived not from Creating them . . . but from the Irresistible Power") sprang from the theoretically indisputable proposition that a never-ending accumulation of property must be based on a never-ending accumulation of power. The philosophical correlative of the inherent instability of a community founded on power is the image of an endless process of history which, in order to be consistent with the constant growth of power, inexorably catches up with individuals, peoples, and finally all mankind. The limitless process of capital accumulation needs the political structure of so "unlimited a Power" that it can protect growing property by constantly growing more powerful. Granted the fundamental dynamism of the new social class, it is perfectly true that "he cannot assure the power and means to live well, which he hath at present, without the acquisition of more." The consistency of this conclusion is in no way altered by the remarkable fact that for some three hundred years there was neither a sovereign who would "convert this Truth of Speculation into the Utility of Practice," nor a bourgeoisie politically conscious and economically mature enough openly to adopt Hobbes's philosophy of power.

This process of never-ending accumulation of power necessary for the protection of a never-ending accumulation of capital determined the "progressive" ideology of the late nineteenth century and foreshadowed the rise of imperialism. Not the naïve delusion of a limitless growth of property, but the realization that power accumulation was the only guarantee for the stability of so-called economic laws, made progress irresistible. The eighteenth-century notion of progress, as conceived in pre-revolutionary France, intended criticism of the past to be a means of mastering the present and controlling the future; progress culminated in the emancipation of man. But this notion had little to do with the endless progress of bourgeois society, which not only did not want the liberty and autonomy of man, but was ready to sacrifice everything and everybody to supposedly superhuman laws of history. "What we call progress is [the] wind . . . [that] drives [the angel of history] irresistibly into the future to which he turns his back while the pile of ruins before him towers to the skies." [39] Only in Marx's dream of a classless society which, in Joyce's words, was to awaken mankind from the nightmare of history, does a last, though utopian, trace of the eighteenth-century concept appear.

[39] Walter Benjamin, "Über den Begriff der Geschichte," *Institut für Sozialforschung,* New York, 1942, mimeographed.—The imperialists themselves were quite aware of the implications of their concept of progress. Said the very representative author from the Civil Services in India who wrote under the pseudonym A. Carthill: "One must always feel sorry for those persons who are crushed by the triumphal car of progress" (*op. cit.,* p. 209).

The imperialist-minded businessman, whom the stars annoyed because he could not annex them, realized that power organized for its own sake would beget more power. When the accumulation of capital had reached its natural, national limits, the bourgeoisie understood that only with an "expansion is everything" ideology, and only with a corresponding power-accumulating process, would it be possible to set the old motor into motion again. At the same moment, however, when it seemed as though the true principle of perpetual motion had been discovered, the specifically optimistic mood of the progress ideology was shaken. Not that anybody began to doubt the irresistibility of the process itself, but many people began to see what had frightened Cecil Rhodes: that the human condition and the limitations of the globe were a serious obstacle to a process that was unable to stop and to stabilize, and could therefore only begin a series of destructive catastrophes once it had reached these limits.

In the imperialistic epoch a philosophy of power became the philosophy of the elite, who quickly discovered and were quite ready to admit that the thirst for power could be quenched only through destruction. This was the essential cause of their nihilism (especially conspicuous in France at the turn, and in Germany in the twenties, of this century) which replaced the superstition of progress with the equally vulgar superstition of doom, and preached automatic annihilation with the same enthusiasm that the fanatics of automatic progress had preached the irresistibility of economic laws. It had taken Hobbes, the great idolator of Success, three centuries to succeed. This was partly because the French Revolution, with its conception of man as lawmaker and *citoyen,* had almost succeeded in preventing the bourgeoisie from fully developing its notion of history as a necessary process. But it was also partly because of the revolutionary implications of the Commonwealth, its fearless breach with Western tradition, which Hobbes did not fail to point out.

Every man and every thought which does not serve and does not conform to the ultimate purpose of a machine whose only purpose is the generation and accumulation of power is a dangerous nuisance. Hobbes judged that the books of the "ancient Greeks and Romans" were as "prejudicial" as the teaching of a Christian "Summum bonum . . . as [it] is spoken of in the Books of the old Morall Philosophers" or the doctrine that "whatsoever a man does against his Conscience, is Sinne" and that "Lawes are the Rules of Just and Unjust." Hobbes's deep distrust of the whole Western tradition of political thought will not surprise us if we remember that he wanted nothing more nor less than the justification of Tyranny which, though it has occurred many times in Western history, has never been honored with a philosophical foundation. That the Leviathan actually amounts to a permanent government of tyranny, Hobbes is proud to admit: "the name of Tyranny signifieth nothing more nor lesse than the name of Soveraignty . . . ; I think the toleration of a professed hatred of Tyranny, is a Toleration of hatred to Commonwealth in generall. . . ."

Since Hobbes was a philosopher, he could already detect in the rise of the bourgeoisie all those antitraditionalist qualities of the new class which would take more than three hundred years to develop fully. His *Leviathan* was not concerned with idle speculation about new political principles or the old search for reason as it governs the community of men; it was strictly a "reckoning of the consequences" that follow from the rise of a new class in society whose existence is essentially tied up with property as a dynamic, new property-producing device. The so-called accumulation of capital which gave birth to the bourgeoisie changed the very conception of property and wealth: they were no longer considered to be the results of accumulation and acquisition but their beginnings; wealth became a never-ending process of getting wealthier. The classification of the bourgeoisie as an owning class is only superficially correct, for a characteristic of this class has been that everybody could belong to it who conceived of life as a process of perpetually becoming wealthier, and considered money as something sacrosanct which under no circumstances should be a mere commodity for consumption.

Property by itself, however, is subject to use and consumption and therefore diminishes constantly. The most radical and the only secure form of possession is destruction, for only what we have destroyed is safely and forever ours. Property owners who do not consume but strive to enlarge their holdings continually find one very inconvenient limitation, the unfortunate fact that men must die. Death is the real reason why property and acquisition can never become a true political principle. A social system based essentially on property cannot possibly proceed toward anything but the final destruction of all property. The finiteness of personal life is as serious a challenge to property as the foundation of society, as the limits of the globe are a challenge to expansion as the foundation of the body politic. By transcending the limits of human life in planning for an automatic continuous growth of wealth beyond all personal needs and possibilities of consumption, individual property is made a public affair and taken out of the sphere of mere private life. Private interests which by their very nature are temporary, limited by man's natural span of life, can now escape into the sphere of public affairs and borrow from them that infinite length of time which is needed for continuous accumulation. This seems to create a society very similar to that of the ants and bees where "the Common good differeth not from the Private; and being by nature enclined to their private, they procure thereby the common benefit."

Since, however, men are neither ants nor bees, the whole thing is a delusion. Public life takes on the deceptive aspect of a total of private interests as though these interests could create a new quality through sheer addition. All the so-called liberal concepts of politics (that is, all the pre-imperialist political notions of the bourgeoisie)—such as unlimited competition regulated by a secret balance which comes mysteriously from the sum total of competing activities, the pursuit of "enlightened self-interest" as an adequate political virtue, unlimited progress inherent in the mere succession of events —have this in common: they simply add up private lives and personal behavior patterns and present the sum as laws of history, or economics, or politics. Liberal concepts, however, while they express the bourgeoisie's instinctive distrust of and its innate hostility to public affairs, are only a temporary compromise between the old standards of Western culture and the new class's faith in property as a dynamic, self-moving principle. The old standards give way to the extent that automatically growing wealth actually replaces political action.

Hobbes was the true, though never fully recognized, philosopher of the bourgeoisie because he realized that acquisition of wealth conceived as a never-ending process can be guaranteed only by the seizure of political power, for the accumulating process must sooner or later force open all existing territorial limits. He foresaw that a society which had entered the path of never-ending acquisition had to engineer a dynamic political organization capable of a corresponding never-ending process of power generation. He even, through sheer force of imagination, was able to outline the main psychological traits of the new type of man who would fit into such a society and its tyrannical body politic. He foresaw the necessary idolatry of power itself by this new human type, that he would be flattered at being called a power-thirsty animal, although actually society would force him to surrender all his natural forces, his virtues and his vices, and would make him the poor meek little fellow who has not even the right to rise against tyranny, and who, far from striving for power, submits to any existing government and does not stir even when his best friend falls an innocent victim to an incomprehensible *raison d'état.*

For a Commonwealth based on the accumulated and monopolized power of all its individual members necessarily leaves each person powerless, deprived of his natural and human capacities. It leaves him degraded into a cog in the power-accumulating machine, free to console himself with sublime thoughts about the ultimate destiny of this machine, which itself is constructed in such a way that it can devour the globe simply by following its own inherent law.

The ultimate destructive purpose of this Commonwealth is at least indicated in the philosophical interpretation of human equality as an "equality of ability" to kill. Living with all other nations "in the condition of a perpetuall war, and upon the confines of battle, with their frontiers armed, and canons planted against their neighbours round about," it has no other law of conduct but the "most conducing to [its] benefit" and will gradually devour weaker structures until it comes to a last war "which provideth for every man, by Victory, or Death."

By "Victory or Death," the Leviathan can indeed overcome all political limitations that go with the existence of other peoples and can envelop the whole earth in its tyranny. But when the last war has come and every man has been provided for, no ultimate peace is established on earth: the power-accumulating machine, without which continual expansion would not have been achieved, needs more material to devour in its never-ending process. If the last victorious Commonwealth cannot proceed to "annex the planets," it can only proceed to destroy itself in order to begin anew the never-ending process of power generation.

III: *The Alliance Between Mob and Capital*

WHEN IMPERIALISM entered the scene of politics with the scramble for Africa in the eighties, it was promoted by businessmen, opposed fiercely by the governments in power, and welcomed by a surprisingly large section of the educated classes.[40] To the last it seemed to be God-sent, a cure for all evils, an easy panacea for all conflicts. And it is true that imperialism in a sense did not disappoint these hopes. It gave a new lease on life to political and social structures which were quite obviously threatened by new social and political forces and which, under other circumstances, without the inter-ference of imperialist developments, would hardly have needed two world wars to disappear.

As matters stood, imperialism spirited away all troubles and produced that deceptive feeling of security, so universal in pre-war Europe, which deceived all but the most sensitive minds. Péguy in France and Chesterton in England knew instinctively that they lived in a world of hollow pretense and that its stability was the greatest pretense of all. Until everything began to crumble, the stability of obviously outdated political structures was a fact, and their stubborn unconcerned longevity seemed to give the lie to those who felt the ground tremble under their feet. The solution of the riddle was imperialism. The answer to the fateful question: why did the European comity of nations allow this evil to spread until everything was destroyed, the good as well as the bad, is that all governments knew very well that their countries were secretly disintegrating, that the body politic was being de-stroyed from within, and that they lived on borrowed time.

Innocently enough, expansion appeared first as the outlet for excess capital production and offered a remedy, capital export.[41] The tremendously increased wealth produced by capitalist production under a social system based on maldistribution had resulted in "oversaving"—that is, the accu-

[40] "The Services offer the cleanest and most natural support to an aggressive foreign policy; expansion of the empire appeals powerfully to the aristocracy and the pro-fessional classes by offering new and ever-growing fields for the honorable and profitable employment of their sons" (J. A. Hobson, "Capitalism and Imperialism in South Africa," *op. cit.*). It was "above all . . . patriotic professors and publicists regardless of political affiliation and unmindful of personal economic interest" who sponsored "the outward imperialistic thrusts of the '70ies and early '80ies" (Hayes, *op. cit.*, p. 220).

[41] For this and the following see J. A. Hobson, *Imperialism,* who as early as 1905 gave a masterly analysis of the driving economic forces and motives as well as of some of its political implications. When, in 1938, his early study was republished, Hobson could rightly state in his introduction to an unchanged text that his book was real proof "that the chief perils and disturbances . . . of today . . . were all latent and discernible in the world of a generation ago. . . . "

mulation of capital which was condemned to idleness within the existing national capacity for production and consumption. This money was actually superfluous, needed by nobody though owned by a growing class of somebodies. The ensuing crises and depressions during the decades preceding the era of imperialism [42] had impressed upon the capitalists the thought that their whole economic system of production depended upon a supply and demand that from now on must come from "outside of capitalist society." [43] Such supply and demand came from inside the nation, so long as the capitalist system did not control all its classes together with its entire productive capacity. When capitalism had pervaded the entire economic structure and all social strata had come into the orbit of its production and consumption system, capitalists clearly had to decide either to see the whole system collapse or to find new markets, that is, to penetrate new countries which were not yet subject to capitalism and therefore could provide a new noncapitalistic supply and demand.

The decisive point about the depressions of the sixties and seventies, which initiated the era of imperialism, was that they forced the bourgeoisie to realize for the first time that the original sin of simple robbery, which centuries ago had made possible the "original accumulation of capital" (Marx) and had started all further accumulation, had eventually to be repeated lest the motor of accumulation suddenly die down. [44] In the face of this danger, which threatened not only the bourgeoisie but the whole nation with a catastrophic breakdown in production, capitalist producers understood that the forms and laws of their production system "from the beginning had been calculated for the whole earth." [45]

[42] The obvious connection between the severe crises in the sixties in England and the seventies on the Continent and imperialism is mentioned in Hayes, *op. cit.*, in a footnote only (on p. 219), and in Schuyler, *op. cit.*, who believes that "a revival of interest in emigration was an important factor in the beginnings of the imperial movement" and that this interest had been caused by "a serious depression in British trade and industry" toward the close of the sixties (p. 280). Schuyler also describes at some length the strong "anti-imperial sentiment of the mid-Victorian era." Unfortunately, Schuyler makes no differentiation between the Commonwealth and the Empire proper, although the discussion of pre-imperialist material might easily have suggested such a differentiation.

[43] Rosa Luxemburg, *Die Akkumulation des Kapitals,* Berlin, 1923, p. 273.

[44] Rudolf Hilferding, *Das Finanzkapital,* Wien, 1910, p. 401, mentions—but does not analyze the implications of—the fact that imperialism "suddenly uses again the methods of the original accumulation of capitalistic wealth."

[45] According to Rosa Luxemburg's brilliant insight into the political structure of imperialism (*op. cit.*, pp. 273 ff., pp. 361 ff.), the "historical process of the accumulation of capital depends in all its aspects upon the existence of noncapitalist social strata," so that "imperialism is the political expression of the accumulation of capital in its competition for the possession of the remainders of the noncapitalistic world." This essential dependence of capitalism upon a noncapitalistic world lies at the basis of all other aspects of imperialism, which then may be explained as the results of oversaving and maldistribution (Hobson, *op. cit.*), as the result of overproduction and the consequent need for new markets (Lenin, *Imperialism, the Last Stage of Capitalism,* 1917), as the result of an undersupply of raw material (Hayes, *op. cit.*), or as capital export in order to equalize the national profit rate (Hilferding, *op. cit.*).

The first reaction to the saturated home market, lack of raw materials, and growing crises, was export of capital. The owners of superfluous wealth first tried foreign investment without expansion and without political control, which resulted in an unparalleled orgy of swindles, financial scandals, and stock-market speculation, all the more alarming since foreign investments grew much more rapidly than domestic ones.[46] Big money resulting from oversaving paved the way for little money, the product of the little fellow's work. Domestic enterprises, in order to keep pace with high profits from foreign investment, turned likewise to fraudulent methods and attracted an increasing number of people who, in the hope of miraculous returns, threw their money out of the window. The Panama scandal in France, the *Gründungsschwindel* in Germany and Austria, became classic examples. Tremendous losses resulted from the promises of tremendous profits. The owners of little money lost so much so quickly that the owners of superfluous big capital soon saw themselves left alone in what was, in a sense, a battlefield. Having failed to change the whole society into a community of gamblers they were again superfluous, excluded from the normal process of production to which, after some turmoil, all other classes returned quietly, if somewhat impoverished and embittered.[47]

Export of money and foreign investment as such are not imperialism and do not necessarily lead to expansion as a political device. As long as the owners of superfluous capital were content with investing "large portions of their property in foreign lands," even if this tendency ran "counter to all past traditions of nationalism," [48] they merely confirmed their alienation from the national body on which they were parasites anyway. Only when they demanded government protection of their investments (after the initial stage of swindle had opened their eyes to the possible use of politics against the risks of gambling) did they re-enter the life of the nation. In this appeal, however, they followed the established tradition of bourgeois society, always to consider political institutions exclusively as an instrument for the protection of individual property.[49] Only the fortunate coincidence of the rise

[46] According to Hilferding, *op. cit.*, p. 409, note, the British income from foreign investment increased ninefold while national income doubled from 1865 to 1898. He assumes a similar though probably less marked increase for German and French foreign investments.

[47] For France see George Lachapelle, *Les Finances de la Troisième République,* Paris, 1937, and D. W. Brogan, *The Development of Modern France,* New York, 1941. For Germany, compare the interesting contemporary testimonies like Max Wirth, *Geschichte der Handelskrisen,* 1873, chapter 15, and A. Schaeffle, "Der 'grosse Boersenkrach' des Jahres 1873" in *Zeitschrift für die gesamte Staatswissenschaft,* 1874, Band 30.

[48] J. A. Hobson, "Capitalism and Imperialism," *op. cit.*

[49] See Hilferding, *op. cit.*, p. 406. "Hence the cry for strong state power by all capitalists with vested interests in foreign countries. . . . Exported capital feels safest when the state power of its own country rules the new domain completely. . . . Its profits should be guaranteed by the state if possible. Thus, exportation of capital favors an imperialist policy." P. 423: "It is a matter of course that the attitude of the bourgeoisie toward the state undergoes a complete change when the political

of a new class of property holders and the industrial revolution had made the bourgeoisie producers and stimulators of production. As long as it fulfilled this basic function in modern society, which is essentially a community of producers, its wealth had an important function for the nation as a whole. The owners of superfluous capital were the first section of the class to want profits without fulfilling some real social function—even if it was the function of an exploiting producer—and whom, consequently, no police could ever have saved from the wrath of the people.

Expansion then was an escape not only for superfluous capital. More important, it protected its owners against the menacing prospect of remaining entirely superfluous and parasitical. It saved the bourgeoisie from the consequences of maldistribution and revitalized its concept of ownership at a time when wealth could no longer be used as a factor in production within the national framework and had come into conflict with the production ideal of the community as a whole.

Older than the superfluous wealth was another by-product of capitalist production: the human debris that every crisis, following invariably upon each period of industrial growth, eliminated permanently from producing society. Men who had become permanently idle were as superfluous to the community as the owners of superfluous wealth. That they were an actual menace to society had been recognized throughout the nineteenth century and their export had helped to populate the dominions of Canada and Australia as well as the United States. The new fact in the imperialist era is that these two superfluous forces, superfluous capital and superfluous working power, joined hands and left the country together. The concept of expansion, the export of government power and annexation of every territory in which nationals had invested either their wealth or their work, seemed the only alternative to increasing losses in wealth and population. Imperialism and its idea of unlimited expansion seemed to offer a permanent remedy for a permanent evil.[50]

Ironically enough, the first country in which superfluous wealth and

power of the state becomes a competitive instrument for the finance capital in the world market. The bourgeoisie had been hostile to the state in its fight against economic mercantilism and political absolutism. . . . Theoretically at least, economic life was to be completely free of state intervention; the state was to confine itself politically to the safeguarding of security and the establishment of civil equality." P. 426: "However, the desire for an expansionist policy causes a revolutionary change in the mentality of the bourgeoisie. It ceases to be pacifist and humanist." P. 470: "Socially, expansion is a vital condition for the preservation of capitalist society; economically, it is the condition for the preservation of, and temporary increase in, the profit rate."

[50] These motives were especially outspoken in German imperialism. Among the first activities of the Alldeutsche Verband (founded in 1891) were efforts to prevent German emigrants from changing their citizenship, and the first imperialist speech of William II, on the occasion of the twenty-fifth anniversary of the foundation of the Reich, contained the following typical passage: "The German Empire has become a World Empire. Thousands of our compatriots live everywhere, in distant parts of the earth. . . . Gentlemen, it is your solemn duty to help me unite this greater German Empire with our native country." Compare also J. A. Froude's statement in note 10.

superfluous men were brought together was itself becoming superfluous. South Africa had been in British possession since the beginning of the century because it assured the maritime road to India. The opening of the Suez Canal, however, and the subsequent administrative conquest of Egypt, lessened considerably the importance of the old trade station on the Cape. The British would, in all probability, have withdrawn from Africa just as all European nations had done whenever their possessions and trade interests in India were liquidated.

The particular irony and, in a sense, symbolical circumstance in the unexpected development of South Africa into the "culture-bed of Imperialism" [51] lies in the very nature of its sudden attractiveness when it had lost all value for the Empire proper: diamond fields were discovered in the seventies and large gold mines in the eighties. The new desire for profit-at-any-price converged for the first time with the old fortune hunt. Prospectors, adventurers, and the scum of the big cities emigrated to the Dark Continent along with capital from industrially developed countries. From now on, the mob, begotten by the monstrous accumulation of capital, accompanied its begetter on those voyages of discovery where nothing was discovered but new possibilities for investment. The owners of superfluous wealth were the only men who could use the superfluous men who came from the four corners of the earth. Together they established the first paradise of parasites whose lifeblood was gold. Imperialism, the product of superfluous money and superfluous men, began its startling career by producing the most superfluous and unreal goods.

It may still be doubtful whether the panacea of expansion would have become so great a temptation for non-imperialists if it had offered its dangerous solutions only for those superfluous forces which, in any case, were already outside the nation's body corporate. The complicity of all parliamentary parties in imperialist programs is a matter of record. The history of the British Labor Party in this respect is an almost unbroken chain of justifications of Cecil Rhodes' early prediction: "The workmen find that although the Americans are exceedingly fond of them, and are just now exchanging the most brotherly sentiments with them yet are shutting out their goods. The workmen also find that Russia, France and Germany locally are doing the same, and the workmen see that if they do not look out they will have no place in the world to trade at all. And so the workmen have become Imperialist and the Liberal Party are following." [52] In Germany, the liberals (and not the Conservative Party) were the actual promoters of that famous naval policy which contributed so heavily to the outbreak of the first World War.[53] The Socialist Party wavered between active

---

[51] E. H. Damce, *The Victorian Illusion*, London, 1928, p. 164: "Africa, which had been included neither in the itinerary of Saxondom nor in the professional philosophers of imperial history, became the culture-bed of British imperialism."

[52] Quoted from Millin, *op. cit.*

[53] "The liberals, and not the Right of Parliament, were the supporters of the naval policy." Alfred von Tirpitz, *Erinnerungen*, 1919. See also Daniel Frymann (pseud. for Heinrich Class), *Wenn ich der Kaiser wär*, 1912: "The true imperial party is the Na-

support of the imperialist naval policy (it repeatedly voted funds for the building of a German navy after 1906) and complete neglect of all questions of foreign policy. Occasional warnings against the *Lumpenproletariat,* and the possible bribing of sections of the working class with crumbs from the imperialist table, did not lead to a deeper understanding of the great appeal which the imperialist programs had to the rank and file of the party. In Marxist terms the new phenomenon of an alliance between mob and capital seemed so unnatural, so obviously in conflict with the doctrine of class struggle, that the actual dangers of the imperialist attempt—to divide mankind into master races and slave races, into higher and lower breeds, into colored peoples and white men, all of which were attempts to unify the people on the basis of the mob—were completely overlooked. Even the breakdown of international solidarity at the outbreak of the first World War did not disturb the complacency of the socialists and their faith in the proletariat as such. Socialists were still probing the economic laws of imperialism when imperialists had long since stopped obeying them, when in overseas countries these laws had been sacrificed to the "imperial factor" or to the "race factor," and when only a few elderly gentlemen in high finance still believed in the inalienable rights of the profit rate.

The curious weakness of popular opposition to imperialism, the numerous inconsistencies and outright broken promises of liberal statesmen, frequently ascribed to opportunism or bribery, have other and deeper causes. Neither opportunism nor bribery could have persuaded a man like Gladstone to break his promise, as the leader of the Liberal Party, to evacuate Egypt when he became Prime Minister. Half consciously and hardly articulately, these men shared with the people the conviction that the national body itself was so deeply split into classes, that class struggle was so universal a characteristic of modern political life, that the very cohesion of the nation was jeopardized. Expansion again appeared as a lifesaver, if and insofar as it could provide a common interest for the nation as a whole, and it is mainly for this reason that imperialists were allowed to become "parasites upon patriotism." [54]

Partly, of course, such hopes still belonged with the old vicious practice of "healing" domestic conflicts with foreign adventures. The difference, however, is marked. Adventures are by their very nature limited in time and space; they may succeed temporarily in overcoming conflicts, although as a rule they fail and tend rather to sharpen them. From the very beginning the imperialist adventure of expansion appeared to be an eternal solution, because expansion was conceived as unlimited. Furthermore, imperialism was not an adventure in the usual sense, because it depended less on nationalist slogans than on the seemingly solid basis of economic interests. In a society of clashing interests, where the common good was identified

tional Liberal Party." Frymann, a prominent German chauvinist during the first World War, even adds with respect to the conservatives: "The aloofness of conservative milieus with regard to race doctrines is also worthy of note."
[54] Hobson, *op. cit.,* p. 61.

with the sum total of individual interests, expansion as such appeared to be a possible common interest of the nation as a whole. Since the owning and dominant classes had convinced everybody that economic interest and the passion for ownership are a sound basis for the body politic, even non-imperialist statesmen were easily persuaded to yield when a common economic interest appeared on the horizon.

These then are the reasons why nationalism developed so clear a tendency toward imperialism, the inner contradiction of the two principles notwithstanding.[55] The more ill-fitted nations were for the incorporation of foreign peoples (which contradicted the constitution of their own body politic), the more they were tempted to oppress them. In theory, there is an abyss between nationalism and imperialism; in practice, it can and has been bridged by tribal nationalism and outright racism. From the beginning, imperialists in all countries preached and boasted of their being "beyond the parties," and the only ones to speak for the nation as a whole. This was especially true of the Central and Eastern European countries · with few or no overseas holdings; there the alliance between mob and capital took place at home and resented even more bitterly (and attacked much more violently) the national institutions and all national parties.[56]

The contemptuous indifference of imperialist politicians to domestic issues was marked everywhere, however, and especially in England. While "parties above parties" like the Primrose League were of secondary influence, imperialism was the chief cause of the degeneration of the two-party system into the Front Bench system, which led to a "diminution of the power of opposition" in Parliament and to a growth of "power of the Cabinet as against the House of Commons."[57] Of course this was also carried through as a policy beyond the strife of parties and particular interests, and by men who claimed to speak for the nation as a whole. Such language was bound to attract and delude precisely those persons who still retained a spark of political idealism. The cry for unity resembled exactly the battle cries which had always led peoples to war; and yet, nobody detected in the universal and permanent instrument of unity the germ of universal and permanent war.

Government officials engaged more actively than any other group in the nationalist brand of imperialism and were chiefly responsible for the confusion of imperialism with nationalism. The nation-states had created and depended upon the civil services as a permanent body of officials who served

---

[55] Hobson, *op. cit.*, was the first to recognize both the fundamental opposition of imperialism and nationalism and the tendency of nationalism to become imperialist. He called imperialism a perversion of nationalism "in which nations . . . transform the wholesome stimulative rivalry of various national types into the cut-throat struggle of competing empires" (p. 9.).

[56] See chapter viii.

[57] Hobson, *op. cit.*, pp. 146 ff.—"There can be no doubt that the power of the Cabinet as against the House of Commons has grown steadily and rapidly and it appears to be still growing," noticed Bryce in 1901, in *Studies in History and Jurisprudence*, 1901, I, 177. For the working of the Front Bench system see also Hilaire Belloc and Cecil Chesterton, *The Party System*, London, 1911.

regardless of class interest and governmental changes. Their professional honor and self-respect—especially in England and Germany—derived from their being servants of the nation as a whole. They were the only group with a direct interest in supporting the state's fundamental claim to independence of classes and factions. That the authority of the nation-state itself depended largely on the economic independence and political neutrality of its civil servants becomes obvious in our time; the decline of nations has invariably started with the corruption of its permanent administration and the general conviction that civil servants are in the pay, not of the state, but of the owning classes. At the close of the century the owning classes had become so dominant that it was almost ridiculous for a state employee to keep up the pretense of serving the nation. Division into classes left them outside the social body and forced them to form a clique of their own. In the colonial services they escaped the actual disintegration of the national body. In ruling foreign peoples in faraway countries, they could much better pretend to be heroic servants of the nation, "who by their services had glorified the British race," [58] than if they had stayed at home. The colonies were no longer simply "a vast system of outdoor relief for the upper classes" as James Mill could still describe them; they were to become the very backbone of British nationalism, which discovered in the domination of distant countries and the rule over strange peoples the only way to serve British, and nothing but British, interests. The services actually believed that "the peculiar genius of each nation shows itself nowhere more clearly than in their system of dealing with subject races." [59]

The truth was that only far from home could a citizen of England, Germany, or France be nothing but an Englishman or German or Frenchman. In his own country he was so entangled in economic interests or social loyalties that he felt closer to a member of his class in a foreign country than to a man of another class in his own. Expansion gave nationalism a new lease on life and therefore was accepted as an instrument of national politics. The members of the new colonial societies and imperialist leagues felt "far removed from the strife of parties," and the farther away they moved the stronger their belief that they "represented only a national purpose." [60] This shows the desperate state of the European nations before imperialism, how fragile their institutions had become, how outdated their social system proved in the face of man's growing capacity to produce. The

[58] Lord Curzon at the unveiling of Lord Cromer's memorial tablet. See Lawrence J. Zetland, *Lord Cromer*, 1932, p. 362.

[59] Sir Hesketh Bell, *op. cit.*, Part I, p. 300.
The same sentiment prevailed in the Dutch colonial services. "The highest task, the task without precedent is that which awaits the East Indian Civil Service official . . . it should be considered as the highest honor to serve in its ranks . . . , the select body which fulfills the mission of Holland overseas." See De Kat Angelino, *Colonial Policy*, Chicago, 1931, II, 129.

[60] The President of the German "Kolonialverein," Hohenlohe-Langenburg, in 1884. See Mary E. Townsend, *Origin of Modern German Colonialism. 1871-1885*, 1921.

means for preservation were desperate too, and in the end the remedy proved worse than the evil—which, incidentally, it did not cure.

The alliance between capital and mob is to be found at the genesis of every consistently imperialist policy. In some countries, particularly in Great Britain, this new alliance between the much-too-rich and the much-too-poor was and remained confined to overseas possessions. The so-called hypocrisy of British policies was the result of the good sense of English statesmen who drew a sharp line between colonial methods and normal domestic policies, thereby avoiding with considerable success the feared boomerang effect of imperialism upon the homeland. In other countries, particularly in Germany and Austria, the alliance took effect at home in the form of pan-movements, and to a lesser extent in France, in a so-called colonial policy. The aim of these "movements" was, so to speak, to im- perialize the whole nation (and not only the "superfluous" part of it), to combine domestic and foreign policy in such a way as to organize the nation for the looting of foreign territories and the permanent degradation of alien peoples.

The rise of the mob out of the capitalist organization was observed early, and its growth carefully and anxiously noted by all great historians of the nineteenth century. Historical pessimism from Burckhardt to Spengler springs essentially from this consideration. But what the historians, sadly pre- occupied with the phenomenon in itself, failed to grasp was that the mob could not be identified with the growing industrial working class, and cer- tainly not with the people as a whole, but that it was composed actually of the refuse of all classes. This composition made it seem that the mob and its representatives had abolished class differences, that those standing out- side the class-divided nation were the people itself (the *Volksgemeinschaft,* as the Nazis would call it) rather than its distortion and caricature. The historical pessimists understood the essential irresponsibility of this new social stratum, and they also correctly foresaw the possibility of converting democracy into a despotism whose tyrants would rise from the mob and lean on it for support. What they failed to understand was that the mob is not only the refuse but also the by-product of bourgeois society, directly produced by it and therefore never quite separable from it. They failed for this reason to notice high society's constantly growing admiration for the underworld, which runs like a red thread through the nineteenth century, its continuous step-by-step retreat on all questions of morality, and its growing taste for the anarchical cynicism of its offspring. At the turn of the century, the Dreyfus Affair showed that underworld and high society in France were so closely bound together that it was difficult definitely to place any of the "heroes" among the Anti-Dreyfusards in either category.

This feeling of kinship, the joining together of begetter and offspring, already classically expressed in Balzac's novels, antedates all practical eco- nomic, political, or social considerations and recalls those fundamental psychological traits of the new type of Western man that Hobbes outlined three hundred years ago. But it is true that it was mainly due to the insights acquired by the bourgeoisie during the crises and depressions which preceded imperialism that high society finally admitted its readiness to accept the revolutionary change in moral standards which Hobbes's "realism" had proposed, and which was now being proposed anew by the mob and its leaders. The very fact that the "original sin" of "original accumulation of capital" would need additional sins to keep the system going was far more effective in persuading the bourgeoisie to shake off the restraints of Western tradition than either its philosopher or its underworld. It finally induced the German bourgeoisie to throw off the mask of hypocrisy and openly confess its relationship to the mob, calling on it expressly to champion its property interests.

It is significant that this should have happened in Germany. In England and Holland the development of bourgeois society had progressed relatively quietly and the bourgeoisie of these countries enjoyed centuries of security and freedom from fear. Its rise in France, however, was interrupted by a great popular revolution whose consequences interfered with the bourgeoisie's enjoyment of supremacy. In Germany, moreover, where the bourgeoisie did not reach full development until the latter half of the nineteenth century, its rise was accompanied from the start by the growth of a revolutionary working-class movement with a tradition nearly as old as its own. It was a matter of course that the less secure a bourgeois class felt in its own country, the more it would be tempted to shed the heavy burden of hypocrisy. High society's affinity with the mob came to light in France earlier than in Germany, but was in the end equally strong in both countries. France, however, because of her revolutionary traditions and her relative lack of industrialization, produced only a relatively small mob, so that her bourgeoisie was finally forced to look for help beyond the frontiers and to ally itself with Hitler Germany.

Whatever the precise nature of the long historical evolution of the bourgeoisie in the various European countries, the political principles of the mob, as encountered in imperialist ideologies and totalitarian movements, betray a surprisingly strong affinity with the political attitudes of bourgeois society, if the latter are cleansed of hypocrisy and untainted by concessions to Christian tradition. What more recently made the nihilistic attitudes of the mob so intellectually attractive to the bourgeoisie is a relationship of principle that goes far beyond the actual birth of the mob.

In other words, the disparity between cause and effect which characterized the birth of imperialism has its reasons. The occasion—superfluous wealth created by overaccumulation, which needed the mob's help to find safe and profitable investment—set in motion a force that had always lain in the basic structure of bourgeois society, though it had been hidden by nobler traditions and by that blessed hypocrisy which La Rochefoucauld called the compliment vice pays to virtue. At the same time, completely unprincipled power politics could not be played until a mass of people was available who were free of all principles and so large numerically that they surpassed the ability of state and society to take care of them. The fact that this mob could be used only by imperialist politicians and inspired only by racial doctrines made it appear as though imperialism alone were able to settle the grave domestic, social, and economic problems of modern times.

The philosophy of Hobbes, it is true, contains nothing of modern race doctrines, which not only stir up the mob, but in their totalitarian form outline very clearly the forms of organization through which humanity could carry the endless process of capital and power accumulation through to its logical end in self-destruction. But Hobbes at least provided political thought with the prerequisite for all race doctrines, that is, the exclusion in principle of the idea of humanity which constitutes the sole regulating idea of international law. With the assumption that foreign politics is necessarily outside of the human contract, engaged in the perpetual war of all against all, which is the law of the "state of nature," Hobbes affords the best possible theoretical foundation for those naturalistic ideologies which hold nations to be tribes, separated from each other by nature, without any connection whatever, unconscious of the solidarity of mankind and having in common only the instinct for self-preservation which man shares with the animal world. If the idea of humanity, of which the most conclusive symbol is the common origin of the human species, is no longer valid, then nothing is more plausible than a theory according to which brown, yellow, or black races are descended from some other species of apes than the white race, and that all together are predestined by nature to war against each other until they have disappeared from the face of the earth.

If it should prove to be true that we are imprisoned in Hobbes's endless process of power accumulation, then the organization of the mob will inevitably take the form of transformation of nations into races, for there is, under the conditions of an accumulating society, no other unifying bond available between individuals who in the very process of power accumulation and expansion are losing all natural connections with their fellow-men.

Racism may indeed carry out the doom of the Western world and, for that matter, of the whole of human civilization. When Russians have become Slavs, when Frenchmen have assumed the role of commanders of a *force noire,* when Englishmen have turned into "white men," as already for a disastrous spell all Germans became Aryans, then this change will itself signify the end of Western man. For no matter what learned scientists may say, race is, politically speaking, not the beginning of humanity but its end, not the origin of peoples but their decay, not the natural birth of man but his unnatural death.

CHAPTER TWO

Race-Thinking Before
Racism

I F RACE-THINKING were a German invention, as it has been sometimes
asserted, then "German thinking" (whatever that may be) was victorious in many parts of the spiritual world long before the Nazis started
their ill-fated attempt at world conquest. Hitlerism exercised its strong
international and inter-European appeal during the thirties because racism,
although a state doctrine only in Germany, had been a powerful trend in
public opinion everywhere. The Nazi political war machine had long been
in motion when in 1939 German tanks began their march of destruction,
since—in political warfare—racism was calculated to be a more powerful
ally than any paid agent or secret organization of fifth columnists.
Strengthened by the experiences of almost two decades in the various capitals, the Nazis were confident that their best "propaganda" would be their
racial policy itself, from which, despite many other compromises and
broken promises, they had never swerved for expediency's sake.[1] Racism
was neither a new nor a secret weapon, though never before had it been
used with this thoroughgoing consistency.

The historical truth of the matter is that race-thinking, with its roots
deep in the eighteenth century, emerged simultaneously in all Western
countries during the nineteenth century. Racism has been the powerful
ideology of imperialistic policies since the turn of our century. It certainly
has absorbed and revived all the old patterns of race opinions which, however, by themselves would hardly have been able to create or, for that
matter, to degenerate into racism as a *Weltanschauung* or an ideology. In
the middle of the last century, race opinions were still judged by the
yardstick of political reason: Tocqueville wrote to Gobineau about the
latter's doctrines, "They are probably wrong and certainly pernicious." [2]
Not until the end of the century were dignity and importance accorded
race-thinking as though it had been one of the major spiritual contribu-
tions of the Western world.[3]

[1] During the German-Russian pact, Nazi propaganda stopped all attacks on "Bolshevism" but never gave up the race-line.

[2] "Lettres de Alexis de Tocqueville et de Arthur de Gobineau," in *Revue des Deux
Mondes,* 1907, Tome 199, Letter of November 17, 1853.

[3] The best historical account of race-thinking in the pattern of a "history of ideas"
is Erich Voegelin, *Rasse und Staat,* Tuebingen, 1933.

Until the fateful days of the "scramble for Africa," race-thinking had been one of the many free opinions which, within the general framework of liberalism, argued and fought each other to win the consent of public opinion.[4] Only a few of them became full-fledged ideologies, that is, systems based upon a single opinion that proved strong enough to attract and persuade a majority of people and broad enough to lead them through the various experiences and situations of an average modern life. For an ideology differs from a simple opinion in that it claims to possess either the key to history, or the solution for all the "riddles of the universe," or the intimate knowledge of the hidden universal laws which are supposed to rule nature and man. Few ideologies have won enough prominence to survive the hard competitive struggle of persuasion, and only two have come out on top and essentially defeated all others: the ideology which interprets history as an economic struggle of classes, and the other that interprets history as a natural fight of races. The appeal of both to large masses was so strong that they were able to enlist state support and establish themselves as official national doctrines. But far beyond the boundaries within which race-thinking and class-thinking have developed into obligatory patterns of thought, free public opinion has adopted them to such an extent that not only intellectuals but great masses of people will no longer accept a presentation of past or present facts that is not in agreement with either of these views.

The tremendous power of persuasion inherent in the main ideologies of our times is not accidental. Persuasion is not possible without appeal to either experiences or desires, in other words to immediate political needs. Plausibility in these matters comes neither from scientific facts, as the various brands of Darwinists would like us to believe, nor from historical laws, as the historians pretend, in their efforts to discover the law according to which civilizations rise and fall. Every full-fledged ideology has been created, continued and improved as a political weapon and not as a theoretical doctrine. It is true that sometimes—and such is the case with racism—an ideology has changed its original political sense, but without immediate contact with political life none of them could be imagined. Their scientific aspect is secondary and arises first from the desire to provide watertight arguments, and second because their persuasive power also got hold of scientists, who no longer were interested in the result of their research but left their laboratories and hurried off to preach to the multitude their new interpretations of life and world.[5] We owe it to these

[4] For the host of nineteenth-century conflicting opinions see Carlton J. H. Hayes, *A Generation of Materialism*, New York, 1941, pp. 111-122.

[5] "Huxley neglected scientific research of his own from the '70's onward, so busy was he in the role of 'Darwin's bulldog' barking and biting at theologians" (Hayes, *op. cit.*, p. 126). Ernst Haeckel's passion for popularizing scientific results which was at least as strong as his passion for science itself, has been stressed recently by an applauding Nazi writer, H. Bruecher, "Ernst Haeckel, Ein Wegbereiter biologischen Staatsdenkens." In *Nationalsozialistische Monatshefte*, 1935, Heft 69.

Two rather extreme examples may be quoted to show what scientists are capable

"scientific" preachers rather than to any scientific findings that today no single science is left into whose categorical system race-thinking has not deeply penetrated. This again has made historians, some of whom have been tempted to hold science responsible for race-thinking, mistake certain either philological or biological research results for causes instead of consequences of race-thinking.[5] The opposite would have come closer to the truth. As a matter of fact, the doctrine that Might is Right needed several centuries (from the seventeenth to the nineteenth) to conquer natural science and produce the "law" of the survival of the fittest. And if, to take another instance, the theory of de Maistre and Schelling about savage tribes as the decaying residues of former peoples had suited the nineteenth-century political devices as well as the theory of progress, we would probably never have heard much of "primitives" and no scientist would have wasted his time looking for the "missing link" between ape and man. The blame is not to be laid on any science as such, but rather on certain scientists who were no less hypnotized by ideologies than their fellow-citizens.

The fact that racism is the main ideological weapon of imperialistic politics is so obvious that it seems as though many students prefer to avoid the beaten track of truism. Instead, an old misconception of racism

of. Both were scholars of good standing, writing during World War I. The German historian of art, Josef Strzygowski, in his *Altai, Iran und Völkerwanderung* (Leipzig, 1917) discovered the Nordic race to be composed of Germans, Ukrainians, Armenians, Persians, Hungarians, Bulgars and Turks (pp. 306-307). The Society of Medicine of Paris not only published a report on the discovery of "polychesia" (excessive defecation) and "bromidrosis" (body odor) in the German race, but proposed urinalysis for the detection of German spies; German urine was "found" to contain 20 per cent non-uric nitrogen as against 15 per cent for other races. See Jacques Barzun, *Race,* New York, 1937, p. 239.

[5] This *quid pro quo* was partly the result of the zeal of students who wanted to put down every single instance in which race has been mentioned. Thereby they mistook relatively harmless authors, for whom explanation by race was a possible and sometimes fascinating opinion, for full-fledged racists. Such opinions, in themselves harmless, were advanced by the early anthropologists as starting points of their investigations. A typical instance is the naïve hypothesis of Paul Broca, noted French anthropologist of the middle of the last century, who assumed that "the brain has something to do with race and the measured shape of the skull is the best way to get at the contents of the brain" (quoted after Jacques Barzun, *op. cit.,* p. 162). It is obvious that this assertion, without the support of a conception of the nature of man, is simply ridiculous.

As for the philologists of the early nineteenth century, whose concept of "Aryanism" has seduced almost every student of racism to count them among the propagandists or even inventors of race-thinking, they are as innocent as innocent can be. When they overstepped the limits of pure research it was because they wanted to include in the same cultural brotherhood as many nations as possible. In the words of Ernest Seillière, *La Philosophie de l'Impérialisme,* 4 vols., 1903-1906: "There was a kind of intoxication: modern civilization believed it had recovered its pedigree . . . and an organism was born which embraced in one and the same fraternity all nations whose language showed some affinity with Sanskrit." (Préface, Tome I, p. xxxv.) In other words, these men were still in the humanistic tradition of the eighteenth century and shared its enthusiasm about strange people and exotic cultures.

as a kind of exaggerated nationalism is still given currency. Valuable works of students, especially in France, who have proved that racism is not only a quite different phenomenon but tends to destroy the body politic of the nation, are generally overlooked. Witnessing the gigantic competition between race-thinking and class-thinking for dominion over the minds of modern men, some have been inclined to see in the one the expression of national and in the other the expression of international trends, to believe the one to be the mental preparation for national wars and the other to be the ideology for civil wars. This has been possible because of the first World War's curious mixture of old national and new imperialistic conflicts, a mixture in which old national slogans proved still to possess a far greater appeal to the masses of all countries involved than any imperialistic aims. The last war, however, with its Quislings and collaborationists everywhere, should have proved that racism can stir up civil conflicts in every country, and is one of the most ingenious devices ever invented for preparing civil war.

For the truth is that race-thinking entered the scene of active politics the moment the European peoples had prepared, and to a certain extent realized, the new body politic of the nation. From the very beginning, racism deliberately cut across all national boundaries, whether defined by geographical, linguistic, traditional, or any other standards, and denied national-political existence as such. Race-thinking, rather than class-thinking, was the ever-present shadow accompanying the development of the comity of European nations, until it finally grew to be the powerful weapon for the destruction of those nations. Historically speaking, racists have a worse record of patriotism than the representatives of all other international ideologies together, and they were the only ones who consistently denied the great principle upon which national organizations of peoples are built, the principle of equality and solidarity of all peoples guaranteed by the idea of mankind.

I: *A "Race" of Aristocrats Against a "Nation" of Citizens*

A STEADILY rising interest in the most different, strange, and even savage peoples was characteristic of France during the eighteenth century. This was the time when Chinese paintings were admired and imitated, when one of the most famous works of the century was named *Lettres Persanes,* and when travelers' reports were the favorite reading of society. The honesty and simplicity of savage and uncivilized peoples were opposed to the sophistication and frivolity of culture. Long before the nineteenth century with its tremendously enlarged opportunities for travel brought the non-European world into the home of every average citizen, eighteenth-century French society had tried to grasp spiritually the content of cultures and countries that lay far beyond European boundaries. A great enthusiasm for "new specimens of mankind" (Herder) filled the hearts of the heroes of the French Revolution who together with the French nation liberated every people of every color under the French flag. This enthusiasm for strange and foreign countries culminated in the message of fraternity, because it was inspired by the desire to prove in every new and surprising "specimen of mankind" the old saying of La Bruyère: *"La raison est de tous les climats."*

Yet it is this nation-creating century and humanity-loving country to which we must trace the germs of what later proved to become the nation-destroying and humanity-annihilating power of racism.[7] It is a remarkable fact that the first author who assumed the coexistence of different peoples with different origins in France, was at the same time the first to elaborate definite class-thinking. The Comte de Boulainvilliers, a French nobleman who wrote at the beginning of the eighteenth century and whose works were published after his death, interpreted the history of France as the history of two different nations of which the one, of Germanic origin, had conquered the older inhabitants, the "Gaules," had imposed its laws upon them, had taken their lands, and had settled down as the ruling class, the "peerage" whose supreme rights rested upon the "right of conquest" and the "necessity of obedience always due to the strongest."[8] Engaged chiefly in finding arguments against the rising political power of the *Tiers Etat* and their spokesmen, the *"nouveau corps"* formed by *"gens de lettres et de lois,"* Boulainvilliers had to fight the monarchy too because the French king wanted no longer to represent the peerage as *primus inter pares* but the nation as a whole; in him, for a while, the new rising class found its most powerful protector. In order to regain uncontested primacy for the nobility, Boulainvilliers proposed that his fellow-noblemen deny a common origin with the French people, break up the unity of the nation, and claim an original and therefore eternal distinction.[9] Much bolder than most of the later defenders of nobility, Boulainvilliers denied any predestined connection with the soil; he conceded that the "Gaules" had been in France longer, that the "Francs" were strangers and barbarians. He based his doctrine solely on the eternal right of conquest and found no difficulty in asserting that "Friesland . . . has been the true cradle of the French nation." Centuries before the actual development of imperialistic racism, following only the inherent logic of his concept, he considered the original inhabitants of France natives in the modern sense, or in his own terms "subjects"—not of

[7] François Hotman, French sixteenth-century author of *Franco-Gallia,* is sometimes held to be a forerunner of eighteenth-century racial doctrines, as by Ernest Seillière, *op. cit.* Against this misconception, Théophile Simar has rightly protested: "Hotman appears, not as an apologist for the Teutons, but as the defender of the people which was oppressed by the monarchy" (*Etude Critique sur la Formation de la doctrine des Races au 18e et son expansion au 19e siècle,* Bruxelles, 1922, p. 20).

[8] *Histoire de l'Ancien Gouvernement de la France,* 1727, Tome I, p. 33.

[9] That the Comte Boulainvilliers' history was meant as a political weapon against the *Tiers Etat* was stated by Montesquieu, *Esprit des Lois,* 1748, XXX, chap. x.

the king—but of all those whose advantage was descent from the conquering people, who by right of birth were to be called "Frenchmen."

Boulainvilliers was deeply influenced by the seventeenth-century might-right doctrines and he certainly was one of the most consistent contemporary disciples of Spinoza, whose *Ethics* he translated and whose *Traité théologico-politique* he analyzed. In his reception and application of Spinoza's political ideas, might was changed into conquest and conquest acted as a kind of unique judgment on the natural qualities and human privileges of men and nations. In this we may detect the first traces of later naturalistic transformations the might-right doctrine was to go through. This view is really corroborated by the fact that Boulainvilliers was one of the outstanding freethinkers of his time, and that his attacks on the Christian Church were hardly motivated by anticlericalism alone.

Boulainvilliers' theory, however, still deals with peoples and not with races; it bases the right of the superior people on a historical deed, conquest, and not on a physical fact—although the historical deed already has a certain influence on the natural qualities of the conquered people. It invents two different peoples within France in order to counteract the new national idea, represented as it was to a certain extent by the absolute monarchy in alliance with the *Tiers Etat*. Boulainvilliers is antinational at a time when the idea of nationhood was felt to be new and revolutionary, but had not yet shown, as it did in the French Revolution, how closely it was connected with a democratic form of government. Boulainvilliers prepared his country for civil war without knowing what civil war meant. He is representative of many of the nobles who did not regard themselves as representative of the nation, but as a separate ruling caste which might have much more in common with a foreign people of the "same society and condition" than with its compatriots. It has been, indeed, these antinational trends that exercised their influence in the milieu of the *émigrés* and finally were absorbed by new and outspoken racial doctrines late in the nineteenth century.

Not until the actual outbreak of the Revolution forced great numbers of the French nobility to seek refuge in Germany and England did Boulainvilliers' ideas show their usefulness as a political weapon. In the meantime, his influence upon the French aristocracy was kept alive, as can be seen in the works of another Comte, the Comte Dubuat-Nançay,[10] who wanted to tie French nobility even closer to its continental brothers. On the eve of the Revolution, this spokesman of French feudalism felt so insecure that he hoped for "the creation of a kind of *Internationale* of aristocracy of barbarian origin,"[11] and since the German nobility was the only one whose help could eventually be expected, here too the true origin of the French nation was supposed to be identical with that of the Germans and the French lower classes, though no longer slaves, were not free by birth but

[10] *Les Origines de l'Ancien Gouvernement de la France, de l'Allemagne et de l'Italie,* 1789.

[11] Seillière, *op. cit.,* p. xxxii.

by *"affranchissement,"* by grace of those who were free by birth, of the nobility. A few years later the French exiles actually tried to form an *internationale* of aristocrats in order to stave off the revolt of those they considered to be a foreign enslaved people. And although the more practical side of these attempts suffered the spectacular disaster of Valmy, *émigrés* like Charles François Dominique de Villiers, who about 1800 opposed the *"Gallo-Romains"* to the Germanics, or like William Alter who a decade later dreamed of a federation of all Germanic peoples,[12] did not admit defeat. It probably never occurred to them that they were actually traitors, so firmly were they convinced that the French Revolution was a "war between foreign peoples"—as François Guizot much later put it.

While Boulainvilliers, with the calm fairness of a less disturbed time, based the rights of nobility solely on the rights of conquest without directly depreciating the very nature of the other conquered nation, the Comte de Montlosier, one of the rather dubious personages among the French exiles, openly expressed his contempt for this "new people risen from slaves . . . (a mixture) of all races and all times." [13] Times obviously had changed and noblemen who no longer belonged to an unconquered race also had to change. They gave up the old idea, so dear to Boulainvilliers and even to Montesquieu, that conquest alone, *fortune des armes,* determined the destinies of men. The Valmy of noble ideologies came when the Abbé Siéyès in his famous pamphlet told the *Tiers Etat* to "send back into the forests of Franconia all those families who preserve the absurd pretension of being descended from the conquering race and of having succeeded to their rights." [14]

It is rather curious that from these early times when French noblemen in their class struggle against the bourgeoisie discovered that they belonged to another nation, had another genealogical origin, and were more closely tied to an international caste than to the soil of France, all French racial theories have supported the Germanism or at least the superiority of the Nordic peoples as against their own countrymen. For if the men of the French Revolution identified themselves mentally with Rome, it was not because they opposed to the "Germanism" of their nobility a "Latinism" of the *Tiers Etat,* but because they felt they were the spiritual heirs of Roman Republicans. This historical claim, in contrast to the tribal identification of the nobility, might have been among the causes that prevented "Latinism" from emerging as a racial doctrine of its own. In any event, paradoxical as it sounds, the fact is that Frenchmen were to insist earlier than Germans

[12] See René Maunier, *Sociologie Coloniale,* Paris, 1932, Tome II, p. 115.

[13] Montlosier, even in exile, was closely connected with the French chief of police, Fouché, who helped him improve the sad financial conditions of a refugee. Later, he served as a secret agent for Napoleon in French society. See Joseph Brugerette, *Le Comte de Montlosier,* 1931, and Simar, *op. cit.,* p. 71.

[14] *Qu'est-ce-que le Tiers Etat?* (1789) published shortly before the outbreak of the Revolution. Translation quoted after J. H. Clapham, *The Abbé Siéyès,* London, 1912, p. 62.

or Englishmen on this *idée fixe* of Germanic superiority.[15] Nor did the
birth of German racial consciousness after the Prussian defeat of 1806,
directed as it was against the French, change the course of racial ideologies
in France. In the forties of the last century, Augustin Thierry still adhered
to the identification of classes and races and distinguished between a
"Germanic nobility" and a "celtic bourgeoisie," [16] and again a nobleman,
the Comte de Rémusat, proclaimed the Germanic origin of the European
aristocracy. Finally, the Comte de Gobineau developed an opinion already
generally accepted among the French nobility into a full-fledged historical
doctrine, claiming to have detected the secret law of the fall of civilizations
and to have exalted history to the dignity of a natural science. With him
race-thinking completed its first stage, and began its second stage whose
influences were to be felt until the twenties of our century.

ii: *Race Unity as a Substitute for National Emancipation*

RACE-THINKING in Germany did not develop before the defeat of the old
Prussian army by Napoleon. It owed its rise to the Prussian patriots and
political romanticism, rather than to the nobility and their spokesmen. In
contrast to the French brand of race-thinking as a weapon for civil war
and for splitting the nation, German race-thinking was invented in an effort
to unite the people against foreign domination. Its authors did not look
for allies beyond the frontiers but wanted to awaken in the people a
consciousness of common origin. This actually excluded the nobility with
their notoriously cosmopolitan relations—which, however, were less characteristic of the Prussian Junkers than of the rest of the European nobility;
at any rate, it excluded the possibility of this race-thinking basing itself
on the most exclusive class of the people.

Since German race-thinking accompanied the long frustrated attempts
to unite the numerous German states, it remained so closely connected, in
its early stages, with more general national feelings that it is rather difficult
to distinguish between mere nationalism and clear-cut racism. Harmless
national sentiments expressed themselves in what we know today to be
racial terms, so that even historians who identify the twentieth-century
German brand of racism with the peculiar language of German nationalism
have strangely been led into mistaking Nazism for German nationalism,
thereby helping to underestimate the tremendous international appeal of
Hitler's propaganda. These particular conditions of German nationalism
changed only when, after 1870, the unification of the nation actually had
taken place and German racism, together with German imperialism, fully
developed. From these early times, however, not a few characteristics sur-

---

[15] "Historical Aryanism has its origin in 18th century feudalism and was supported
by 19th century Germanism" observes Seillière, *op. cit.*, p. ii.
[16] *Lettres sur l'histoire de France* (1840).

vived which have remained significant for the specifically German brand of race-thinking.

In contrast to France, Prussian noblemen felt their interests to be closely connected with the position of the absolute monarchy and, at least since the time of Frederick II, they sought recognition as the legitimate representatives of the nation as a whole. With the exception of the few years of Prussian reforms (from 1808-1812), the Prussian nobility was not frightened by the rise of a bourgeois class that might have wanted to take over the government, nor did they have to fear a coalition between the middle classes and the ruling house. The Prussian king, until 1809 the greatest landlord of the country, remained *primus inter pares* despite all efforts of the Reformers. Race-thinking, therefore, developed outside the nobility, as a weapon of certain nationalists who wanted the union of all German-speaking peoples and therefore insisted on a common origin. They were liberals in the sense that they were rather opposed to the exclusive rule of the Prussian Junkers. As long as this common origin was defined by common language, one can hardly speak of race-thinking.[17]

It is noteworthy that only after 1814 is this common origin described frequently in terms of "blood relationship," of family ties, of tribal unity, of unmixed origin. These definitions, which appear almost simultaneously in the writings of the Catholic Josef Goerres and nationalistic liberals like Ernst Moritz Arndt or F. L. Jahn, bear witness to the utter failure of the hopes of rousing true national sentiments in the German people. Out of the failure to raise the people to nationhood, out of the lack of common historical memories and the apparent popular apathy to common destinies in the future, a naturalistic appeal was born which addressed itself to tribal instincts as a possible substitute for what the whole world had seen to be the glorious power of French nationhood. The organic doctrine of a history for which "every race is a separate, complete whole"[18] was invented by men who needed ideological definitions of national unity as a substitute for political nationhood. It was a frustrated nationalism that led to Arndt's statement that Germans—who apparently were the last to develop an organic unity—had the luck to be of pure, unmixed stock, a "genuine people."[19]

Organic naturalistic definitions of peoples are an outstanding characteristic of German ideologies and German historism. They nevertheless are not yet actual racism, for the same men who speak in these "racial" terms still uphold the central pillar of genuine nationhood, the equality of all peoples. Thus, in the same article in which Jahn compares the laws of peoples with

[17] This is the case for instance in Friedrich Schlegel's *Philosophische Vorlesungen aus den Jahren 1804-1806,* II, 357. The same holds true for Ernst Moritz Arndt. See Alfred P. Pundt, *Arndt and the National Awakening in Germany,* New York, 1935, pp. 116 f. Even Fichte, the favorite modern scapegoat for German race-thinking, hardly ever went beyond the limits of nationalism.

[18] Joseph Goerres, in *Rheinischer Merkur,* 1814, No. 25.

[19] In *Phantasien zur Berichtigung der Urteile über künftige deutsche Verfassungen,* 1815.

the laws of animal life, he insists on the genuine equal plurality of peoples in whose complete multitude alone mankind can be realized.[20] And Arndt, who later was to express strong sympathies with the national liberation movements of the Poles and the Italians, exclaimed: "Cursed be anyone who would subjugate and rule foreign peoples." [21] Insofar as German national feelings had not been the fruit of a genuine national development but rather the reaction to foreign occupation,[22] national doctrines were of a peculiar negative character, destined to create a wall around the people, to act as substitutes for frontiers which could not be clearly defined either geographically or historically.

If, in the early form of French aristocracy, race-thinking had been invented as an instrument of internal division and had turned out to be a weapon for civil war, this early form of German race-doctrine was invented as a weapon of internal national unity and turned out to be a weapon for national wars. As the decline of the French nobility as an important class in the French nation would have made this weapon useless if the foes of the Third Republic had not revived it, so upon the accomplishment of German national unity the organic doctrine of history would have lost its meaning had not modern imperialistic schemers wanted to revive it, in order to appeal to the people and to hide their hideous faces under the respectable cover of nationalism. The same does not hold true for another source of German racism which, though seemingly more remote from the scene of politics, had a far stronger genuine bearing upon later political ideologies.

Political romanticism has been accused of inventing race-thinking, as it has been and could be accused of inventing every other possible irresponsible opinion. Adam Mueller and Friedrich Schlegel are symptomatic in the highest degree of a general playfulness of modern thought in which almost any opinion can gain ground temporarily. No real thing, no historical event, no political idea was safe from the all-embracing and all-destroying mania by which these first literati could always find new and original opportunities for new and fascinating opinions. "The world must be romanticized," as Novalis put it, wanting "to bestow a high sense upon the common, a mysterious appearance upon the ordinary, the dignity of the unknown upon

[20] "Animals of mixed stock have no real generative power; similarly, hybrid peoples have no folk propagation of their own. . . . The ancestor of humanity is dead, the original race is extinct. That is why each dying people is a misfortune for humanity. . . . Human nobility cannot express itself in one people alone." In *Deutsches Volkstum*, 1810.

The same instance is expressed by Goerres, who despite his naturalistic definition of people ("all members are united by a common tie of blood"), follows a true national principle when he states: "No branch has a right to dominate the other" (*op. cit.*).

[21] *Blick aus der Zeit auf die Zeit*, 1814.—Translation quoted from Alfred P. Pundt, *op. cit.*

[22] "Not until Austria and Prussia had fallen after a vain struggle did I really begin to love Germany . . . as Germany succumbed to conquest and subjection it became to me one and indissoluble," writes E. M. Arndt in his *Erinnerungen aus Schweden*, 1818, p. 82. Translation quoted from Pundt, *op. cit.*, p. 151.

the well-known." [23] One of these romanticized objects was the people, an object that could be changed at a moment's notice into the state, or the family, or nobility, or anything else that either—in the earlier days—happened to cross the minds of one of these intellectuals or—later when, growing older, they had learned the reality of daily bread—happened to be asked for by some paying patron.[24] Therefore it is almost impossible to study the development of any of the free competing opinions of which the nineteenth century is so amazingly full, without coming across romanticism in its German form.

What these first modern intellectuals actually prepared was not so much the development of any single opinion but the general mentality of modern German scholars; these latter have proved more than once that hardly an ideology can be found to which they would not willingly submit if the only reality—which even a romantic can hardly afford to overlook—is at stake, the reality of their position. For this peculiar behavior, romanticism provided the most excellent pretext in its unlimited idolization of the "personality" of the individual, whose very arbitrariness became the proof of genius. Whatever served the so-called productivity of the individual, namely, the entirely arbitrary game of his "ideas," could be made the center of a whole outlook on life and world.

This inherent cynicism of romantic personality-worship has made possible certain modern attitudes among intellectuals. They were fairly well represented by Mussolini, one of the last heirs of this movement, when he described himself as at the same time "aristocrat and democrat, revolutionary and reactionary, proletarian and antiproletarian, pacifist and antipacifist." The ruthless individualism of romanticism never meant anything more serious than that "everybody is free to create for himself his own ideology." What was new in Mussolini's experiment was the "attempt to carry it out with all possible energy." [25]

Because of this inherent "relativism" the direct contribution of romanticism to the development of race-thinking can almost be neglected. In the anarchic game whose rules entitle everybody at any given time to at least one personal and arbitrary opinion, it is almost a matter of course that every conceivable opinion should be formulated and duly printed. Much more characteristic than this chaos was the fundamental belief in personality as an ultimate aim in itself. In Germany, where the conflict between the nobility and the rising middle class was never fought out on the political scene, personality worship developed as the only means of gaining at least some kind of social emancipation. The governing class of the country frankly showed its traditional contempt for business and its dislike for association with merchants in spite of the latter's growing wealth and importance, so that it

[23] "Neue Fragmentensammlung" (1798) in *Schriften*, Leipzig, 1929, Tome II, p. 335.
[24] For the romantic attitude in Germany see Carl Schmitt, *Politische Romantik*, München, 1925.
[25] Mussolini, "Relativismo e Fascismo," in *Diuturna*, Milano, 1924. The translation quoted from F. Neumann, *Behemoth*, 1942, pp. 462-463.

was not easy to find the means of winning some kind of self-respect. The classic German *Bildungsroman, Wilhelm Meister,* in which the middle-class hero is educated by noblemen and actors because the bourgeois in his own social sphere is without "personality," is evidence enough of the hopelessness of the situation.

German intellectuals, though they hardly promoted a political fight for the middle classes to which they belonged, fought an embittered and, unfortunately, highly successful battle for social status. Even those who had written in defense of nobility still felt their own interests at stake when it came to social ranks. In order to enter competition with rights and qualities of birth, they formulated the new concept of the "innate personality" which was to win general approval within bourgeois society. Like the title of the heir of an old family, the "innate personality" was given by birth and not acquired by merit. Just as the lack of common history for the formation of the nation had been artificially overcome by the naturalistic concept of organic development, so, in the social sphere, nature itself was supposed to supply a title when political reality had refused it. Liberal writers soon boasted of "true nobility" as opposed to the shabby titles of Baron or others which could be given and taken away, and asserted, by implication, that their natural privileges, like "force or genius," could not be retraced to any human deed.[26]

The discriminatory point of this new social concept was immediately affirmed. During the long period of mere social antisemitism, which introduced and prepared the discovery of Jew-hating as a political weapon, it was the lack of "innate personality," the innate lack of tact, the innate lack of productivity, the innate disposition for trading, etc., which separated the behavior of his Jewish colleague from that of the average businessman. In its feverish attempt to summon up some pride of its own against the caste arrogance of the Junkers, without, however, daring to fight for political leadership, the bourgeoisie from the very beginning wanted to look down not so much on other lower classes of their own, but simply on other peoples. Most significant for these attempts is the small literary work of Clemens Brentano[27] which was written for and read in the ultranationalistic club of Napoleon-haters that gathered together in 1808 under the name of "Die Christlich-Deutsche Tischgesellschaft." In his highly sophisticated and witty manner, Brentano points out the contrast between the "innate personality," the genial individual, and the "philistine" whom he immediately identifies with Frenchmen and Jews. Thereafter, the German bourgeois would at least try to attribute to other peoples all the qualities which the nobility despised as typically bourgeois—at first to the French, later to the English, and always to the Jews. As for the mysterious qualities which an "innate person-

---

[26] See the very interesting pamphlet against the nobility by the liberal writer Buchholz, *Untersuchungen ueber den Geburtsadel,* Berlin, 1807, p. 68: "True nobility . . . cannot be given or taken away; for, like power and genius, it sets itself and exists by itself."

[27] Clemens Brentano, *Der Philister vor, in und nach der Geschichte,* 1811.

ality" received at birth, they were exactly the same as those the real Junkers claimed for themselves.

Although in this way standards of nobility contributed to the rise of race-thinking, the Junkers themselves did hardly anything for the shaping of this mentality. The only Junker of this period to develop a political theory of his own, Ludwig von der Marwitz, never used racial terms. According to him, nations were separated by language—a spiritual and not a physical difference—and although he was violently opposed to the French Revolution, he spoke like Robespierre when it came to the possible aggression of one nation against another: "Who aims at expanding his frontiers should be considered a disloyal betrayer among the whole European republic of states." [28] It was Adam Mueller who insisted on purity of descent as a test of nobility, and it was Haller who went beyond the obvious fact that the powerful rule those deprived of power by stating it as a natural law that the weak should be dominated by the strong. Noblemen, of course, applauded enthusiastically when they learned that their usurpation of power was not only legal but in accordance with natural laws, and it was a consequence of bourgeois definitions that during the course of the nineteenth century they avoided "mesalliances" more carefully than ever before.[29]

This insistence on common tribal origin as an essential of nationhood, formulated by German nationalists during and after the war of 1814, and the emphasis laid by the romantics on the innate personality and natural nobility prepared the way intellectually for race-thinking in Germany. From the former sprang the organic doctrine of history with its natural laws; from the latter arose at the end of the century the grotesque homunculus of the superman whose natural destiny it is to rule the world. As long as these trends ran side by side, they were but temporary means of escape from political realities. Once welded together, they formed the very basis for racism as a full-fledged ideology. This, however, did not happen first in Germany, but in France, and was not accomplished by middle-class intellectuals but by a highly gifted and frustrated nobleman, the Comte de Gobineau.

III: *The New Key to History*

IN 1853, Count Arthur de Gobineau published his *Essai sur l'Inégalité des Races Humaines* which, only some fifty years later, at the turn of the century, was to become a kind of standard work for race theories in history.

[28] "Entwurf eines Friedenspaktes." In Gerhard Ramlow, *Ludwig von der Marwitz und die Anfänge konservativer Politik und Staatsauffassung in Preussen,* Historische Studien, Heft 185, p. 92.

[29] See Sigmund Neumann, *Die Stufen des preussischen Konservatismus,* Historische Studien, Heft 190, Berlin, 1930. Especially pp. 48, 51, 64, 82. For Adam Mueller, see *Elemente der Staatskunst,* 1809.

The first sentence of the four-volume work—"The fall of civilization is the most striking and, at the same time, the most obscure of all phenomena of history" [30]—indicates clearly the essentially new and modern interest of its author, the new pessimistic mood which pervades his work and which is the ideological force that was capable of uniting all previous factors and conflicting opinions. True, from time immemorial, mankind has wanted to know as much as possible about past cultures, fallen empires, extinct peoples; but nobody before Gobineau thought of finding one single reason, one single force according to which civilization always and everywhere rises and falls. Doctrines of decay seem to have some very intimate connection with race-thinking. It certainly is no coincidence that another early "believer in race," Benjamin Disraeli, was equally fascinated by the fall of cultures, while on the other hand Hegel, whose philosophy was concerned in great part with the dialectical law of development in history, was never interested in the rise and fall of cultures as such or in any law which would explain the death of nations: Gobineau demonstrated precisely such a law. Without Darwinism or any other evolutionist theory to influence him, this historian boasted of having introduced history into the family of natural sciences, detected the natural law of all courses of events, reduced all spiritual utterances or cultural phenomena to something "that by virtue of exact science our eyes can see, our ears can hear, our hands can touch."

The most surprising aspect of the theory, set forth in the midst of the optimistic nineteenth century, is the fact that the author is fascinated by the fall and hardly interested in the rise of civilizations. At the time of writing the *Essai* Gobineau gave but little thought to the possible use of his theory as a weapon in actual politics, and therefore had the courage to draw the inherent sinister consequences of his law of decay. In contrast to Spengler, who predicts only the fall of Western culture, Gobineau foresees with "scientific" precision nothing less than the definite disappearance of Man—or, in his words, of the human race—from the face of the earth. After four volumes of rewriting human history, he concludes: "One might be tempted to assign a total duration of 12 to 14 thousand years to human rule over the earth, which era is divided into two periods: the first has passed away and possessed the youth . . . the second has begun and will witness the declining course down toward decrepitude."

It has rightly been observed that Gobineau, thirty years before Nietzsche, was concerned with the problem of *"décadence."* [31] There is, however, this difference, that Nietzsche possessed the basic experience of European decadence, writing as he did during the climax of this movement with Baudelaire in France, Swinburne in England, and Wagner in Germany, whereas Gobineau was hardly aware of the variety of the modern *taedium vitae,* and must be regarded as the last heir of Boulainvilliers and the French

[30] Translation quoted from *The Inequality of Human Races,* translated by Adrien Collins, 1915.

[31] See Robert Dreyfus, "La vie et les prophéties du Comte de Gobineau," Paris, 1905, in *Cahiers de la quinzaine,* Ser. 6, Cah. 16, p. 56.

exiled nobility who, without psychological complications, simply (and rightly) feared for the fate of aristocracy as a caste. With a certain naïveté he accepted almost literally the eighteenth-century doctrines about the origin of the French people: the bourgeois are the descendants of Gallic-Roman slaves, noblemen are Germanic.[32] The same is true for his insistence on the international character of nobility. A more modern aspect of his theories is revealed in the fact that he possibly was an impostor (his French title being more than dubious), that he exaggerated and overstrained the older doctrines until they became frankly ridiculous—he claimed for himself a genealogy which led over a Scandinavian pirate to Odin: "I, too, am of the race of Gods."[33] But his real importance is that in the midst of progress-ideologies he prophesied doom, the end of mankind in a slow natural catastrophe. When Gobineau started his work, in the days of the bourgeois king, Louis Philippe, the fate of nobility appeared sealed. Nobility no longer needed to fear the victory of the *Tiers Etat,* it had already occurred and they could only complain. Their distress, as expressed by Gobineau, sometimes comes very near to the great despair of the poets of decadence who, a few decades later, sang the frailty of all things human— *les neiges d'antan,* the snows of yesteryear. As far as Gobineau himself was concerned, this affinity is rather incidental; but it is interesting to note that once this affinity was established, nothing could prevent very respectable intellectuals at the turn of the century, like Robert Dreyfus in France or Thomas Mann in Germany, from taking this descendant of Odin seriously. Long before the horrible and the ridiculous had merged into the humanly incomprehensible mixture that is the hallmark of our century, the ridiculous had lost its power to kill.

It is also to the peculiar pessimistic mood, to the active despair of the last decades of the century that Gobineau owed his belated fame. This, however, does not necessarily mean that he himself was a forerunner of the generation of "the merry dance of death and trade" (Joseph Conrad). He was neither a statesman who believed in business nor a poet who praised death. He was only a curious mixture of frustrated nobleman and romantic intellectual who invented racism almost by accident. This was when he saw that he could not simply accept the old doctrines of the two peoples within France and that, in view of changed circumstances, he had to revise the old line that the best men necessarily are at the top of society. In sad contrast to his teachers, he had to explain why the best men, noblemen, could not even hope to regain their former position. Step by step, he identified the fall of his caste with the fall of France, then of Western civilization, and then of the whole of mankind. Thus he made that discovery, for which he was so much admired by later writers and biographers, that the fall of civilizations is due to a degeneration of race and the decay of race is due to a mixture of blood. This implies that in every mixture the lower race is always dom-

<hr>

[32] *Essai,* Tome II, Book IV, p. 445, and the article "Ce qui est arrivé à la France en 1870," in *Europe,* 1923.

[33] J. Duesberg, "Le Comte de Gobineau," in *Revue Générale,* 1939.

inant. This kind of argumentation, almost commonplace after the turn of
the century, did not fit in with the progress-doctrines of Gobineau's contemporaries, who soon acquired another *idée fixe,* the "survival of the
fittest." The liberal optimism of the victorious bourgeoisie wanted a new
edition of the might-right theory, not the key to history or the proof of inevitable decay. Gobineau tried in vain to get a wider audience by taking a
side in the American slave issue and by conveniently building his whole
system on the basic conflict between white and black. He had to wait almost
fifty years to become a success among the elite, and not until the first World
War with its wave of death-philosophies could his works claim wide popularity.[34]

What Gobineau was actually looking for in politics was the definition and
creation of an "elite" to replace the aristocracy. Instead of princes, he
proposed a "race of princes," the Aryans, who he said were in danger of
being submerged by the lower non-Aryan classes through democracy. The
concept of race made it possible to organize the "innate personalities" of
German romanticism, to define them as members of a natural aristocracy
destined to rule over all others. If race and mixture of races are the all-
determining factors for the individual—and Gobineau did not assume the
existence of "pure" breeds—it is possible to pretend that physical superiori-
ties might evolve in every individual no matter what his present social situation, that every exceptional man belongs to the "true surviving sons of . . .
the Merovings," the "sons of kings." Thanks to race, an "elite" would be
formed which could lay claim to the old prerogatives of feudal families, and
this only by asserting that they felt like noblemen; the acceptance of the
race ideology as such would become conclusive proof that an individual was
"well-bred," that "blue blood" ran through his veins and that a superior
origin implied superior rights. From one political event, therefore, the decline
of the nobility, the Count drew two contradictory consequences—the decay
of the human race and the formation of a new natural aristocracy. But he did
not live to see the practical application of his teachings which resolved their
inherent contradictions—the new race-aristocracy actually began to effect
the "inevitable" decay of mankind in a supreme effort to destroy it.

Following the example of his forerunners, the exiled French noblemen,
Gobineau saw in his race-elite not only a bulwark against democracy but
also against the "Canaan monstrosity" of patriotism.[35] And since France
still happened to be the *"patrie" par excellence,* for her government—

[34] See the Gobineau memorial issue of the French review *Europe,* 1923. Especially
the article of Clément Serpeille de Gobineau, "Le Gobinisme et la pensée moderne."
"Yet it was not until . . . the middle of the war that I thought the *Essai sur les
Races* was inspired by a productive hypothesis, the only one that could explain certain
events happening before our eyes. . . . I was surprised to note that this opinion was
almost unanimously shared. After the war, I noticed that for nearly the whole younger
generation the works of Gobineau had become a revelation."

[35] *Essai,* Tome II, Book IV, p. 440 and note on p. 445: "The word *patrie* . . . has
regained its significance only since the Gallo-Roman strata rose and assumed a political role. With their triumph, patriotism has again become a virtue."

whether kingdom or Empire or Republic—was still based upon the essential
equality of men, and since, worst of all, she was the only country of his
time in which even people with black skin could enjoy civil rights, it was
natural for Gobineau to give allegiance not to the French people, but to
the English, and later, after the French defeat of 1871, to the Germans.[36]
Nor can this lack of dignity be called accidental and this opportunism an
unhappy coincidence. The old saying that nothing succeeds like success
reckons with people who are used to various and arbitrary opinions. Ideolo-
gists who pretend to possess the key to reality are forced to change and
twist their opinions about single cases according to the latest events and can
never afford to come into conflict with their ever-changing deity, reality.
It would be absurd to ask people to be reliable who by their very convictions
must justify any given situation.

It must be conceded that up to the time when the Nazis, in establishing
themselves as a race-elite, frankly bestowed their contempt on all peoples,
including the German, French racism was the most consistent, for it never
fell into the weakness of patriotism. (This attitude did not change even
during the last war; true, the *"essence aryenne"* no longer was a monopoly
of the Germans but rather of the Anglo-Saxons, the Swedes, and the Nor-
mans, but nation, patriotism, and law were still considered to be "prejudices,
fictitious and nominal values.") [37] Even Taine believed firmly in the superior
genius of the "Germanic nation," [38] and Ernest Renan was probably the
first to oppose the "Semites" to the "Aryans" in a decisive *"division du genre
humain,"* although he held civilization to be the great superior force which
destroys local originalities as well as original race differences.[39] All the loose
race talk that is so characteristic of French writers after 1870,[40] even if they
are not racists in any strict sense of the word, follows antinational, pro-
Germanic lines.

If the consistent antinational trend of Gobinism served to equip the
enemies of French democracy and, later, of the Third Republic, with real
or fictitious allies beyond the frontiers of their country, the specific amalgamation of the race and "elite" concepts equipped the international intelli-

[36] See Seillière, *op. cit.*, Tome I: *Le Comte de Gobineau et l'Aryanisme historique*,
p. 32: "In the *Essai* Germany is hardly Germanic, Great Britain is Germanic to a
much higher degree. . . . Certainly, Gobineau later changed his mind, but under the
influence of success." It is interesting to note that for Seillière who during his studies
became an ardent adherent of Gobinism—"the intellectual climate to which probably
the lungs of the 20th century will have to adapt themselves"—success appeared as
quite a sufficient reason for Gobineau's suddenly revised opinion.

[37] Examples could be multiplied. The quotation is taken from Camille Spiess,
Impérialismes. Gobinisme en France, Paris, 1917.

[38] For Taine's stand see John S. White, "Taine on Race and Genius," in *Social Research*, February, 1943.

[39] In Gobineau's opinion, the Semites were a white hybrid race bastardized by a
mixture with blacks. For Renan see *Histoire Générale et Système comparé des Langues*,
1863, Part I, pp. 4, 503, and *passim*. The same distinction in his *Langues Sémitiques*,
I, 15.

[40] This has been very well exposed by Jacques Barzun, *op. cit.*

gentsia with new and exciting psychological toys to play with on the great playground of history. Gobineau's *"fils des rois"* were close relatives of the romantic heroes, saints, geniuses and supermen of the late nineteenth century, all of whom can hardly hide their German romantic origin. The inherent irresponsibility of romantic opinions received a new stimulant from Gobineau's mixture of races, because this mixture showed a historical event of the past which could be traced in the depths of one's own self. This meant that inner experiences could be given historical significance, that one's own self had become the battlefield of history. "Since I read the *Essai,* every time some conflict stirred up the hidden sources of my being, I have felt that a relentless battle went on in my soul, the battle between the black, the yellow, the Semite and the Aryans." [41] Significant as this and similar confessions may be of the state of mind of modern intellectuals, who are the true heirs of romanticism whatever opinion they happen to hold, they nevertheless indicate the essential harmlessness and political innocence of people who probably could have been forced into line by each and every ideology.

IV: *The "Rights of Englishmen" vs. the Rights of Men*

WHILE THE SEEDS of German race-thinking were planted during the Napoleonic wars, the beginnings of the later English development appeared during the French Revolution and may be traced back to the man who violently denounced it as the "most astonishing [crisis] that has hitherto happened in the world"—to Edmund Burke.[42] The tremendous influence his work has exercised not only on English but also on German political thought is well known. The fact, however, must be stressed because of resemblances between German and English race-thinking as contrasted with the French brand. These resemblances stem from the fact that both countries had defeated the Tricolor and therefore showed a certain tendency to discriminate against the ideas of *Liberté-Egalité-Fraternité* as foreign inventions. Social inequality being the basis of English society, British Conservatives felt not a little uncomfortable when it came to the "rights of men." According to opinions widely held by nineteenth-century Tories, inequality belonged to the English national character. Disraeli found "something better than the Rights of Men in the rights of Englishmen" and to Sir James Stephen "few things in history [seemed] so beggarly as the degree to which the French allowed themselves to be excited about such things." [43] This is one of the reasons why they could afford to develop race-thinking

---

[41] This surprising gentleman is none other than the well-known writer and historian Elie Faure, "Gobineau et le Problème des Races," in *Europe,* 1923.

[42] *Reflections on the Revolution in France,* 1790, Everyman's Library Edition, New York, p. 8.

[43] *Liberty, Equality, Fraternity,* 1873, p. 254. For Lord Beaconsfield see Benjamin Disraeli, *Lord George Bentinck,* 1853, p. 184.

along national lines until the end of the nineteenth century, whereas the same opinions in France showed their true antinational face from the very beginning.

Burke's main argument against the "abstract principles" of the French Revolution is contained in the following sentence: "It has been the uniform policy of our constitution to claim and assert our liberties, as an *entailed inheritance* derived to us from our forefathers, and to be transmitted to our posterity; as an estate specially belonging to the people of this kingdom, without any reference whatever to any other more general or prior right." The concept of inheritance, applied to the very nature of liberty, has been the ideological basis from which English nationalism received its curious touch of race-feeling ever since the French Revolution. Formulated by a middle-class writer, it signified the direct acceptance of the feudal concept of liberty as the sum total of privileges inherited together with title and land. Without encroaching upon the rights of the privileged class within the English nation, Burke enlarged the principle of these privileges to include the whole English people, establishing them as a kind of nobility among nations. Hence he drew his contempt for those who claimed their franchise as the rights of men, rights which he saw fit to claim only as "the rights of Englishmen."

In England nationalism developed without serious attacks on the old feudal classes. This has been possible because the English gentry, from the seventeenth century on and in ever-increasing numbers, had assimilated the higher ranks of the bourgeoisie, so that sometimes even the common man could attain the position of a lord. By this process much of the ordinary caste arrogance of nobility was taken away and a considerable sense of responsibility for the nation as a whole was created; but by the same token, feudal concepts and mentality could influence the political ideas of the lower classes more easily than elsewhere. Thus, the concept of inheritance was accepted almost unchanged and applied to the entire British "stock." The consequence of this assimilation of noble standards was that the English brand of race-thinking was almost obsessed with inheritance theories and their modern equivalent, eugenics.

Ever since the European peoples made practical attempts to include all the peoples of the earth in their conception of humanity, they have been irritated by the great physical differences between themselves and the peoples they found on other continents.[44] The eighteenth-century enthusiasm for the diversity in which the all-present identical nature of man and reason could find expression provided a rather thin cover of argument to the crucial question, whether the Christian tenet of the unity and equality of all men, based upon common descent from one original set of parents, would be kept

[44] A significant if moderate echo of this inner bewilderment can be found in many an eighteenth-century traveling report. Voltaire thought it important enough to make a special note in his *Dictionnaire Philosophique:* "We have seen, moreover, how different the races are who inhabit this globe, and how great must have been the surprise of the first Negro and the first white man who met" (Article: *Homme*).

in the hearts of men who were faced with tribes which, as far as we know, never had found by themselves any adequate expression of human reason or human passion in either cultural deeds or popular customs, and which had developed human institutions only to a very low level. This new problem which appeared on the historical scene of Europe and America with the more intimate knowledge of African tribes had already caused, and this especially in America and some British possessions, a relapse into forms of social organization which were thought to have been definitely liquidated by Christianity. But even slavery, though actually established on a strict racial basis, did not make the slave-holding peoples race-conscious before the nineteenth century. Throughout the eighteenth century, American slave-holders themselves considered it a temporary institution and wanted to abolish it gradually. Most of them probably would have said with Jefferson: "I tremble when I think that God is just."

In France, where the problem of black tribes had been met with the desire to assimilate and educate, the great scientist Leclerc de Buffon had given a first classification of races which, based upon the European peoples and classifying all others by their differences, had taught equality by strict juxtaposition.[45] The eighteenth century, to use Tocqueville's admirably precise phrase, "believed in the variety of races but in the unity of the human species." [46] In Germany, Herder had refused to apply the "ignoble word" race to men, and even the first cultural historian of mankind to make use of the classification of different species, Gustav Klemm,[47] still respected the idea of mankind as the general framework for his investigations.

But in America and England, where people had to solve a problem of living together after the abolition of slavery, things were considerably less easy. With the exception of South Africa—a country which influenced Western racism only after the "scramble for Africa" in the eighties—these nations were the first to deal with the race problem in practical politics. The abolition of slavery sharpened inherent conflicts instead of finding a solution for existing serious difficulties. This was especially true in England where the "rights of Englishmen" were not replaced by a new political orientation which might have declared the rights of men. The abolition of slavery in the British possessions in 1834 and the discussion preceding the American Civil War, therefore, found in England a highly confused public opinion which was fertile soil for the various naturalistic doctrines which arose in those decades.

The first of these was represented by the polygenists who, challenging the Bible as a book of pious lies, denied any relationship between human "races"; their main achievement was the destruction of the idea of the natural law as the uniting link between all men and all peoples. Although it did not stipulate predestined racial superiority, polygenism arbitrarily isolated all peoples from one another by the deep abyss of the physical impos-

---

[45] *Histoire Naturelle*, 1769-89.
[46] *Op. cit.*, letter of May 15, 1852.
[47] *Allgemeine Kulturgeschichte der Menschheit*, 1843-1852.

sibility of human understanding and communication. Polygenism explains why "East is East and West is West; And never the twain shall meet," and helped much to prevent intermarriage in the colonies and to promote discrimination against individuals of mixed origin. According to polygenism, these people are not true human beings; they belong to no single race, but are a kind of monster whose "every cell is the theater of a civil war." [48]

Lasting as the influence of polygenism on English race-thinking proved to be in the long run, in the nineteenth century it was soon to be beaten in the field of public opinion by another doctrine. This doctrine also started from the principle of inheritance but added to it the political principle of the nineteenth century, progress, whence it arrived at the opposite but far more convincing conclusion that man is related not only to man but to animal life, that the existence of lower races shows clearly that gradual differences alone separate man and beast and that a powerful struggle for existence dominates all living things. Darwinism was especially strengthened by the fact that it followed the path of the old might-right doctrine. But while this doctrine, when used exclusively by aristocrats, had spoken the proud language of conquest, it was now translated into the rather bitter language of people who had known the struggle for daily bread and fought their way to the relative security of upstarts.

Darwinism met with such overwhelming success because it provided, on the basis of inheritance, the ideological weapons for race as well as class rule and could be used for, as well as against, race discrimination. Politically speaking, Darwinism as such was neutral, and it has led, indeed, to all kinds of pacifism and cosmopolitanism as well as to the sharpest forms of imperialistic ideologies. [49] In the seventies and eighties of the last century, Darwinism was still almost exclusively in the hands of the utilitarian anticolonial party in England. And the first philosopher of evolution, Herbert Spencer, who treated sociology as part of biology, believed natural selection to benefit the evolution of mankind and to result in everlasting peace. For political discussion, Darwinism offered two important concepts: the struggle for existence with optimistic assertion of the necessary and automatic "survival of the fittest," and the indefinite possibilities which seemed to lie in the evolution of man out of animal life and which started the new "science" of eugenics.

The doctrine of the necessary survival of the fittest, with its implication that the top layers in society eventually are the "fittest," died as the conquest doctrine had died, namely, at the moment when the ruling classes in England or the English domination in colonial possessions were no longer absolutely secure, and when it became highly doubtful whether those who were "fittest" today would still be the fittest tomorrow. The other part of Darwinism, the genealogy of man from animal life, unfortunately survived. Eugenics promised to overcome the troublesome uncertainties of the survival doctrine ac-

---

[48] A. Carthill, *The Lost Dominion*, 1924, p. 158.

[49] See Friedrich Brie, *Imperialistische Strömungen in der englischen Literatur*, Halle, 1928.

cording to which it was impossible either to predict who would turn out to be the fittest or to provide the means for the nations to develop everlasting fitness. This possible consequence of applied eugenics was stressed in Germany in the twenties as a reaction to Spengler's *Decline of the West*.[50] The process of selection had only to be changed from a natural necessity which worked behind the backs of men into an "artificial," consciously applied physical tool. Bestiality had always been inherent in eugenics, and Ernst Haeckel's early remark that mercy-death would save "useless expenses for family and state" is quite characteristic.[51] Finally the last disciples of Darwinism in Germany decided to leave the field of scientific research altogether, to forget about the search for the missing link between man and ape, and started instead their practical efforts to change man into what the Darwinists thought an ape is.

But before Nazism, in the course of its totalitarian policy, attempted to change man into a beast, there were numerous efforts to develop him on a strictly hereditary basis into a god.[52] Not only Herbert Spencer, but all the early evolutionists and Darwinists "had as strong a faith in humanity's angelic future as in man's simian origin." [53] Selected inheritance was believed to result in "hereditary genius," [54] and again aristocracy was held to be the natural outcome, not of politics, but of natural selection, of pure breeding. To transform the whole nation into a natural aristocracy from which choice

[50] See, for instance, Otto Bangert, *Gold oder Blut,* 1927. "Therefore a civilization can be eternal," p. 17.

[51] In *Lebenswunder,* 1904, pp. 128 ff.

[52] Almost a century before evolutionism had donned the cloak of science, warning voices foretold the inherent consequences of a madness that was then merely in the stage of pure imagination. Voltaire, more than once, had played with evolutionary opinions—see chiefly "Philosophie Générale: Métaphysique, Morale et Théologie," *Oeuvres Complètes,* 1785, Tome 40, pp. 16 ff.—In his *Dictionnaire Philosophique,* Article "Chaîne des Etres Créés," he wrote: "At first, our imagination is pleased at the imperceptible transition of crude matter to organized matter, of plants to zoophytes, of these zoophytes to animals, of these to man, of man to spirits, of these spirits clothed with a small aerial body to immaterial substances; and . . . to God Himself. . . . But the most perfect spirit created by the Supreme Being, can he become God? Is there not an infinity between God and him? . . . Is there not obviously a void between the monkey and man?"

[53] Hayes, *op. cit.,* p. 11. Hayes rightly stresses the strong practical morality of all these early materialists. He explains "this curious divorce of morals from beliefs" by "what later sociologists have described as a time lag" (p. 130). This explanation, however, appears rather weak if one recalls that other materialists who, like Haeckel in Germany or Vacher de Lapouge in France, had left the calm of studies and research for propaganda activities, did not greatly suffer from such a time lag; that, on the other hand, their contemporaries who were not tinged by their materialistic doctrines, such as Barrès and Co. in France, were very practical adherents of the perverse brutality which swept France during the Dreyfus Affair. The sudden decay of morals in the Western world seems to be caused less by an autonomous development of certain "ideas" than by a series of new political events and new political and social problems which confronted a bewildered and confused humanity.

[54] Such was the title of the widely read book of Fr. Galton, published in 1869, which caused a flood of literature about the same topic in the following decades.

exemplars would develop into geniuses and supermen, was one of the many
"ideas" produced by frustrated liberal intellectuals in their dreams of replacing the old governing classes by a new "elite" through nonpolitical
means. At the end of the century, writers treated political topics in terms
of biology and zoology as a matter of course, and zoologists wrote "Biological Views of our Foreign Policy" as though they had detected an in-
fallible guide for statesmen.[55] All of them put forward new ways to control
and regulate the "survival of the fittest" in accordance with the national interests of the English people.[56]

The most dangerous aspect of these evolutionist doctrines is that they
combined the inheritance concept with the insistence on personal achievement and individual character which had been so important for the self-
respect of the nineteenth-century middle class. This middle class wanted
scientists who could prove that the great men, not the aristocrats, were the
true representatives of the nation, in whom the "genius of the race" was
personified. These scientists provided an ideal escape from political responsibility when they "proved" the early statement of Benjamin Disraeli
that the great man is "the personification of race, its choice exemplar." The
development of this "genius" found its logical end when another disciple
of evolutionism simply declared: "The Englishman is the Overman and the
history of England is the history of his evolution." [57]

It is as significant for English as it was for German race-thinking that it
originated among middle-class writers and not the nobility, that it was born
of the desire to extend the benefits of noble standards to all classes and that
it was nourished by true national feelings. In this respect, Carlyle's ideas on
the genius and hero were really more the weapons of a "social reformer"
than the doctrines of the "Father of British Imperialism," a very unjust
accusation, indeed.[58] His hero worship which earned him wide audiences in
both England and in Germany, had the same sources as the personality
worship of German romanticism. It was the same assertion and glorification
of the innate greatness of the individual character independent of his social
environment. Among the men who influenced the colonial movement from

[55] "A Biological View of Our Foreign Policy" was published by P. Charles Michel in
Saturday Review, London, February, 1896. The most important works of this kind are:
Thomas Huxley, *The Struggle for Existence in Human Society,* 1888. His main thesis:
The fall of civilizations is necessary only as long as birthrate is uncontrolled. Benjamin
Kidd, *Social Evolution,* 1894. John B. Crozier, *History of Intellectual Development on
the Lines of Modern Evolution,* 1897-1901. Karl Pearson (*National Life,* 1901), Professor of Eugenics at London University, was among the first to describe progress as a
kind of impersonal monster which devours everything that happens to be in its way.
Charles H. Harvey, *The Biology of British Politics,* 1904, argues that by strict control
of the "struggle for life" within the nation, a nation could become all-powerful for the
inevitable fight with other people for existence.

[56] See especially K. Pearson, *op. cit.* But Fr. Galton had already stated: "I wish to
emphasize the fact that the improvement of the natural gifts of future generations of
the human race is largely under our control" (*op. cit.,* ed. 1892, p. xxvi).

[57] *Testament of John Davidson,* 1908.

[58] C. A. Bodelsen, *Studies in Mid-Victorian Imperialism,* 1924, pp. 22 ff.

the middle of the nineteenth century until the outbreak of actual imperialism
at its end, not one has escaped the influence of Carlyle, but not one can be
accused of preaching outspoken racism. Carlyle himself, in his essay on the
"Nigger Question" is concerned with means to help the West Indies produce
"heroes." Charles Dilke, whose *Greater Britain* (1869) is sometimes taken
as the beginning of imperialism,[59] was an advanced radical who glorified the
English colonists as being part of the British nation, as against those who
would look down upon them and their lands as mere colonies. J. R. Seeley,
whose *Expansion of England* (1883) sold 80,000 copies in less than two
years, still respects the Hindus as a foreign people and distinguishes them
clearly from "barbarians." Even Froude, whose admiration for the Boers,
the first white people to be converted clearly to the tribal philosophy of
racism, might appear suspect, opposed too many rights for South Africa
because "self-government in South Africa meant the government of the
natives by the European colonists and that is not self-government." [60]

Very much as in Germany, English nationalism was born and stimulated
by a middle class which had never entirely emancipated itself from the
nobility and therefore bore the first germs of race-thinking. But unlike
Germany, whose lack of unity made necessary an ideological wall to substitute for historical or geographical facts, the British Isles were completely
separated from the surrounding world by natural frontiers and England as
a nation had to devise a theory of unity among people who lived in far-flung
colonies beyond the seas, separated from the mother country by thousands
of miles. The only link between them was common descent, common origin,
common language. The separation of the United States had shown that these
links in themselves do not guarantee domination; and not only America,
other colonies too, though not with the same violence, showed strong
tendencies toward developing along different constitutional lines from the
mother country. In order to save these former British nationals, Dilke, influenced by Carlyle, spoke of "Saxondom," a word that seemed able to win
back even the people of the United States, to whom one-third of his book is
devoted. Being a radical, Dilke could act as though the War of Independence
had not been a war between two nations, but the English form of eighteenth-
century civil war, in which he belatedly sided with the Republicans. For
here lies one of the reasons for the surprising fact that social reformers and
radicals were the promoters of nationalism in England: they wanted to keep
the colonies not only because they thought they were necessary outlets for
the lower classes; they actually wanted to retain the influence on the mother
country which these more radical sons of the British Isles exercised. This
motif is strong with Froude, who wished "to retain the colonies because he
thought it possible to reproduce in them a simpler state of society and a
nobler way of life than were possible in industrial England," [61] and it had a

[59] E. H. Damce, *The Victorian Illusion*, 1928. "Imperialism began with a book . . .
Dilke's Greater Britain."

[60] "Two Lectures on South Africa," in *Short Studies on Great Subjects*, 1867-1882.

[61] C. A. Bodelsen, *op. cit.*, p. 199.

definite impact on Seeley's *Expansion of England:* "When we have accustomed ourselves to contemplate the whole Empire together and we call it *all*
England we shall see that there too is a United States." Whatever later political writers may have used "Saxondom" for, in Dilke's work it had a genuine
political meaning for a nation that was no longer held together by a limited
country. "The idea which in all the length of my travels has been at once my
fellow and my guide—the key wherewith to unlock the hidden things of
strange new lands—is the conception . . . of the grandeur of our race
already girdling the earth, which it is destined perhaps, eventually to over-
spread" (Preface). For Dilke, common origin, inheritance, "grandeur of
race" were neither physical facts nor the key to history but a much-needed
guide in the present world, the only reliable link in a boundless space.

Because English colonists had spread all over the earth, it happened that
the most dangerous concept of nationalism, the idea of "national mission,"
was especially strong in England. Although national mission as such developed for a long while untinged by racial influences in all countries where
peoples aspired to nationhood, it proved finally to have a peculiarly close
affinity to race-thinking. The above-quoted English nationalists may be considered borderline cases in the light of later experience. In themselves, they
were not more harmful than, for example, Auguste Comte in France when
he expressed the hope for a united, organized, regenerated humanity under
the leadership—*présidence*—of France.[62] They do not give up the idea of
mankind, though they think England is the supreme guarantee for humanity.
They could not help but overstress this nationalistic concept because of its
inherent dissolution of the bond between soil and people implied in the mission idea, a dissolution which for English politics was not a propagated
ideology but an established fact with which every statesman had to reckon.
What separates them definitely from later racists is that none of them was
ever seriously concerned with discrimination against other peoples as lower
races, if only for the reason that the countries they were talking about,
Canada and Australia, were almost empty and had no serious population
problem.

It is, therefore, not by accident that the first English statesman who repeatedly stressed his belief in races and race superiority as a determining
factor of history and politics was a man who without particular interest in
the colonies and the English colonists—"the colonial deadweight which we
do not govern"—wanted to extend British imperial power to Asia and,
indeed, forcefully strengthened the position of Great Britain in the only
colony with a grave population and cultural problem. It was Benjamin
Disraeli who made the Queen of England the Empress of India; he was
the first English statesman who regarded India as the cornerstone of an
Empire and who wanted to cut the ties which linked the English people
to the nations of the Continent.[63] Thereby he laid one of the foundation

[62] In his *Discours sur l'Ensemble du Positivisme,* 1848, pp. 384 ff.
[63] "Power and influence we should exercise in Asia; consequently in Western
Europe" (W. F. Monypenny and G. E. Buckle, *The Life of Benjamin Disraeli, Earl of*

stones for a fundamental change in British rule in India. This colony had been governed with the usual ruthlessness of conquerors—men whom Burke had called "the breakers of the law in India." It was now to receive a carefully planned administration which aimed at the establishment of a permanent government by administrative measures. This experiment has brought England very close to the danger against which Burke had warned, that the "breakers of the law in India" might become "the makers of law for England." [64] For all those, to whom there was "no transaction in the history of England of which we have more just cause to be proud . . . than the establishment of the Indian Empire," held liberty and equality to be "big names for a small thing." [65]

The policy introduced by Disraeli signified the establishment of an exclusive caste in a foreign country whose only function was rule and not colonization. For the realization of this conception which Disraeli did not live to see accomplished, racism would indeed be an indispensable tool. It foreshadowed the menacing transformation of the people from a nation into an "unmixed race of a first-rate organization" that felt itself to be "the aristocracy of nature"—to repeat in Disraeli's own words quoted above.[66]

What we have followed so far is the story of an opinion in which we see only now, after all the terrible experiences of our times, the first dawn of racism. But although racism has revived elements of race-thinking in every country, it is not the history of an idea endowed by some "immanent logic" with which we were concerned. Race-thinking was a source of convenient arguments for varying political conflicts, but it never possessed any kind of monopoly over the political life of the respective nations; it sharpened and exploited existing conflicting interests or existing political problems, but it never created new conflicts or produced new categories of political thinking. Racism sprang from experiences and political constellations which were still unknown and would have been utterly strange even to such devoted defenders of "race" as Gobineau or Disraeli. There is an abyss between the men of brilliant and facile conceptions and men of brutal deeds and active bestiality which no intellectual explanation is able to bridge. It is highly probable that the thinking in terms of race would have disappeared in due time together with other irresponsible opinions of the nineteenth century, if the "scramble for Africa" and the new era of imperialism had not exposed Western humanity to new and shocking experiences. Imperialism

---

Beaconsfield, New York, 1929, II, 210). But "If ever Europe by her shortsightedness falls into an inferior and exhausted state, for England there will remain an illustrious future" (*Ibid.*, I, Book IV, ch. 2). For "England is no longer a mere European power . . . she is really more an Asiatic power than a European." (*Ibid.*, II, 201).

[64] Burke, *op. cit.*, pp. 42-43: "The power of the House of Commons . . . is indeed great; and long may it be able to preserve its greatness . . . and it will do so, as long as it can keep the breaker of the law in India from becoming the maker of law for England."

[65] Sir James F. Stephen, *op. cit.*, p. 253, and *passim;* see also his "Foundations of the Government of India," 1883, in *The Nineteenth Century*, LXXX.

[66] For Disraeli's racism, compare chapter iii.

would have necessitated the invention of racism as the only possible "explanation" and excuse for its deeds, even if no race-thinking had ever existed in the civilized world.

Since, however, race-thinking did exist, it proved to be a powerful help to racism. The very existence of an opinion which could boast of a certain tradition served to hide the destructive forces of the new doctrine which, without this appearance of national respectability or the seeming sanction of tradition, might have disclosed its utter incompatibility with all Western political and moral standards of the past, even before it was allowed to destroy the comity of European nations.

CHAPTER THREE

Race and Bureaucracy

T WO NEW DEVICES for political organization and rule over foreign peoples were discovered during the first decades of imperialism. One was race as a principle of the body politic, and the other bureaucracy as a principle of foreign domination. Without race as a substitute for the nation, the scramble for Africa and the investment fever might well have remained the purposeless "dance of death and trade" (Joseph Conrad) of all gold rushes. Without bureaucracy as a substitute for government, the British possession of India might well have been left to the recklessness of the "breakers of law in India" (Burke) without changing the political climate of an entire era.

Both discoveries were actually made on the Dark Continent. Race was the emergency explanation of human beings whom no European or civilized man could understand and whose humanity so frightened and humiliated the immigrants that they no longer cared to belong to the same human species. Race was the Boers' answer to the overwhelming monstrosity of Africa—a whole continent populated and overpopulated by savages—an explanation of the madness which grasped and illuminated them like "a flash of lightning in a serene sky: 'Exterminate all the brutes.' " [1] This answer resulted in the most terrible massacres in recent history, the Boers' extermination of Hottentot tribes, the wild murdering by Carl Peters in German Southeast Africa, the decimation of the peaceful Congo population —from 20 to 40 million reduced to 8 million people; and finally, perhaps worst of all, it resulted in the triumphant introduction of such means of pacification into ordinary, respectable foreign policies. What head of a civilized state would ever before have uttered the exhortation of William II to a German expeditionary contingent fighting the Boxer insurrection in 1900: "Just as the Huns a thousand years ago, under the leadership of Attila, gained a reputation by virtue of which they still live in history, so may the German name become known in such a manner in China that no Chinese will ever again dare to look askance at a German." [2]

[1] Joseph Conrad, "Heart of Darkness" in *Youth and Other Tales*, 1902, is the most illuminating work on actual race experience in Africa.

[2] Quoted from Carlton J. Hayes, *A Generation of Materialism*, New York, 1941, p. 338.—An even worse case is of course that of Leopold II of Belgium, responsible for the blackest pages in the history of Africa. "There was only one man who could be accused of the outrages which reduced the native population [of the Congo] from between 20 to 40 million in 1890 to 8,500,000 in 1911—Leopold II." See Selwyn James, *South of the Congo*, New York, 1943, p. 305.

While race, whether as a home-grown ideology in Europe or an emergency explanation for shattering experiences, has always attracted the worst elements in Western civilization, bureaucracy was discovered by and first attracted the best, and sometimes even the most clear-sighted, strata of the European intelligentsia. The administrator who ruled by reports [3] and decrees in more hostile secrecy than any oriental despot grew out of a tradition of military discipline in the midst of ruthless and lawless men; for a long time he had lived by the honest, earnest boyhood ideals of a modern knight in shining armor sent to protect helpless and primitive people. And he fulfilled this task, for better or worse, as long as he moved in a world dominated by the old "trinity—war, trade and piracy" (Goethe), and not in a complicated game of far-reaching investment policies which demanded the domination of one people, not as before for the sake of its own riches, but for the sake of another country's wealth. Bureaucracy was the organization of the great game of expansion in which every area was considered a stepping-stone to further involvements and every people an instrument for further conquest.

Although in the end racism and bureaucracy proved to be interrelated in many ways, they were discovered and developed independently. No one who in one way or the other was implicated in their perfection ever came to realize the full range of potentialities of power accumulation and destruction that this combination alone provided. Lord Cromer, who in Egypt changed from an ordinary British chargé d'affaires into an imperialist bureaucrat, would no more have dreamed of combining administration with massacre ("administrative massacres" as Carthill bluntly put it forty years later), than the race fanatics of South Africa thought of organizing massacres for the purpose of establishing a circumscribed, rational political community (as the Nazis did in the extermination camps).

I: *The Phantom World of the Dark Continent*

UP TO THE END of the last century, the colonial enterprises of the seafaring European peoples produced two outstanding forms of achievement: in recently discovered and sparsely populated territories, the founding of new settlements which adopted the legal and political institutions of the mother country; and in well-known though exotic countries in the midst of foreign peoples, the establishment of maritime and trade stations whose only function was to facilitate the never very peaceful exchange of the treasures of the world. Colonization took place in America and Australia, the two continents that, without a culture and a history of their own, had fallen into the hands of Europeans. Trade stations were characteristic of Asia where for centuries Europeans had shown no ambition for permanent rule or inten-

[3] See A. Carthill's description of the "Indian system of government by reports" in *The Lost Dominion*, 1924, p. 70.

tions of conquest, decimation of the native population, and permanent settlement.[4] Both forms of overseas enterprise evolved in a long steady process which extended over almost four centuries, during which the settlements gradually achieved independence, and the possession of trade stations shifted among the nations according to their relative weakness or strength in Europe.

The only continent Europe had not touched in the course of its colonial history was the Dark Continent of Africa. Its northern shores, populated by Arabic peoples and tribes, were well known and had belonged to the European sphere of influence in one way or another since the days of antiquity. Too well populated to attract settlers, and too poor to be exploited, these regions suffered all kinds of foreign rule and anarchic neglect, but oddly enough never—after the decline of the Egyptian Empire and the destruction of Carthage—achieved authentic independence and reliable political organization. European countries tried time and again, it is true, to reach beyond the Mediterranean to impose their rule on Arabic lands and their Christianity on Moslem peoples, but they never attempted to treat North African territories like overseas possessions. On the contrary, they frequently aspired to incorporate them into the respective mother country. This age-old tradition, still followed in recent times by Italy and France, was broken in the eighties when England went into Egypt to protect the Suez Canal without any intention either of conquest or incorporation. The point is not that Egypt was wronged but that England (a nation that did not lie on the shores of the Mediterranean) could not possibly have been interested in Egypt as such, but needed her only because there were treasures in India.

While imperialism changed Egypt from a country occasionally coveted for her own sake into a military station for India and a stepping-stone for further expansion, the exact opposite happened to South Africa. Since the seventeenth century, the significance of the Cape of Good Hope had depended upon India, the center of colonial wealth; any nation that established trade stations there needed a maritime station on the Cape, which was then abandoned when trade in India was liquidated. At the end of the eighteenth century, the British East India Company defeated Portugal, Holland, and France and won a trade monopoly in India; the occupation of South Africa followed as a matter of course. If imperialism had simply continued the old trends of colonial trade (which is so frequently mistaken for imperialism), England would have liquidated her position in South Africa with the opening of the Suez Canal in 1869.[5] Although today South Africa belongs to the

---

[4] It is important to bear in mind that colonization of America and Australia was accompanied by comparatively short periods of cruel liquidation because of the natives' numerical weakness, whereas "in understanding the genesis of modern South African society it is of the greatest importance to know that the land beyond the Cape's borders was not the open land which lay before the Australian squatter. It was already an area of settlement, of settlement by a great Bantu population." See C. W. de Kiewiet, *A History of South Africa, Social and Economic* (Oxford, 1941), p. 59.

[5] "As late as 1884 the British Government had still been willing to diminish its authority and influence in South Africa" (De Kiewiet, *op. cit.,* p. 113).

Commonwealth, it was always different from the other dominions; fertility and sparseness of population, the main prerequisites for definite settlement, were lacking, and a single effort to settle 5,000 unemployed Englishmen at the beginning of the nineteenth century proved a failure. Not only did the streams of emigrants from the British Isles consistently avoid South Africa throughout the nineteenth century, but South Africa is the only dominion from which a steady stream of emigrants has gone back to England in recent times.[6] South Africa, which became the "culture-bed of Imperialism" (Damce), was never claimed by England's most radical defenders of "Saxon-dom" and it did not figure in the visions of her most romantic dreamers of an Asiatic Empire. This in itself shows how small the real influence of pre-imperialist colonial enterprise and overseas settlement was on the development of imperialism itself. If the Cape colony had remained within the framework of pre-imperialist policies, it would have been abandoned at the exact moment when it actually became all-important.

Although the discoveries of gold mines and diamond fields in the seventies and eighties would have had little consequence in themselves if they had not accidentally acted as a catalytic agent for imperialist forces, it remains remarkable that the imperialists' claim to have found a permanent solution to the problem of superfluity was initially motivated by a rush for the most superfluous raw material on earth. Gold hardly has a place in human production and is of no importance compared with iron, coal, oil, and rubber; instead, it is the most ancient symbol of mere wealth. In its uselessness in industrial production it bears an ironical resemblance to the superfluous money that financed the digging of gold and to the superfluous men who did the digging. To the imperialists' pretense of having discovered a permanent savior for a decadent society and antiquated political organization, it added its own pretense of apparently eternal stability and independence of all functional determinants. It was significant that a society about to part with all traditional absolute values began to look for an absolute value in the world of economics where, indeed, such a thing does not and cannot exist, since everything is functional by definition. This delusion of an absolute value has made the production of gold since ancient times the business of

[6] The following table of British immigration to and emigration from South Africa between 1924 and 1928 shows that Englishmen had a stronger inclination to leave the country than other immigrants and that, with one exception, each year showed a greater number of British people leaving the country than coming in:

Year	British Immigration	Total Immigration	British Emigration	Total Emigration
1924	3.724	5.265	5.275	5.857
1925	2.400	5.426	4.019	4.483
1926	4.094	6.575	3.512	3.799
1927	3.681	6.595	3.717	3.988
1928	3.285	7.050	3.409	4.127
Total	17.184	30.911	19.932	22.254

These figures are quoted from Leonard Barnes, *Caliban in Africa. An Impression of Colour Madness*, Philadelphia, 1931, p. 59, note.

adventurers, gamblers, criminals, of elements outside the pale of normal, sane society. The new turn in the South African gold rush was that here the luck-hunters were not distinctly outside civilized society but, on the contrary, very clearly a by-product of this society, an inevitable residue of the capitalist system and even the representatives of an economy that relentlessly produced a superfluity of men and capital.

The superfluous men, "the Bohemians of the four continents" [7] who came rushing down to the Cape, still had much in common with the old adventurers. They too felt "Ship me somewheres east of Suez where the best is like the worst, / Where there aren't no Ten Commandments, an' a man can raise a thirst." The difference was not their morality or immorality, but rather that the decision to join this crowd "of all nations and colors" [8] was no longer up to them; that they had not stepped out of society but had been spat out by it; that they were not enterprising beyond the permitted limits of civilization but simply victims without use or function. Their only choice had been a negative one, a decision against the workers' movements, in which the best of the superfluous men or of those who were threatened with superfluity established a kind of countersociety through which men could find their way back into a human world of fellowship and purpose. They were nothing of their own making, they were like living symbols of what had happened to them, living abstractions and witnesses of the absurdity of human institutions. They were not individuals like the old adventurers, they were the shadows of events with which they had nothing to do.

Like Mr. Kurtz in Conrad's "Heart of Darkness," they were "hollow to the core," "reckless without hardihood, greedy without audacity and cruel without courage." They believed in nothing and "could get (themselves) to believe anything—anything." Expelled from a world with accepted social values, they had been thrown back upon themselves and still had nothing to fall back upon except, here and there, a streak of talent which made them as dangerous as Kurtz if they were ever allowed to return to their homelands. For the only talent that could possibly burgeon in their hollow souls was the gift of fascination which makes a "splendid leader of an extreme party." The more gifted were walking incarnations of resentment like the German Carl Peters (possibly the model for Kurtz), who openly admitted that he "was fed up with being counted among the pariahs and wanted to belong to a master race." [9] But gifted or not, they were all "game for anything from pitch and toss to wilful murder" and to them their fellow-men were "no more one way or another than that fly there." Thus they brought with them, or they learned quickly, the code of manners which befitted the coming type of murderer to whom the only unforgivable sin is to lose his temper.

There were, to be sure, authentic gentlemen among them, like Mr. Jones of Conrad's *Victory,* who out of boredom were willing to pay any price to

[7] J. A. Froude, "Leaves from a South African Journal" (1874), in *Short Studies on Great Subjects,* 1867-1882, Vol. IV.

[8] *Ibid.*

[9] Quoted from Paul Ritter, *Kolonien im deutschen Schrifttum,* 1936, Preface.

inhabit the "world of hazard and adventure," or like Mr. Heyst, who was drunk with contempt for everything human until he drifted "like a detached leaf . . . without ever catching on to anything." They were irresistibly attracted by a world where everything was a·joke, which could teach them "the Great Joke" that is "the mastery of despair." The perfect gentleman and the perfect scoundrel came to know each other well in the "great wild jungle without law," and they found themselves "well-matched in their enormous dissimilarity, identical souls in different disguises." We have seen the behavior of high society during the Dreyfus Affair and watched Disraeli discover the social relationship between vice and crime; here, too, we have essentially the same story of high society falling in love with its own underworld, and of the criminal feeling elevated when by civilized coldness, the avoidance of "unnecessary exertion," and good manners he is allowed to create a vicious, refined atmosphere around his crimes. This refinement, the very contrast between the brutality of the crime and the manner of carrying it out, becomes the bridge of deep understanding between himself and the perfect gentleman. But what, after all, took decades to achieve in Europe, because of the delaying effect of social ethical values, exploded with the suddenness of a short circuit in the phantom world of colonial adventure.

Outside all social restraint and hypocrisy, against the backdrop of native life, the gentleman and the criminal felt not only the closeness of men who share the same color of skin, but the impact of a world of infinite possibilities for crimes committed in the spirit of play, for the combination of horror and laughter, that is for the full realization of their own phantom-like existence. Native life lent these ghostlike events a seeming guarantee against all consequences because anyhow it looked to these men like a "mere play of shadows. A play of shadows, the dominant race could walk through unaffected and disregarded in the pursuit of its incomprehensible aims and needs."

The world of native savages was a perfect setting for men who had escaped the reality of civilization. Under a merciless sun, surrounded by an entirely hostile nature, they were confronted with human beings who, living without the future of a purpose and the past of an accomplishment, were as incomprehensible as the inmates of a madhouse. "The prehistoric man was cursing us, praying to us, welcoming us—who could tell? We were cut off from the comprehension of our surroundings; we glided past like phantoms, wondering and secretly appalled, as sane men would be, before an enthusiastic outbreak in a madhouse. We could not understand because we were too far and could not remember, because we were traveling in the night of first ages, of those ages that are gone leaving hardly a sign—and no memories. The earth seemed unearthly, . . . and the men . . . No, they were not inhuman. Well, you know, that was the worst of it—this suspicion of their not being inhuman. It would come slowly to one. They howled and leaped, and spun, and made horrid faces; but what thrilled you was just the thought of their humanity—like yours—the thought of your remote kinship with this wild and passionate uproar" ("Heart of Darkness").

It is strange that, historically speaking, the existence of "prehistoric men" had so little influence on Western man before the scramble for Africa. It is, however, a matter of record that nothing much had happened as long as savage tribes, outnumbered by European settlers, had been exterminated, as long as shiploads of Negroes were imported as slaves into the Europe-determined world of the United States, or even as long as only individuals had drifted into the interior of the Dark Continent where the savages were numerous enough to constitute a world of their own, a world of folly, to which the European adventurer added the folly of the ivory hunt. Many of these adventurers had gone mad in the silent wilderness of an overpopulated continent where the presence of human beings only underlined utter solitude, and where an untouched, overwhelmingly hostile nature that nobody had ever taken the trouble to change into human landscape seemed to wait in sublime patience "for the passing away of the fantastic invasion" of man. But their madness had remained a matter of individual experience and without consequences.

This changed with the men who arrived during the scramble for Africa. These were no longer lonely individuals; "all Europe had contributed to the making of (them)." They concentrated on the southern part of the continent where they met the Boers, a Dutch splinter group which had been almost forgotten by Europe, but which now served as a natural introduction to the challenge of new surroundings. The response of the superfluous men was largely determined by the response of the only European group that ever, though in complete isolation, had to live in a world of black savages.

The Boers are descended from Dutch settlers who in the middle of the seventeenth century were stationed at the Cape to provide fresh vegetables and meat for ships on their voyage to India. A small group of French Huguenots was all that followed them in the course of the next century, so that it was only with the help of a high birthrate that the little Dutch splinter grew into a small people. Completely isolated from the current of European history, they set out on a path such "as few nations have trod before them, and scarcely one trod with success." [10]

The two main material factors in the development of the Boer people were the extremely bad soil which could be used only for extensive cattle-raising, and the very large black population which was organized in tribes and lived as nomad hunters.[11] The bad soil made close settlement impossible and prevented the Dutch peasant settlers from following the village organization of their homeland. Large families, isolated from each other by broad spaces of wilderness, were forced into a kind of clan organization and only the ever-present threat of a common foe, the black tribes which by far outnumbered

---

[10] Lord Selbourne in 1907: "The white people of South Africa are committed to such a path as few nations have trod before them, and scarcely one trod with success." See Kiewiet, *op. cit.,* chapter 6.

[11] See especially chapter iii of Kiewiet, *op. cit.*

the white settlers, deterred these clans from active war against each other. The solution to the double problem of lack of fertility and abundance of natives was slavery.[12]

Slavery, however, is a very inadequate word to describe what actually happened. First of all, slavery, though it domesticated a certain part of the savage population, never got hold of all of them, so the Boers were never able to forget their first horrible fright before a species of men whom human pride and the sense of human dignity could not allow them to accept as fellow-men. This fright of something like oneself that still under no circumstances ought to be like oneself remained at the basis of slavery and became the basis for a race society.

Mankind remembers the history of peoples but has only legendary knowledge of prehistoric tribes. The word "race" has a precise meaning only when and where peoples are confronted with such tribes of which they have no historical record and which do not know any history of their own. Whether these represent "prehistoric man," the accidentally surviving specimens of the first forms of human life on earth, or whether they are the "posthistoric" survivors of some unknown disaster which ended a civilization we do not know. They certainly appeared rather like the survivors of one great catastrophe which might have been followed by smaller disasters until catastrophic monotony seemed to be a natural condition of human life. At any rate, races in this sense were found only in regions where nature was particularly hostile. What made them different from other human beings was not at all the color of their skin but the fact that they behaved like a part of nature, that they treated nature as their undisputed master, that they had not created a human world, a human reality, and that therefore nature had remained, in all its majesty, the only overwhelming reality—compared to which they appeared to be phantoms, unreal and ghostlike. They were, as it were, "natural" human beings who lacked the specifically human character, the specifically human reality, so that when European men massacred them they somehow were not aware that they had committed murder.

Moreover, the senseless massacre of native tribes on the Dark Continent was quite in keeping with the traditions of these tribes themselves. Extermination of hostile tribes had been the rule in all African native wars, and it was not abolished when a black leader happened to unite several tribes under his leadership. King Tchaka, who at the beginning of the nineteenth century united the Zulu tribes in an extraordinarily disciplined and warlike organization, established neither a people nor a nation of Zulus. He only succeeded in exterminating more than one million members of weaker tribes.[13] Since discipline and military organization by themselves

---

[12] "Slaves and Hottentots together provoked remarkable changes in the thought and habits of the colonists, for climate and geography were not alone in forming the distinctive traits of the Boer race. Slaves and droughts, Hottentots and isolation, cheap labor and land, combined to create the institutions and habits of South African society. The sons and daughters born to sturdy Hollanders and Huguenots learned to look upon the labour of the field and upon all hard physical toil as the functions of a servile race" (Kiewiet, *op. cit.*, p. 21).

[13] See James, *op. cit.*, p. 28.

cannot establish a political body, the destruction remained an unrecorded episode in an unreal, incomprehensible process which cannot be accepted by man and therefore is not remembered by human history.

Slavery in the case of the Boers was a form of adjustment of a European people to a black race,[14] and only superficially resembled those historical instances when it had been a result of conquest or slave trade. No body politic, no communal organization kept the Boers together, no territory was definitely colonized, and the black slaves did not serve any white civilization. The Boers had lost both their peasant relationship to the soil and their civilized feeling for human fellowship. "Each man fled the tyranny of his neighbor's smoke" [15] was the rule of the country, and each Boer family repeated in complete isolation the general pattern of Boer experience among black savages and ruled over them in absolute lawlessness, unchecked by "kind neighbors ready to cheer you or to fall on you stepping delicately between the butcher and the policeman, in the holy terror of scandal and gallows and lunatic asylums" (Conrad). Ruling over tribes and living parasitically from their labor, they came to occupy a position very similar to that of the native tribal leaders whose domination they had liquidated. The natives, at any rate, recognized them as a higher form of tribal leadership, a kind of natural deity to which one has to submit; so that the divine role of the Boers was as much imposed by their black slaves as assumed freely by themselves. It is a matter of course that to these white gods of black slaves each law meant only deprivation of freedom, government only restriction of the wild arbitrariness of the clan.[16] In the natives the Boers discovered the only "raw material" which Africa provided in abundance and they used them not for the production of riches but for the mere essentials of human existence.

The black slaves in South Africa quickly became the only part of the population that actually worked. Their toil was marked by all the known disadvantages of slave labor, such as lack of initiative, laziness, neglect of tools, and general inefficiency. Their work therefore barely sufficed to keep their masters alive and never reached the comparative abundance which nurtures civilization. It was this absolute dependence on the work of others and complete contempt for labor and productivity in any form that transformed the Dutchman into the Boer and gave his concept of race a distinctly economic meaning.[17]

[14] "The true history of South African colonization describes the growth, not of a settlement of Europeans, but of a totally new and unique society of different races and colours and cultural attainments, fashioned by conflicts of racial heredity and the oppositions of unequal social groups" (Kiewiet, *op. cit.,* p. 19).

[15] Kiewiet, *op. cit.,* p. 19.

[16] "[The Boers'] society was rebellious, but it was not revolutionary" (*ibid.,* p. 58).

[17] "Little effort was made to raise the standard of living or increase the opportunities of the class of slaves and servants. In this manner, the limited wealth of the Colony became the privilege of its white population. . . . Thus early did South Africa learn that a self-conscious group may escape the worst effects of life in a poor and unprosperous land by turning distinctions of race and colour into devices for social and economic discrimination" (*ibid.,* p. 22).

The Boers were the first European group to become completely alienated from the pride which Western man felt in living in a world created and fabricated by himself.[18] They treated the natives as raw material and lived on them as one might live on the fruits of wild trees. Lazy and unproductive, they agreed to vegetate on essentially the same level as the black tribes had vegetated for thousands of years. The great horror which had seized European men at their first confrontation with native life was stimulated by precisely this touch of inhumanity among human beings who apparently were as much a part of nature as wild animals. The Boers lived on their slaves exactly the way natives had lived on an unprepared and unchanged nature. When the Boers, in their fright and misery, decided to use these savages as though they were just another form of animal life, they embarked upon a process which could only end with their own degeneration into a white race living beside and together with black races from whom in the end they would differ only in the color of their skin.

The poor whites in South Africa, who in 1923 formed 10 per cent of the total white population[19] and whose standard of living does not differ much from that of the Bantu tribes, are today a warning example of this possibility. Their poverty is almost exclusively the consequence of their contempt for work and their adjustment to the way of life of black tribes. Like the blacks, they deserted the soil if the most primitive cultivation no longer yielded the little that was necessary or if they had exterminated the animals of the region.[20] Together with their former slaves, they came to the gold and diamond centers, abandoning their farms whenever the black workers departed. But in contrast to the natives who were immediately hired as cheap unskilled labor, they demanded and were granted charity as the right of a white skin, having lost all consciousness that normally men do not earn a living by the color of their skin.[21] Their race consciousness today is violent

[18] The point is that, for instance, in "the West Indies such a large proportion of slaves as were held at the Cape would have been a sign of wealth and a source of prosperity"; whereas "at the Cape slavery was the sign of an unenterprising economy . . . whose labour was wastefully and inefficiently used" (*ibid.*). It was chiefly this that led Barnes (*op. cit.,* p. 107) and many other observers to the conclusion: "South Africa is thus a foreign country, not only in the sense that its standpoint is definitely un-British, but also in the much more radical sense that its very *raison d'etre,* as an attempt at an organised society, is in contradiction to the principles on which the states of Christendom are founded."

[19] This corresponded to as many as 160,000 individuals (Kiewiet, *op. cit.,* p. 181). James (*op. cit.,* p. 43) estimated the number of poor whites in 1943 at 500,000 which would correspond to about 20 per cent of the white population.

[20] "The poor white Afrikaaner population, living on the same subsistence level as the Bantus, is primarily the result of the Boers' inability or stubborn refusal to learn agricultural science. Like the Bantu, the Boer likes to wander from one area to another, tilling the soil until it is no longer fertile, shooting the wild game until it ceases to exist" (*ibid.*).

[21] "Their race was their title of superiority over the natives, and to do manual labour conflicted with the dignity conferred upon them by their race. . . . Such an aversion degenerated, in those who were most demoralized, into a claim to charity as a right" (Kiewiet, *op. cit.,* p. 216).

not only because they have nothing to lose save their membership in the
white community, but also because the race concept seems to define their
own condition much more adequately than it does that of their former
slaves, who are well on the way to becoming workers, a normal part of
human civilization.

Racism as a ruling device was used in this society of whites and blacks
before imperialism exploited it as a major political idea. Its basis, and its
excuse, were still experience itself, a horrifying experience of something alien
beyond imagination or comprehension; it was tempting indeed simply to
declare that these were not human beings. Since, however, despite all ideological explanations the black men stubbornly insisted on retaining their
human features, the "white men" could not but reconsider their own humanity and decide that they themselves were more than human and obviously
chosen by God to be the gods of black men. This conclusion was logical and
unavoidable if one wanted to deny radically all common bonds with savages;
in practice it meant that Christianity for the first time could not act as a
decisive curb on the dangerous perversions of human self-consciousness, a
premonition of its essential ineffectiveness in other more recent race societies.[22] The Boers simply denied the Christian doctrine of the common
origin of men and changed those passages of the Old Testament which did
not yet transcend the limits of the old Israelite national religion into a superstition which could not even be called a heresy.[23] Like the Jews, they firmly
believed in themselves as the chosen people,[24] with the essential difference
that they were chosen not for the sake of divine salvation of mankind, but for
the lazy domination over another species that was condemned to an equally
lazy drudgery.[25] This was God's will on earth as the Dutch Reformed Church
proclaimed it and still proclaims it today in sharp and hostile contrast to
the missionaries of all other Christian denominations.[26]

[22] The Dutch Reformed Church has been in the forefront of the Boers' struggle
against the influence of Christian missionaries on the Cape. In 1944, however, they
went one step farther and adopted "without a single voice of dissent" a motion opposing the marriage of Boers with English-speaking citizens. (According to the Cape
Times, editorial of July 18, 1944. Quoted from New Africa, Council on African Affairs. Monthly Bulletin, October, 1944.)

[23] Kiewiet (op. cit., p. 181) mentions "the doctrine of racial superiority which was
drawn from the Bible and reinforced by the popular interpretation which the nineteenth century placed upon Darwin's theories."

[24] "The God of the Old Testament has been to them almost as much a national
figure as He has been to the Jews. . . . I recall a memorable scene in a Cape Town
club, where a bold Briton, dining by chance with three or four Dutchmen, ventured
to observe that Christ was a non-European and that, legally speaking, he would have
been a prohibited immigrant in the Union of South Africa. The Dutchmen were so
electrified at the remark that they nearly fell off their chairs" (Barnes, op. cit., p. 33).

[25] "For the Boer farmer the separation and the degradation of the natives are or-
dained by God, and it is crime and blasphemy to argue to the contrary" (Norman Bentwich, "South Africa. Dominion of Racial Problems." In Political Quarterly, 1939,
Vol. X, No. 3).

[26] "To this day the missionary is to the Boer the fundamental traitor, the white man
who stands for black against white" (S. Gertrude Millin, Rhodes, London, 1933, p. 38).

Boer racism, unlike the other brands, has a touch of authenticity and, so to speak, of innocence. A complete lack of literature and other intellectual achievement is the best witness to this statement.[27] It was and remains a desperate reaction to desperate living conditions which was inarticulate and inconsequential as long as it was left alone. Things began to happen only with the arrival of the British, who showed little interest in their newest colony which in 1849 was still called a military station (as opposed to either a colony or a plantation). But their mere presence—that is, their contrasting attitude toward the natives whom they did not consider a different animal species, their later attempts (after 1834) to abolish slavery, and above all their efforts to impose fixed boundaries upon landed property—provoked the stagnant Boer society into violent reactions. It is characteristic of the Boers that these reactions followed the same, repeated pattern throughout the nineteenth century: Boer farmers escaped British law by treks into the interior wilderness of the country, abandoning without regret their homes and their farms. Rather than accept limitations upon their possessions, they left them altogether.[28] This does not mean that the Boers did not feel at home wherever they happened to be; they felt and still feel much more at home in Africa than any subsequent immigrants, but in Africa and not in any specific limited territory. Their fantastic treks, which threw the British administration into consternation, showed clearly that they had transformed themselves into a tribe and had lost the European's feeling for a territory, a *patria* of his own. They behaved exactly like the black tribes who had also roamed the Dark Continent for centuries—feeling at home wherever the horde happened to be, and fleeing like death every attempt at definite settlement.

Rootlessness is characteristic of all race organizations. What the European "movements" consciously aimed at, the transformation of the people into a horde, can be watched like a laboratory test in the Boers' early and sad attempt. While rootlessness as a conscious aim was based primarily upon

[27] "Because they had little art, less architecture, and no literature, they depended upon their farms, their Bibles, and their blood to set them off sharply against the native and the outlander" (Kiewiet, *op. cit.*, p. 121).

[28] "The true Vortrekker hated a boundary. When the British Government insisted on fixed boundaries for the Colony and for farms within it, something was taken from him. . . . It was best surely to betake themselves across the border where there were water and free land and no British Government to disallow Vagrancy Laws and where white men could not be haled to court to answer the complaints of their servants" (*Ibid.*, pp. 54-55). "The Great Trek, a movement unique in the history of colonization" (p. 58) "was the defeat of the policy of more intensive settlement. The practice which required the area of an entire Canadian township for the settlement of ten families was extended through all of South Africa. It made for ever impossible the segregation of white and black races in separate areas of settlement. . . . By taking the Boers beyond the reach of British law, the Great Trek enabled them to establish 'proper' relations with the native population" (p. 56). "In later years, the Great Trek was to become more than a protest; it was to become a rebellion against the British administration, and the foundation stone of the Anglo-Boer racialism of the twentieth century" (James, *op. cit.*, p. 28).

hatred of a world that had no place for "superfluous" men, so that its destruction could become a supreme political goal, the rootlessness of the
Boers was a natural result of early emancipation from work and complete
lack of a human-built world. The same striking similarity prevails between
the "movements" and the Boers' interpretation of "chosenness." But while
the Pan-German, Pan-Slav, or Polish Messianic movements' chosenness was
a more or less conscious instrument for domination, the Boers' perversion
of Christianity was solidly rooted in a horrible reality in which miserable
"white men" were worshipped as divinities by equally unfortunate "black
men." Living in an environment which they had no power to transform into
a civilized world, they could discover no higher value than themselves. The
point, however, is that no matter whether racism appears as the natural
result of a catastrophe or as the conscious instrument for bringing it about,
it is always closely tied to contempt for labor, hatred of territorial limitation, general rootlessness, and an activistic faith in one's own divine chosenness.

Early British rule in South Africa, with its missionaries, soldiers, and
explorers, did not realize that the Boers' attitudes had some basis in reality.
They did not understand that absolute European supremacy—in which they,
after all, were as interested as the Boers—could hardly be maintained except
through racism because the permanent European settlement was so hopelessly outnumbered; [29] they were shocked "if Europeans settled in Africa
were to act like savages themselves because it was the custom of the country," [30] and to their simple utilitarian minds it seemed folly to sacrifice productivity and profit to the phantom world of white gods ruling over black
shadows. Only with the settlement of Englishmen and other Europeans during the gold rush did they gradually adjust to a population which could not
be lured back into European civilization even by profit motives, which had
lost contact even with the lower incentives of European man when it had
cut itself off from his higher motives, because both lose their meaning and
appeal in a society where nobody wants to achieve anything and everyone
has become a god.

II: *Gold and Race*

THE DIAMOND FIELDS of Kimberley and the gold mines of the Witwatersrand
happened to lie in this phantom world of race, and "a land that had seen
boat-load after boat-load of emigrants for New Zealand and Australia pass
it unheeding by now saw men tumbling on to its wharves and hurrying

[29] In 1939, the total population of the Union of South Africa amounted to 9,500,000
of whom 7,000,000 were natives and 2,500,000 Europeans. Of the latter, more than
1,250,000 were Boers, about one-third were British, and 100,000 were Jews. See Norman Bentwich, *op. cit.*
[30] J. A. Froude, *op. cit.*, p. 375.

up country to the mines. Most of them were English, but among them was more than a sprinkling from Riga and Kiev, Hamburg and Frankfort, Rotterdam and San Francisco." [31] All of them belonged to "a class of persons who prefer adventure and speculation to settled industry, and who do not work well in the harness of ordinary life. . . . [There were] diggers from America and Australia, German speculators, traders, saloonkeepers, professional gamblers, barristers . . . , ex-officers of the army and navy, younger sons of good families . . . a marvelous motley assemblage among whom money flowed like water from the amazing productiveness of the mine." They were joined by thousands of natives who first came to "steal diamonds and to lag their earnings out in rifles and powder," [32] but quickly started to work for wages and became the seemingly inexhaustible cheap labor supply when the "most stagnant of colonial regions suddenly exploded into activity." [33]

The abundance of natives, of cheap labor, was the first and perhaps most important difference between this gold rush and others of its type. It was soon apparent that the mob from the four corners of the earth would not even have to do the digging; at any rate, the permanent attraction of South Africa, the permanent resource that tempted the adventurers to permanent settlement, was not the gold but this human raw material which promised a permanent emancipation from work.[34] The Europeans served solely as supervisors and did not even produce skilled labor and engineers, both of which had constantly to be imported from Europe.

Second in importance only, for the ultimate outcome, was the fact that this gold rush was not simply left to itself but was financed, organized, and connected with the ordinary European economy through the accumulated superfluous wealth and with the help of Jewish financiers. From the very beginning "a hundred or so Jewish merchants who have gathered like eagles over their prey" [35] actually acted as middlemen through whom European capital was invested in the gold mining and diamond industries.

The only section of the South African population that did not have and did not want to have a share in the suddenly exploding activities of the country were the Boers. They hated all these *uitlanders,* who did not care for citizenship but who needed and obtained British protection, thereby seemingly strengthening British government influence on the Cape. The Boers reacted as they had always reacted, they sold their diamond-laden possessions in Kimberley and their farms with gold mines near Johannesburg and trekked once more into the interior wilderness. They did not understand that this new influx was different from the British missionaries, government officials, or ordinary settlers, and they realized only when it was too late

[31] Kiewiet, *op. cit.,* p. 119.
[32] Froude, *op. cit.,* p. 400.
[33] Kiewiet, *op. cit.,* p. 119.
[34] "What an abundance of rain and grass was to New Zealand mutton, what a plenty of cheap grazing land was to Australian wool, what the fertile prairie acres were to Canadian wheat, cheap native labour was to South African mining and industrial enterprise" (Kiewiet, *op. cit.,* p. 96).
[35] J. A. Froude, *ibid.*

and they had already lost their share in the riches of the gold hunt that the new idol of Gold was not at all irreconcilable with their idol of Blood, that the new mob was as unwilling to work and as unfit to establish a civilization as they were themselves, and would therefore spare them the British officials' annoying insistence on law and the Christian missionaries' irritating concept of human equality.

The Boers feared and fled what actually never happened, namely, the industrialization of the country. They were right insofar as normal production and civilization would indeed have destroyed automatically the way of life of a race society. A normal market for labor and merchandise would have liquidated the privileges of race. But gold and diamonds, which soon provided a living for half of South Africa's population, were not merchandise in the same sense and were not produced in the same way as wool in Australia, meat in New Zealand, or wheat in Canada. The irrational, non-functional place of gold in the economy made it independent of rational production methods which, of course, could never have tolerated the fantastic disparities between black and white wages. Gold, an object for speculation and essentially dependent in value upon political factors, became the "lifeblood" of South Africa [36] but it could not and did not become the basis of a new economic order.

The Boers also feared the mere presence of the *uitlanders* because they mistook them for British settlers. The *uitlanders,* however, came solely in order to get rich quickly, and only those remained who did not quite succeed or who, like the Jews, had no country to return to. Neither group cared very much to establish a community after the model of European countries, as British settlers had done in Australia, Canada, and New Zealand. It was Barnato who happily discovered that "the Transvaal Government is like no other government in the world. It is indeed not a government at all, but an unlimited company of some twenty thousand shareholders." [37] Similarly, it was more or less a series of misunderstandings which finally led to the British-Boer war, which the Boers wrongly believed to be "the culmination of the British Government's lengthy quest for a united South Africa," while it was actually prompted mainly by investment interests.[38] When the Boers lost the war, they lost no more than they had already deliberately abandoned, that is, their share in the riches; but they definitely won the consent of all other European elements, including the British government, to the lawless-

[36] "The goldmines are the life-blood of the Union . . . one half of the population obtained their livelihood directly or indirectly from the goldmining industry, and . . . one half of the finances of the government were derived directly or indirectly from gold mining" (Kiewiet, *op. cit.,* p. 155).

[37] See Paul H. Emden, *Jews of Britain, A Series of Biographies,* London, 1944, chapter "From Cairo to the Cape."

[38] Kiewiet (*op. cit.,* pp. 138-39) mentions, however, also another "set of circumstances": "Any attempt by the British Government to secure concessions or reforms from the Transvaal Government made it inevitably the agent of the mining magnates. . . . Great Britain gave its support, whether this was clearly realized in Downing Street or not, to capital and mining investments."

ness of a race society.[39] Today, all sections of the population, British or Afrikander, organized workers or capitalists, agree on the race question,[40] and whereas the rise of Nazi Germany and its conscious attempt to transform the German people into a race strengthened the political position of the Boers considerably, Germany's defeat has not weakened it.

The Boers hated and feared the financiers more than the other foreigners. They somehow understood that the financier was a key figure in the combination of superfluous wealth and superfluous men, that it was his function to turn the essentially transitory gold hunt into a much broader and more permanent business.[41] The war with the British, moreover, soon demonstrated an even more decisive aspect; it was quite obvious that it had been prompted by foreign investors who demanded the government's protection of their tremendous profits in faraway countries as a matter of course—as though armies engaged in a war against foreign peoples were nothing but native police forces involved in a fight with native criminals. It made little difference to the Boers that the men who introduced this kind of violence into the shadowy affairs of the gold and diamond production were no longer the financiers, but those who somehow had risen from the mob itself and, like Cecil Rhodes, believed less in profits than in expansion for expansion's sake.[42] The financiers, who were mostly Jews and only the representatives, not the owners, of the superfluous capital, had neither the necessary political influence nor enough economic power to introduce political purposes and the use of violence into speculation and gambling.

Without doubt the financiers, though finally not the decisive factor in

[39] "Much of the hesitant and evasive conduct of British statesmanship in the generation before the Boer War could be attributed to the indecision of the British Government between its obligation to the natives and its obligation to the white communities. . . . Now, however, the Boer War compelled a decision on native policy. In the terms of the peace the British Government promised that no attempt would be made to alter the political status of the natives before self-government had been granted to the ex-Republics. In that epochal decision the British Government receded from its humanitarian position and enabled the Boer leaders to win a signal victory in the peace negotiations which marked their military defeat. Great Britain abandoned the effort to exercise a control over the vital relations between white and black. Downing Street had surrendered to the frontiers" (Kiewiet, *op. cit.,* pp. 143-44).

[40] "There is . . . an entirely erroneous notion that the Africaaners and the English-speaking people of South Africa still disagree on how to treat the natives. On the contrary, it is one of the few things on which they do agree" (James, *op. cit.,* p. 47).

[41] This was mostly due to the methods of Alfred Beit who had arrived in 1875 to buy diamonds for a Hamburg firm. "Till then only speculators had been shareholders in mining ventures. . . . Beit's method attracted the genuine investor also" (Emden, *op. cit.*).

[42] Very characteristic in this respect was Barnato's attitude when it came to the amalgamation of his business with the Rhodes group. "For Barnato the amalgamation was nothing but a financial transaction in which he wanted to make money. . . . He therefore desired that the company should have nothing to do with politics. Rhodes however was not merely a business man. . . ." This shows how very wrong Barnato was when he thought that "if I had received the education of Cecil Rhodes there would not have been a Cecil Rhodes" (*ibid.*).

imperialism, were remarkably representative of it in its initial period.[43] They had taken advantage of the overproduction of capital and its accompanying complete reversal of economic and moral values. Instead of mere trade in goods and mere profit from production, trade in capital itself emerged on an unprecedented scale. This alone would have given them a prominent position; in addition profits from investments in foreign countries soon increased at a much more rapid rate than trade profits, so that traders and merchants lost their primacy to the financier.[44] The main economic characteristic of the financier is that he earns his profits not from production and exploitation or exchange of merchandise or normal banking, but solely through commissions. This is important in our context because it gives him that touch of unreality, of phantom-like existence and essential futility even in a normal economy, that are typical of so many South African events. The financiers certainly did not exploit anybody and they had least control over the course of their business ventures, whether these turned out to be common swindles or sound enterprises belatedly confirmed.

It is also significant that it was precisely the mob element among the Jewish people who turned into financiers. It is true that the discovery of gold mines in South Africa had coincided with the first modern pogroms in Russia, so that a trickle of Jewish emigrants went to South Africa. There, however, they would hardly have played a role in the international crowd of desperadoes and fortune hunters if a few Jewish financiers had not been there ahead of them and taken an immediate interest in the newcomers who clearly could represent them in the population.

The Jewish financiers came from practically every country on the continent where they had been, in terms of class, as superfluous as the other South African immigrants. They were quite different from the few established families of Jewish notables whose influence had steadily decreased after 1820, and into whose ranks they could therefore no longer be assimilated. They belonged in that new caste of Jewish financiers which, from the seventies and eighties on, we find in all European capitals, where they had come, mostly after having left their countries of origin, in order to try their luck in the international stock-market gamble. This they did everywhere to the great dismay of the older Jewish families, who were too weak to stop the unscrupulousness of the newcomers and therefore only too glad if the latter decided to transfer the field of their activities overseas. In other words, the Jewish financiers had become as superfluous in legitimate Jewish banking as the wealth they represented had become superfluous in legitimate

[43] Compare chapter v, note 34.

[44] The increase in profits from foreign investment and a relative decrease of foreign trade profits characterizes the economic side of imperialism. In 1899, it was estimated that Great Britain's whole foreign and colonial trade had brought her an income of only 18 million pounds, while in the same year profits from foreign investment amounted to 90 or 100 million pounds. See J. A. Hobson, *Imperialism*, London, 1938, pp. 53 ff. It is obvious that investment demanded a much more conscious long-range policy of exploitation than mere trade.

industrial enterprise and the fortune hunters in the world of legitimate labor. In South Africa itself, where the merchant was about to lose his status within the country's economy to the financier, the new arrivals, the Barnatos, Beits, Sammy Marks, removed the older Jewish settlers from first position much more easily than in Europe.[45] In South Africa, though hardly anywhere else, they were the third factor in the initial alliance between capital and mob; to a large extent, they set the alliance into motion, handled the influx of capital and its investment in the gold mines and diamond fields, and soon became more conspicuous than anybody else.

The fact of their Jewish origin added an undefinable symbolic flavor to the role of the financiers—a flavor of essential homelessness and rootlessness —and thus served to introduce an element of mystery, as well as to symbolize the whole affair. To this must be added their actual international connections, which naturally stimulated the general popular delusions concerning Jewish political power all over the world. It is quite comprehensible that all the fantastic notions of a secret international Jewish power—notions which originally had been the result of the closeness of Jewish banking capital to the state's sphere of business—became even more virulent here than on the European continent. Here, for the first time Jews were driven into the midst of a race society and almost automatically singled out by the Boers from all other "white" people for special hatred, not only as the representatives of the whole enterprise, but as a different "race," the embodiment of a devilish principle introduced into the normal world of "blacks" and "whites." This hatred was all the more violent as it was partly caused by the suspicion that the Jews with their own older and more authentic claim would be harder than anyone else to convince of the Boers' claim to chosenness. While Christianity simply denied the principle as such, Judaism seemed a direct challenge and rival. Long before the Nazis consciously built up an antisemitic movement in South Africa, the race issue had invaded the conflict between the *uitlander* and the Boers in the form of antisemitism,[46] which is all the more noteworthy since the importance of Jews in the South African gold and diamond economy did not survive the turn of the century.

As soon as the gold and diamond industries reached the stage of imperialist development where absentee shareholders demand their governments' political protection, it turned out that the Jews could not hold their important economic position. They had no home government to turn to and their position in South African society was so insecure that much more was at stake for them than a mere decrease in influence. They could preserve economic

---

[45] Early Jewish settlers in South Africa in the eighteenth and the first part of the nineteenth century were adventurers; traders and merchants followed them after the middle of the century, among whom the most prominent turned to industries such as fishing, sealing, and whaling (De Pass Brothers) and ostrich breeding (the Mosenthal family). Later, they were almost forced into the Kimberley diamond industries where, however, they never achieved such pre-eminence as Barnato and Beit.

[46] Ernst Schultze, "Die Judenfrage in Sued-Afrika," in *Der Weltkampf*, October, 1938, Vol. XV, No. 178.

security and permanent settlement in South Africa, which they needed more than any other group of *uitlanders,* only if they achieved some status in society—which in this case meant admission to exclusive British clubs. They were forced to trade their influence against the position of a gentleman, as Cecil Rhodes very bluntly put it when he bought his way into the Barnato Diamond Trust, after having amalgamated his De Beers Company with Alfred Beit's Company.[47] But these Jews had more to offer than just economic power; it was thanks to them that Cecil Rhodes, as much a newcomer and adventurer as they, was finally accepted by England's respectable banking business with which the Jewish financiers after all had better connections than anybody else.[48] "Not one of the English banks would have lent a single shilling on the security of gold shares. It was the unbounded confidence of these diamond men from Kimberley that operated like a magnet upon their co-religionists at home." [49]

The gold rush became a full-fledged imperialist enterprise only after Cecil Rhodes had dispossessed the Jews, taken investment policies from England's into his own hands, and had become the central figure on the Cape. Seventy-five per cent of the dividends paid to shareholders went abroad, and a large majority of them to Great Britain. Rhodes succeeded in interesting the British government in his business affairs, persuaded them that expansion and export of the instruments of violence was necessary to protect investments, and that such a policy was a holy duty of every national government. On the other hand, he introduced on the Cape itself that typically imperialist economic policy of neglecting all industrial enterprises which were not owned by absentee shareholders, so that finally not only the gold mining companies but the government itself discouraged the exploitation of abundant base metal deposits and the production of consumers' goods.[50] With the initiation of this policy, Rhodes introduced the most potent factor in the eventual appeasement of the Boers; the neglect of all authentic industrial enterprise was the most solid guarantee for the avoidance of normal capitalist development and thus against a normal end of race society.

It took the Boers several decades to understand that imperialism was

[47] Barnato sold his shares to Rhodes in order to be introduced to the Kimberley Club. "This is no mere money transaction," Rhodes is reported to have told Barnato, "I propose to make a gentleman of you." Barnato enjoyed his life as a gentleman for eight years and then committed suicide. See Millin, *op. cit.,* pp. 14, 85.

[48] "The path from one Jew [in this case, Alfred Beit from Hamburg] to another is an easy one. Rhodes went to England to see Lord Rothschild and Lord Rothschild approved of him" (*ibid.*).

[49] Emden, *op. cit.*

[50] "South Africa concentrated almost all its peacetime industrial energy on the production of gold. The average investor put his money into gold because it offered the quickest and biggest returns. But South Africa also has tremendous deposits of iron ore, copper, asbestos, manganese, tin, lead, platinum, chrome, mica and graphite. These, along with the coal mines and the handful of factories producing consumer goods, were known as 'secondary' industries. The investing public's interest in them was limited. And development of these secondary industries was discouraged by the gold-mining companies and to a large extent by the government" (James, *op. cit.,* p. 333).

nothing to be afraid of, since it would neither develop the country as Australia and Canada had been developed, nor draw profits from the country
at large, being quite content with a high turnover of investments in one
specific field. Imperialism therefore was willing to abandon the so-called
laws of capitalist production and their egalitarian tendencies, so long as
profits from specific investments were safe. This led eventually to the abolition of the law of mere profitableness and South Africa became the first
example of a phenomenon that occurs whenever the mob becomes the
dominant factor in the alliance between mob and capital.

In one respect, the most important one, the Boers remained the undisputed
masters of the country: whenever rational labor and production policies
came into conflict with race considerations, the latter won. Profit motives
were sacrificed time and again to the demands of a race society, frequently
at a terrific price. The rentability of the railroads was destroyed overnight
when the government dismissed 17,000 Bantu employees and paid whites
wages that amounted to 200 per cent more; [51] expenses for municipal government became prohibitive when native municipal employees were replaced
with whites; the Color Bar Bill finally excluded all black workers from
mechanical jobs and forced industrial enterprise to a tremendous increase
of production costs. The race world of the Boers had nobody to fear any
more, least of all white labor, whose trade unions complained bitterly that
the Color Bar Bill did not go far enough.[52]

At first glance, it is surprising that a violent antisemitism survived the
disappearance of the Jewish financiers as well as the successful indoctrination
with racism of all parts of the European population. The Jews were certainly
no exception to this rule; they adjusted to racism as well as everybody else
and their behavior toward black people was beyond reproach.[53] Yet they
had, without being aware of it and under pressure of special circumstances,
broken with one of the most powerful traditions of the country.

The first sign of "anormal" behavior came immediately after the Jewish
financiers had lost their position in the gold and diamond industries. They
did not leave the country but settled down permanently [54] into a unique posi-

[51] James, op. cit., pp. 111-112. "The Government reckoned that this was a good example for private employers to follow . . . and public opinion soon forced changes
in the hiring policies of many employers."

[52] James, op. cit., p. 108.

[53] Here again, a definite difference between the earlier settlers and the financiers
can be recognized until the end of the nineteenth century. Saul Salomon, for instance,
a Negrophilist member of the Cape Parliament, was a descendant of a family which
had settled in South Africa in the early nineteenth century. Emden, op. cit.

[54] Between 1924 and 1930, 12,319 Jews immigrated to South Africa while only
461 left the country. These figures are very striking if one considers that the total
immigration for the same period after deduction of emigrants amounted to 14,241
persons. (See Schultze, op. cit.) If we compare these figures with the immigration
table of note 6, it follows that Jews constituted roughly one-third of the total immigration to South Africa in the twenties, and that they, in sharp contrast to all other

tion for a white group: they neither belonged to the "lifeblood" of Africa nor to the "poor white trash." Instead they started almost immediately to build up those industries and professions which according to South African opinion are "secondary" because they are not connected with gold.[55] Jews became manufacturers of furniture and clothes, shopkeepers and members of the professions, physicians, lawyers, and journalists. In other words, no matter how well they thought they were adjusted to the mob conditions of the country and its race attitude, Jews had broken its most important pattern by introducing into South African economy a factor of normalcy and productivity, with the result that when Mr. Malan introduced into Parliament a bill to expel all Jews from the Union he had the enthusiastic support of all poor whites and of the whole Afrikander population.[56]

This change in the economic function, the transformation of South African Jewry from representing the most shadowy characters in the shadow world of gold and race into the only productive part of the population, came like an oddly belated confirmation of the original fears of the Boers. They had hated the Jews not so much as the middlemen of superfluous wealth or the representatives of the world of gold; they had feared and despised them as the very image of the *uitlanders* who would try to change the country into a normal producing part of Western civilization, whose profit motives, at least, would mortally endanger the phantom world of race. And when the Jews were finally cut off from the golden lifeblood of the *uitlanders* and could not leave the country as all other foreigners would have done in similar circumstances, developing "secondary" industries instead, the Boers turned out to be right. The Jews, entirely by themselves and without being the image of anything or anybody, had become a real menace to race society. As matters stand today, the Jews have against them the concerted hostility of all those who believe in race or gold—and that is practically the whole European population in South Africa. Yet they cannot and will not make common cause with the only other group which slowly and gradually is being won away from race society: the black workers who are becoming more and more aware of their humanity under the impact of regular labor and urban life. Although they, in contrast to the "whites," do have a genuine race origin, they have made no fetish of race, and the abolition of race society means only the promise of their liberation.

In contrast to the Nazis, to whom racism and antisemitism were major political weapons for the destruction of civilization and the setting up of a new body politic, racism and antisemitism are a matter of course and a

---

categories of *uitlanders*, settled there permanently; their share in the annual emigration is less than 2 per cent.

[55] "Rabid Afrikaaner nationalist leaders have deplored the fact that there are 102,000 Jews in the Union; most of them are white-collar workers, industrial employers, shopkeepers, or members of the professions. The Jews did much to build up the secondary industries of South Africa—*i.e.*, industries other than gold and diamond mining—concentrating particularly on the manufacture of clothes and furniture" (James, *op. cit.*, p. 46).

[56] *Ibid.*, pp. 67-68.

natural consequence of the status quo in South Africa. They did not need Nazism in order to be born and they influenced Nazism only in an indirect way.

There were, however, real and immediate boomerang effects of South Africa's race society on the behavior of European peoples: since cheap Indian and Chinese labor had been madly imported to South Africa whenever her interior supply was temporarily halted,[57] a change of attitude toward colored people was felt immediately in Asia where, for the first time, people were treated in almost the same way as those African savages who had frightened Europeans literally out of their wits. The difference was only that there could be no excuse and no humanly comprehensible reason for treating Indians and Chinese as though they were not human beings. In a certain sense, it is only here that the real crime began, because here everyone ought to have known what he was doing. It is true that the race notion was somewhat modified in Asia; "higher and lower breeds," as the "white man" would say when he started to shoulder his burden, still indicate a scale and the possibility of gradual development, and the idea somehow escapes the concept of two entirely different species of animal life. On the other hand, since the race principle supplanted the older notion of alien and strange peoples in Asia, it was a much more consciously applied weapon for domination and exploitation than in Africa.

Less immediately significant but of greater importance for totalitarian governments was the other experience in Africa's race society, that profit motives are not holy and can be overruled, that societies can function according to principles other than economic, and that such circumstances may favor those who under conditions of rationalized production and the capitalist system would belong to the underprivileged. South Africa's race society taught the mob the great lesson of which it had always had a confused premonition, that through sheer violence an underprivileged group could create a class lower than itself, that for this purpose it did not even need a revolution but could band together with groups of the ruling classes, and that foreign or backward peoples offered the best opportunities for such tactics.

The full impact of the African experience was first realized by leaders of the mob, like Carl Peters, who decided that they too had to belong to a master race. African colonial possessions became the most fertile soil for the flowering of what later was to become the Nazi elite. Here they had seen with their own eyes how peoples could be converted into races and how, simply by taking the initiative in this process, one might push one's own people into the position of the master race. Here they were cured of the

---

[57] More than 100,000 Indian coolies were imported to the sugar plantations of Natal in the nineteenth century. These were followed by Chinese laborers in the mines who numbered about 55,000 in 1907. In 1910, the British government ordered the repatriation of all Chinese mine laborers, and in 1913 it prohibited any further immigration from India or any other part of Asia. In 1931, 142,000 Asiatics were still in the Union and treated like African natives. (See also Schultze, *op. cit.*)

illusion that the historical process is necessarily "progressive," for if it was the course of older colonization to trek to something, the "Dutchman trekked away from everything," [58] and if "economic history once taught that man had developed by gradual steps from a life of hunting to pastoral pursuits and finally to a settled and agricultural life," the story of the Boers clearly demonstrated that one could also come "from a land that had taken the lead in a thrifty and intensive cultivation . . . [and] gradually become a herdsman and a hunter." [59] These leaders understood very well that precisely because the Boers had sunk back to the level of savage tribes they remained their undisputed masters. They were perfectly willing to pay the price, to recede to the level of a race organization, if by so doing they could buy lordship over other "races." And they knew from their experiences with people gathered from the four corners of the earth in South Africa that the whole mob of the Western civilized world would be with them.[60]

III: *The Imperialist Character*

OF THE TWO main political devices of imperialist rule, race was discovered in South Africa and bureaucracy in Algeria, Egypt, and India; the former was originally the barely conscious reaction to tribes of whose humanity European man was ashamed and frightened, whereas the latter was a consequence of that administration by which Europeans had tried to rule foreign peoples whom they felt to be hopelessly their inferiors and at the same time in need of their special protection. Race, in other words, was an escape into an irresponsibility where nothing human could any longer exist, and bureaucracy was the result of a responsibility that no man can bear for his fellowman and no people for another people.

The exaggerated sense of responsibility in the British administrators of India who succeeded Burke's "breakers of law" had its material basis in the fact that the British Empire had actually been acquired in a "fit of absentmindedness." Those, therefore, who were confronted with the accomplished fact and the job of keeping what had become theirs through an accident, had to find an interpretation that could change the accident into a kind of willed act. Such historical changes of fact have been carried through by legends

[58] Barnes, *op. cit.*, p. 13.

[59] Kiewiet, *op. cit.*, p. 13.

[60] "When economists declared that higher wages were a form of bounty, and that protected labour was uneconomical, the answer was given that the sacrifice was well made if the unfortunate elements in the white population ultimately found an assured footing in modern life." "But it has not been in South Africa alone that the voice of the conventional economist has gone unheeded since the end of the Great War. . . . In a generation which saw England abandon free trade, America leave the gold standard, the Third Reich embrace autarchy, . . . South Africa's insistence that its economic life must be organized to secure the dominant position of the white race is not seriously out of place" (Kiewiet, *op. cit.*, pp. 224 and 245).

since ancient times, and legends dreamed up by the British intelligentsia have played a decisive role in the formation of the bureaucrat and the secret agent of the British services.

Legends have always played a powerful role in the making of history. Man, who has not been granted the gift of undoing, who is always an unconsulted heir of other men's deeds, and who is always burdened with a responsibility that appears to be the consequence of an unending chain of events rather than conscious acts, demands an explanation and interpretation of the past in which the mysterious key to his future destiny seems to be concealed. Legends were the spiritual foundations of every ancient city, empire, people, promising safe guidance through the limitless spaces of the future. Without ever relating facts reliably, yet always expressing their true significance, they offered a truth beyond realities, a remembrance beyond memories.

Legendary explanations of history always served as belated corrections of facts and real events, which were needed precisely because history itself would hold man responsible for deeds he had not done and for consequences he had never foreseen. The truth of the ancient legends—what gives them their fascinating actuality many centuries after the cities and empires and peoples they served have crumbled to dust—was nothing but the form in which past events were made to fit the human condition in general and political aspirations in particular. Only in the frankly invented tale about events did man consent to assume his responsibility for them, and to consider past events *his* past. Legends made him master of what he had not done, and capable of dealing with what he could not undo. In this sense, legends are not only among the first memories of mankind, but actually the true beginning of human history.

The flourishing of historical and political legends came to a rather abrupt end with the birth of Christianity. Its interpretation of history, from the days of Adam to the Last Judgment, as one single road to redemption and salvation, offered the most powerful and all-inclusive legendary explanation of human destiny. Only after the spiritual unity of Christian peoples gave way to the plurality of nations, when the road to salvation became an uncertain article of individual faith rather than a universal theory applicable to all happenings, did new kinds of historical explanations emerge. The nineteenth century has offered us the curious spectacle of an almost simultaneous birth of the most varying and contradictory ideologies, each of which claimed to know the hidden truth about otherwise incomprehensible facts. Legends, however, are not ideologies; they do not aim at universal explanation but are always concerned with concrete facts. It seems rather significant that the growth of national bodies was nowhere accompanied by a foundation legend, and that a first unique attempt in modern times was made precisely when the decline of the national body had become obvious and imperialism seemed to take the place of old-fashioned nationalism.

The author of the imperialist legend is Rudyard Kipling, its topic is the

British Empire, its result the imperialist character (imperialism was the
only school of character in modern politics). And while the legend of the
British Empire has little to do with the realities of British imperialism, it
forced or deluded into its services the best sons of England. For legends attract the very best in our times, just as ideologies attract the average, and the
whispered tales of gruesome secret powers behind the scenes attract the very
worst.

No doubt, no political structure could have been more evocative of
legendary tales and justifications than the British Empire, than the British
people's drifting from the conscious founding of colonies into ruling and
dominating foreign peoples all over the world.

The foundation legend, as Kipling tells it, starts from the fundamental
reality of the people of the British Isles.[61] Surrounded by the sea, they need
and win the help of the three elements of Water, Wind, and Sun through the
invention of the Ship. The ship made the always dangerous alliance with the
elements possible and made the Englishman master of the world. "You'll
win the world," says Kipling, "without anyone *caring* how you did it: you'll
keep the world without anyone *knowing* how you did it: and you'll carry the
world on your backs without anyone *seeing* how you did it. But neither you
nor your sons will get anything out of that little job except Four Gifts—one
for the Sea, one for the Wind, one for the Sun and one for the Ship that
carries you. . . . For, winning the world, and keeping the world, and carrying the world on their backs—on land, or on sea, or in the air—your sons
will always have the Four Gifts. Long-headed and slow-spoken and heavy
—damned heavy—in the hand, will they be; and always a little bit to wind-
ward of every enemy—that they may be a safeguard to all who pass on the
seas on their lawful occasions."

What brings the little tale of the "First Sailor" so close to ancient foundation legends is that it presents the British as the only politically mature
people, caring for law and burdened with the welfare of the world, in the
midst of barbarian tribes who neither care nor know what keeps the world
together. Unfortunately this presentation lacked the innate truth of ancient
legends; the world cared and knew and saw how they did it and no such
tale could ever have convinced the world that they did not "get anything out
of that little job." Yet there was a certain reality in England herself which
corresponded to Kipling's legend and made it at all possible, and that was
the existence of such virtues as chivalry, nobility, bravery, even though they
were utterly out of place in a political reality ruled by Cecil Rhodes or Lord
Curzon.

The fact that the "white man's burden" is either hypocrisy or racism has
not prevented a few of the best Englishmen from shouldering the burden in
earnest and making themselves the tragic and quixotic fools of imperialism.
As real in England as the tradition of hypocrisy is another less obvious one
which one is tempted to call a tradition of dragon-slayers who went enthusiastically into far and curious lands to strange and naïve peoples to slay the

[61] Rudyard Kipling, "The First Sailor," in *Humorous Tales*, 1891.

numerous dragons that had plagued them for centuries. There is more than a grain of truth in Kipling's other tale, "The Tomb of His Ancestor," [62] in which the Chinn family "serve India generation after generation, as dolphins follow in line across the open sea." They shoot the deer that steals the poor man's crop, teach him the mysteries of better agricultural methods, free him from some of his more harmful superstitions and kill lions and tigers in grand style. Their only reward is indeed a "tomb of ancestors" and a family legend, believed by the whole Indian tribe, according to which "the revered ancestor . . . has a tiger of his own—a saddle tiger that he rides round the country whenever he feels inclined." Unfortunately, this riding around the countryside is "a sure sign of war or pestilence or—or something," and in this particular case it is a sign of vaccination. So that Chinn the Youngest, a not very important underling in the hierarchy of the Army Services, but all-important as far as the Indian tribe is concerned, has to shoot the beast of his ancestor so that people can be vaccinated without fear of "war or pestilence or something."

As modern life goes, the Chinns indeed "are luckier than most folks." Their chance is that they were born into a career that gently and naturally leads them to the realization of the best dreams of youth. When other boys have to forget "noble dreams," they happen to be just old enough to translate them into action. And when after thirty years of service they retire, their steamer will pass "the outward bound troopship, carrying his son eastward to the family duty," so that the power of old Mr. Chinn's existence as a government-appointed and army-paid dragon-slayer can be imparted to the next generation. No doubt, the British government pays them for their services, but it is not at all clear in whose service they eventually land. There is a strong possibility that they really serve this particular Indian tribe, generation after generation, and it is consoling all around that at least the tribe itself is convinced of this. The fact that the higher services know hardly anything of little Lieutenant Chinn's strange duties and adventures, that they are hardly aware of his being a successful reincarnation of his grandfather, gives his dreamlike double existence an undisturbed basis in reality. He is simply at home in two worlds, separated by water- and gossip-tight walls. Born in "the heart of the scrubby tigerish country" and educated among his own people in peaceful, well-balanced, ill-informed England, he is ready to live permanently with two peoples and is rooted in and well acquainted with the tradition, language, superstition, and prejudices of both. At a moment's notice he can change from the obedient underling of one of His Majesty's soldiers into an exciting and noble figure in the natives' world, a well-beloved protector of the weak, the dragon-slayer of old tales.

The point is that these queer quixotic protectors of the weak who played their role behind the scenes of official British rule were not so much the product of a primitive people's naïve imagination as of dreams which contained the best of European and Christian traditions, even when they had

[62] In *The Day's Work,* 1898.

already deteriorated into the futility of boyhood ideals. It was neither His Majesty's soldier nor the British higher official who could teach the natives something of the greatness of the Western world. Only those who had never been able to outgrow their boyhood ideals and therefore had enlisted in the colonial services were fit for the task. Imperialism to them was nothing but an accidental opportunity to escape a society in which a man had to forget his youth if he wanted to grow up. English society was only too glad to see them depart to faraway countries, a circumstance which permitted the toleration and even the furtherance of boyhood ideals in the public school system; the colonial services took them away from England and prevented, so to speak, their converting the ideals of their boyhood into the mature ideas of men. Strange and curious lands attracted the best of England's youth since the end of the nineteenth century, deprived her society of the most honest and the most dangerous elements, and guaranteed, in addition to this bliss, a certain conservation, or perhaps petrification, of boyhood noblesse which preserved *and* infantilized Western moral standards.

Lord Cromer, secretary to the Viceroy and financial member in the pre-imperialist government of India, still belonged in the category of British dragon-slayers. Led solely by "the sense of sacrifice" for backward populations and "the sense of duty" [63] to the glory of Great Britain that "has given birth to a class of officials who have both the desire and the capacity to govern," [64] he declined in 1894 the post of Viceroy and refused ten years later the position of Secretary of State for Foreign Affairs. Instead of such honors, which would have satisfied a lesser man, he became the little-publicized and all-powerful British Consul General in Egypt from 1883 to 1907. There he became the first imperialist administrator, certainly "second to none among those who by their services have glorified the British race"; [65] perhaps the last to die in undisturbed pride: "Let these suffice for Britain's meed— / No nobler price was ever won, / The blessings of a people freed / The consciousness of duty done." [66]

Cromer went to Egypt because he realized that "the Englishman straining far over to hold his loved India [has to] plant a firm foot on the banks of the Nile." [67] Egypt was to him only a means to an end, a necessary expansion for the sake of security for India. At almost the same moment it happened that another Englishman set foot on the African continent, though at its opposite end and for opposite reasons: Cecil Rhodes went to South Africa and saved the Cape colony after it had lost all importance for the Englishman's "loved India." Rhodes's ideas on expansion were far more advanced

[63] Lawrence J. Zetland, *Lord Cromer*, 1932, p. 16.
[64] Lord Cromer, "The Government of Subject Races" in *Edinburgh Review*, January, 1908.
[65] Lord Curzon at the unveiling of the memorial tablet for Cromer. See Zetland, *op. cit.*, p. 362.
[66] Quoted from a long poem by Cromer. See Zetland, *op. cit.*, pp. 17-18.
[67] From a letter Lord Cromer wrote in 1882. *Ibid.*, p. 87.

than those of his more respectable colleague in the north; to him expansion did not need to be justified by such sensible motives as the holding of what one already possessed. "Expansion was everything" and India, South Africa, and Egypt were equally important or unimportant as stepping-stones in an expansion limited only by the size of the earth. There certainly was an abyss between the vulgar megalomaniac and the educated man of sacrifice and duty; yet they arrived at roughly identical results and were equally responsible for the "Great Game" of secrecy, which was no less insane and no less detrimental to politics than the phantom world of race.

The outstanding similarity between Rhodes's rule in South Africa and Cromer's domination of Egypt was that both regarded the countries not as desirable ends in themselves but merely as means for some supposedly higher purpose. They were similar therefore in their indifference and aloofness, in their genuine lack of interest in their subjects, an attitude which differed as much from the cruelty and arbitrariness of native despots in Asia as from the exploiting carelessness of conquerors, or the insane and anarchic oppression of one race tribe through another. As soon as Cromer started to rule Egypt for the sake of India, he lost his role of protector of "backward peoples" and could no longer sincerely believe that "the self-interest of the subject-races is the principal basis of the whole Imperial fabric." [68]

Aloofness became the new attitude of all members of the British services; it was a more dangerous form of governing than despotism and arbitrariness because it did not even tolerate that last link between the despot and his subjects, which is formed by bribery and gifts. The very integrity of the British administration made despotic government more inhuman and inaccessible to its subjects than Asiatic rulers or reckless conquerors had ever been.[69] Integrity and aloofness were symbols for an absolute division of interests to the point where they are not even permitted to conflict. In comparison, exploitation, oppression, or corruption look like safeguards of human dignity, because exploiter and exploited, oppressor and oppressed, corruptor and corrupted still live in the same world, still share the same goals, fight each other for the possession of the same things; and it is this *tertium comparationis* which aloofness destroyed. Worst of all was the fact that the aloof administrator was hardly aware that he had invented a new form of government but actually believed that his attitude was conditioned by "the forcible contact with a people living on a lower plane." So, instead of believing in his individual superiority with some degree of essentially harmless vanity, he felt that he belonged to "a nation which had reached a comparatively high plane of civilization" [70] and therefore held his position by right of birth, regardless of personal achievements.

Lord Cromer's career is fascinating because it embodies the very turning

[68] Lord Cromer, *op. cit.*

[69] Bribery "was perhaps the most human institution among the barbed-wire entanglements of the Russian order." Moissaye J. Olgin, *The Soul of the Russian Revolution*, New York, 1917.

[70] Zetland, *op. cit.*, p. 89.

point from the older colonial to imperialist services. His first reaction to his duties in Egypt was a marked uneasiness and concern about a state of affairs which was not "annexation" but a "hybrid form of government to which no name can be given and for which there is no precedent." [71] In 1885, after two years of service, he still harbored serious doubts about a system in which he was the nominal British Consul General and the actual ruler of Egypt and wrote that a "highly delicate mechanism [whose] efficient working depends very greatly on the judgment and ability of a few individuals . . . can . . . be justified [only] if we are able to keep before our eyes the possibility of evacuation. . . . If that possibility becomes so remote as to be of no practical account . . . it would be better for us . . . to arrange . . . with the other Powers that we should take over the government of the country, guarantee its debt, etc." [72] No doubt Cromer was right, and either, occupation or evacuation, would have normalized matters. But that "hybrid form of government" without precedent was to become characteristic of all imperialist enterprise, with the result that a few decades afterwards everybody had lost Cromer's early sound judgment about possible and impossible forms of government, just as there was lost Lord Selbourne's early insight that a race society as a way of life was unprecedented. Nothing could better characterize the initial stage of imperialism than the combination of these two judgments on conditions in Africa: a way of life without precedent in the south, a government without precedent in the north.

In the following years, Cromer reconciled himself to the "hybrid form of government"; in his letters he began to justify it and to expound the need for the government without name and precedent. At the end of his life, he laid down (in his essay on "The Government of Subject Races") the main lines of what one may well call a philosophy of the bureaucrat.

Cromer started by recognizing that "personal influence" without a legal or written political treaty could be enough for "sufficiently effective supervision over public affairs" [73] in foreign countries. This kind of informal influence was preferable to a well-defined policy because it could be altered at a moment's notice and did not necessarily involve the home government in case of difficulties. It required a highly trained, highly reliable staff whose loyalty and patriotism were not connected with personal ambition or vanity and who would even be required to renounce the human aspiration of having their names connected with their achievements. Their greatest passion would have to be for secrecy ("the less British officials are talked about the better"),[74] for a role behind the scenes; their greatest contempt would be directed at publicity and people who love it.

Cromer himself possessed all these qualities to a very high degree; his wrath was never more strongly aroused than when he was "brought out of

[71] From a letter Lord Cromer wrote in 1884. *Ibid.*, p. 117.
[72] In a letter to Lord Granville, a member of the Liberal Party, in 1885. *Ibid.*, p. 219.
[73] From a letter to Lord Rosebery in 1886. *Ibid.*, p. 134.
[74] *Ibid.*, p. 352.

[his] hiding place," when "the reality which before was only known to a few behind the scenes [became] patent to all the world." [75] His pride was indeed to "remain more or less hidden [and] to pull the strings." [76] In exchange, and in order to make his work possible at all, the bureaucrat has to feel safe from control—the praise as well as the blame, that is—of all public institutions, either Parliament, the "English Departments," or the press. Every growth of democracy or even the simple functioning of existing democratic institutions can only be a danger, for it is impossible to govern "a people by a people—the people of India by the people of England." [77] Bureaucracy is always a government of experts, of an "experienced minority" which has to resist as well as it knows how the constant pressure from "the inexperienced majority." Each people is fundamentally an inexperienced majority and can therefore not be trusted with such a highly specialized matter as politics and public affairs. Bureaucrats, moreover, are not supposed to have general ideas about political matters at all; their patriotism should never lead them so far astray that they believe in the inherent goodness of political principles in their own country; that would only result in their cheap "imitative" application "to the government of backward populations," which, according to Cromer, was the principal defect of the French system.[78]

Nobody will ever pretend that Cecil Rhodes suffered from a lack of vanity. According to Jameson, he expected to be remembered for at least four thousand years. Yet, despite all his appetite for self-glorification, he hit upon the same idea of rule through secrecy as the overmodest Lord Cromer. Extremely fond of drawing up wills, Rhodes insisted in all of them (over the course of two decades of his public life) that his money should be used to found "a secret society . . . to carry out his scheme," which was to be "organized like Loyola's, supported by the accumulated wealth of those whose aspiration is a desire to do something," so that eventually there would be "between two and three thousand men in the prime of life scattered all over the world, each one of whom would have had impressed upon his mind in the most susceptible period of his life the dream of the Founder, each one of whom, moreover, would have been especially—mathematically— selected towards the Founder's purpose." [79] More farsighted than Cromer,

[75] From a letter to Lord Rosebery in 1893. *Ibid.,* pp. 204-205.
[76] From a letter to Lord Rosebery in 1893. *Ibid.,* p. 192.
[77] From a speech by Cromer in Parliament after 1904. *Ibid.,* p. 311.
[78] During the negotiations and considerations of the administrative pattern for the annexation of the Sudan, Cromer insisted on keeping the whole matter outside the sphere of French influence; he did this not because he wanted to secure a monopoly in Africa for England but much rather because he had "the utmost want of confidence in their administrative system as applied to subject races" (from a letter to Salisbury in 1899, *Ibid.,* p. 248).
[79] Rhodes drew up six wills (the first was already composed in 1877), all of which mention the "secret society." For extensive quotes, see Basil Williams, *Cecil Rhodes,* London, 1921, and Millin, *op. cit.,* pp. 128 and 331. The citations are upon the authority of W. T. Stead.

Rhodes opened the society at once to all members of the "Nordic race" [80] so that the aim was not so much the growth and glory of Great Britain—her occupation of the "entire continent of Africa, the Holy Land, the valley of the Euphrates, the islands of Cyprus and Candia, the whole of South America, the islands of the Pacific, . . . the whole of the Malay Archipelago, the seaboards of China and Japan [and] the ultimate recovery of the United States" [81]—as the expansion of the "Nordic race" which, organized in a secret society, would establish a bureaucratic government over all peoples of the earth.

What overcame Rhodes's monstrous innate vanity and made him discover the charms of secrecy was the same thing that overcame Cromer's innate sense of duty: the discovery of an expansion which was not driven by the specific appetite for a specific country but conceived as an endless process in which every country would serve only as stepping-stone for further expansion. In view of such a concept, the desire for glory can no longer be satisfied by the glorious triumph over a specific people for the sake of one's own people, nor can the sense of duty be fulfilled through the consciousness of specific services and the fulfillment of specific tasks. No matter what individual qualities or defects a man may have, once he has entered the maelstrom of an unending process of expansion, he will, as it were, cease to be what he was and obey the laws of the process, identify himself with anonymous forces that he is supposed to serve in order to keep the whole process in motion; he will think of himself as mere function, and eventually consider such functionality, such an incarnation of the dynamic trend, his highest possible achievement. Then, as Rhodes was insane enough to say, he could indeed "do nothing wrong, what he did became right. It was his duty to do what he wanted. He felt himself a god—nothing less." [82] But Lord Cromer sanely pointed out the same phenomenon of men degrading themselves voluntarily into mere instruments or mere functions when he called the bureaucrats "instruments of incomparable value in the execution of a policy of Imperialism." [83]

It is obvious that these secret and anonymous agents of the force of expansion felt no obligation to man-made laws. The only "law" they obeyed was the "law" of expansion, and the only proof of their "lawfulness" was success. They had to be perfectly willing to disappear into complete oblivion once failure had been proved, if for any reason they were no longer "instruments of incomparable value." As long as they were successful, the feeling of embodying forces greater than themselves made it relatively easy to resign and even to despise applause and glorification. They were monsters of conceit in their success and monsters of modesty in their failure.

[80] It is well known that Rhodes's "secret society" ended as the very respectable Rhodes Scholarship Association to which even today not only Englishmen but members of all "Nordic races," such as Germans, Scandinavians, and Americans, are admitted.

[81] Basil Williams, *op. cit.*, p. 51.

[82] Millin, *op. cit.*, p. 92.   [83] Cromer, *op. cit.*

96 IMPERIALISM

At the basis of bureaucracy as a form of government, and of its inherent replacement of law with temporary and changing decrees, lies this superstition of a possible and magic identification of man with the forces of history. The ideal of such a political body will always be the man behind the scenes who pulls the strings of history. Cromer finally shunned every "written instrument, or, indeed, anything which is tangible" [84] in his relationships with Egypt—even a proclamation of annexation—in order to be free to obey only the law of expansion, without obligation to a man-made treaty. Thus does the bureaucrat shun every general law, handling each situation separately by decree, because a law's inherent stability threatens to establish a permanent community in which nobody could possibly be a god because all would have to obey a law.

The two key figures in this system, whose very essence is aimless process, are the bureaucrat on one side and the secret agent on the other. Both types, as long as they served only British imperialism, never quite denied that they were descended from dragon-slayers and protectors of the weak and therefore never drove bureaucratic regimes to their inherent extremes. A British bureaucrat almost two decades after Cromer's death knew "administrative massacres" could keep India within the British Empire, but he knew also how utopian it would be to try to get the support of the hated "English Departments" for an otherwise quite realistic plan.[85] Lord Curzon, Viceroy of India, showed nothing of Cromer's noblesse and was quite characteristic of a society that increasingly inclined to accept the mob's race standards if they were offered in the form of fashionable snobbery.[86] But snobbery is incompatible with fanaticism and therefore never really efficient.

The same is true of the members of the British Secret Service. They too are of illustrious origin—what the dragon-slayer was to the bureaucrat, the adventurer is to the secret agent—and they too can rightly lay claim to a

[84] From a letter of Lord Cromer to Lord Rosebery in 1886. Zetland, *op. cit.,* p. 134.
[85] "The Indian system of government by reports was . . . suspect [in England]. There was no trial by jury in India and the judges were all paid servants of the Crown, many of them removable at pleasure. . . . Some of the men of formal law felt rather uneasy as to the success of the Indian experiment. 'If,' they said, 'despotism and bureaucracy work so well in India, may not that be perhaps at some time used as an argument for introducing something of the same system here?'" The government of India, at any rate, "knew well enough that it would have to justify its existence and its policy before public opinion in England, and it well knew that that public opinion would never tolerate oppression" (A. Carthill, *op. cit.,* pp. 70 and 41-42).
[86] Harold Nicolson in his *Curzon: The Last Phase 1919-1925,* Boston-New York, 1934, tells the following story: "Behind the lines in Flanders was a large brewery in the vats of which the private soldiers would bathe on returning from the trenches. Curzon was taken to see this dantesque exhibit. He watched with interest those hundred naked figures disporting themselves in the steam. 'Dear me!,' he said, 'I had no conception that the lower classes had such white skins.' Curzon would deny the authenticity of this story but loved it none the less" (pp. 47-48).

foundation legend, the legend of the Great Game as told by Rudyard Kipling in *Kim.*

Of course every adventurer knows what Kipling means when he praises Kim because "what he loved was the game for its own sake." Every person still able to wonder at "this great and wonderful world" knows that it is hardly an argument against the game when "missionaries and secretaries of charitable societies could not see the beauty of it." Still less, it seems, have those a right to speak who think it "a sin to kiss a white girl's mouth and a virtue to kiss a black man's shoe." [87] Since life itself ultimately has to be lived and loved for its own sake, adventure and love of the game for its own sake easily appear to be a most intensely human symbol of life. It is this underlying passionate humanity that makes *Kim* the only novel of the imperialist era in which a genuine brotherhood links together the "higher and lower breeds," in which Kim, "a Sahib and the son of a Sahib," can rightly talk of "us" when he talks of the "chain-men," "all on one lead-rope." There is more to this "we"—strange in the mouth of a believer in imperialism—than the all-enveloping anonymity of men who are proud to have "no name, but only a number and a letter," more than the common pride of having "a price upon [one's] head." What makes them comrades is the common experience of being—through danger, fear, constant surprise, utter lack of habits, constant preparedness to change their identities—symbols of life itself, symbols, for instance, of happenings all over India, immediately sharing the life of it all as "it runs like a shuttle throughout all Hind," and therefore no longer "alone, one person, in the middle of it all," trapped, as it were, by the limitations of one's own individuality or nationality. Playing the Great Game, a man may feel as though he lives the only life worth while because he has been stripped of everything which may still be considered to be accessory. Life itself seems to be left, in a fantastically intensified purity, when man has cut himself off from all ordinary social ties, family, regular occupation, a definite goal, ambitions, and the guarded place in a community to which he belongs by birth. "When every one is dead the Great Game is finished. Not before." When one is dead, life is finished, not before, not when one happens to achieve whatever he may have wanted. That the game has no ultimate purpose makes it so dangerously similar to life itself.

Purposelessness is the very charm of Kim's existence. Not for the sake of England did he accept his strange duties, nor for the sake of India, nor for any other worthy or unworthy cause. Imperialist notions like expansion for expansion's or power for power's sake might have suited him, but he would not have cared particularly and certainly would not have constructed any such formula. He stepped into his peculiar way of "theirs not to reason why, theirs but to do and die" without even asking the first question. He was tempted only by the basic endlessness of the game and by secrecy as

[87] Carthill, *op. cit.,* p. 88.

such. And secrecy again seems like a symbol of the basic mysteriousness of life.

Somehow it was not the fault of the born adventurers, of those who by their very nature dwelt outside society and outside all political bodies, that they found in imperialism a political game that was endless by definition; they were not supposed to know that in politics an endless game can end only in catastrophe and that political secrecy hardly ever ends in anything nobler than the vulgar duplicity of a spy. The joke on these players of the Great Game was that their employers knew what they wanted and used their passion for anonymity for ordinary spying. But this triumph of the profit-hungry investors was temporary, and they were duly cheated when a few decades later they met the players of the game of totalitarianism, a game played without ulterior motives like profit and therefore played with such murderous efficiency that it devoured even those who financed it.

Before this happened, however, the imperialists had destroyed the best man who ever turned from an adventurer (with a strong mixture of dragon-slayer) into a secret agent, Lawrence of Arabia. Never again was the experiment of secret politics made more purely by a more decent man. Lawrence experimented fearlessly upon himself, and then came back and believed that he belonged to the "lost generation." He thought this was because "the old men came out again and took from us our victory" in order to "re-make [the world] in the likeness of the former world they knew." [88] Actually the old men were quite inefficient even in this, and handed their victory, together with their power, down to other men of the same "lost generation," who were neither older nor so dissimilar to Lawrence. The only difference was that Lawrence still clung fast to a morality which, however, had already lost all objective bases and consisted only of a kind of private and necessarily quixotic attitude of chivalry.

Lawrence was seduced into becoming a secret agent in Arabia because of his strong desire to leave the world of dull respectability whose continuity had become simply meaningless, because of his disgust with the world as well as with himself. What attracted him most in Arab civilization was its "gospel of bareness . . . [which] involves apparently a sort of moral bareness too," which "has refined itself clear of household gods." [89] What he tried to avoid most of all after he had returned to English civilization was living a life of his own, so that he ended with an apparently incomprehensible enlistment as a private in the British army, which obviously was the only institution in which a man's honor could be identified with the loss of his individual personality.

When the outbreak of the first World War sent T. E. Lawrence to the Arabs of the Near East with the assignment to rouse them into a rebellion against their Turkish masters and make them fight on the British side, he

---

[88] T. E. Lawrence, *Seven Pillars of Wisdom*, Introduction (first edition, 1926) which was omitted on the advice of George Bernard Shaw from the later edition. See T. E. Lawrence, *Letters*, edited by David Garnett, New York, 1939, pp. 262 ff.

[89] From a letter written in 1918. *Letters*, p. 244.

came into the very midst of the Great Game. He could achieve his purpose only if a national movement was stirred up among Arab tribes, a national movement that ultimately was to serve British imperialism. Lawrence had to behave as though the Arab national movement were his prime interest, and he did it so well that he came to believe in it himself. But then again he did not belong, he was ultimately unable "to think their thought" and to "assume their character." [90] Pretending to be an Arab, he could only lose his "English self" [91] and was fascinated by the complete secrecy of self-effacement rather than fooled by the obvious justifications of benevolent rule over backward peoples that Lord Cromer might have used. One generation older and sadder than Cromer, he took great delight in a role that demanded a reconditioning of his whole personality until he fitted into the Great Game, until he became the incarnation of the force of the Arab national movement, until he lost all natural vanity in his mysterious alliance with forces necessarily bigger than himself, no matter how big he could have been, until he acquired a deadly "contempt, not for other men, but for all they do" on their own initiative and not in alliance with the forces of history.

When, at the end of the war, Lawrence had to abandon the pretenses of a secret agent and somehow recover his "English self," [92] he "looked at the West and its conventions with new eyes: they destroyed it all for me." [93] From the Great Game of incalculable bigness, which no publicity had glorified or limited and which had elevated him, in his twenties, above kings and prime ministers because he had "made 'em or played with them," [94] Lawrence came home with an obsessive desire for anonymity and the deep conviction that nothing he could possibly still do with his life would ever satisfy him. This conclusion he drew from his perfect knowledge that it was not he who had been big, but only the role he had aptly assumed, that his bigness had been the result of the Game and not a product of himself. Now he did not "want to be big any more" and, determined that he was not "going to be respectable again," he thus was indeed "cured . . . of any desire ever to do anything for myself." [95] He had been the phantom of a force, and he became a phantom among the living when the force, the function, was taken away from him. What he was frantically looking for was another role to play, and this incidentally was the "game" about which

[90] T. E. Lawrence, *Seven Pillars of Wisdom*, Garden City, 1938, chapter i.

[91] *Ibid.*

[92] How ambiguous and how difficult a process this must have been is illustrated by the following anecdote: "Lawrence had accepted an invitation to dinner at Claridge's and a party afterwards at Mrs. Harry Lindsay's. He shirked the dinner, but came to the party in Arab dresses." This happened in 1919. *Letters*, p. 272, note 1.

[93] Lawrence, *op. cit.*, ch. i.

[94] Lawrence wrote in 1929: "Anyone who had gone up so fast as I went . . . and had seen so much of the inside of the top of the world might well lose his aspirations, and get weary of the ordinary motives of action, which had moved him till he reached the top. I wasn't King or Prime Minister, but I made 'em, or played with them, and after that there wasn't much more, in that direction, for me to do" (*Letters*, p. 653).

[95] *Ibid.*, pp. 244, 447, 450. Compare especially the letter of 1918 (p. 244) with the two letters to George Bernard Shaw of 1923 (p. 447) and 1928 (p. 616).

George Bernard Shaw inquired so kindly but uncomprehendingly, as though he spoke from another century, not understanding why a man of such great achievements should not own up to them.[96] Only another role, another function would be strong enough to prevent himself and the world from identifying him with his deeds in Arabia, from replacing his old self with a new personality. He did not want to become "Lawrence of Arabia," since, fundamentally, he did not want to regain a new self after having lost the old. His greatness was that he was passionate enough to refuse cheap compromises and easy roads into reality and respectability, that he never lost his awareness that he had been only a function and had played a role and therefore "must not benefit in any way from what he had done in Arabia. The honors which he had won were refused. The jobs offered on account of his reputation had to be declined nor would he allow himself to exploit his success by profiting from writing a single paid piece of journalism under the name of Lawrence." [97]

The story of T. E. Lawrence in all its moving bitterness and greatness was not simply the story of a paid official or a hired spy, but precisely the story of a real agent or functionary, of somebody who actually believed he had entered—or been driven into—the stream of historical necessity and become a functionary or agent of the secret forces which rule the world. "I had pushed my go-cart into the eternal stream, and so it went faster than the ones that are pushed cross-stream or up-stream. I did not believe finally in the Arab movement: but thought it necessary in its time and place." [98] Just as Cromer had ruled Egypt for the sake of India, or Rhodes South Africa for the sake of further expansion, Lawrence had acted for some ulterior unpredictable purpose. The only satisfaction he could get out of this, lacking the calm good conscience of some limited achievement, came from the sense of functioning itself, from being embraced and driven by some big movement. Back in London and in despair, he would try to find some substitute for this kind of "self-satisfaction" and would "only get it out of hot speed on a motor-bike." [99] Although Lawrence had not yet been seized by the fanaticism of an ideology of movement, probably because he was too well educated for the superstitions of his time, he had already experienced that fascination, based on despair of all possible human responsibility, which the eternal stream and its eternal movement exert. He drowned himself in it and nothing was left of him but some inexplicable decency and a pride in having "pushed the right way." "I am still puzzled as to how far the individual counts: a lot, I fancy, if he pushes the right way." [100] This, then, is the end of the real pride of Western man who no longer counts as an end in himself, no longer does "a thing of himself nor a thing so clean

[96] George Bernard Shaw, asking Lawrence in 1928 "What is your game *really?*", suggested that his role in the army or his looking for a job as a night-watchman (for which he could "get good references") were not authentic.
[97] Garnett, *op. cit.*, p. 264.   [99] *Ibid.*, in 1924, p. 456.
[98] *Letters*, in 1930, p. 693.   [100] *Ibid.*, p. 693.

as to be his own" [101] by giving laws to the world, but has a chance only "if he pushes the right way," in alliance with the secret forces of history and necessity—of which he is but a function.

When the European mob discovered what a "lovely virtue" a white skin could be in Africa,[102] when the English conqueror in India became an administrator who no longer believed in the universal validity of law, but was convinced of his own innate capacity to rule and dominate, when the dragon-slayers turned into either "white men" of "higher breeds" or into bureaucrats and spies, playing the Great Game of endless ulterior motives in an endless movement; when the British Intelligence Services (especially after the first World War) began to attract England's best sons, who preferred serving mysterious forces all over the world to serving the common good of their country, the stage seemed to be set for all possible horrors. Lying under anybody's nose were many of the elements which gathered together could create a totalitarian government on the basis of racism. "Administrative massacres" were proposed by Indian bureaucrats while African officials declared that "no ethical considerations such as the rights of man will be allowed to stand in the way" of white rule.[103]

The happy fact is that although British imperialist rule sank to some level of vulgarity, cruelty played a lesser role between the two World Wars than ever before and a minimum of human rights was always safeguarded. It is this moderation in the midst of plain insanity that paved the way for what Churchill has called "the liquidation of His Majesty's Empire" and that eventually may turn out to mean the transformation of the English nation into a Commonwealth of English peoples.

[101] Lawrence, *op. cit.*, chapter i.
[102] Millin, *op. cit.*, p. 15.
[103] As put by Sir Thomas Watt, a citizen of South Africa, of British descent. See Barnes, *op. cit.*, p. 230.

CHAPTER FOUR: Continental Imperialism: the Pan-Movements

N AZISM AND BOLSHEVISM owe more to Pan-Germanism and Pan-Slavism
(respectively) than to any other ideology or political movement. This
is most evident in foreign policies, where the strategies of Nazi Germany
and Soviet Russia have followed so closely the well-known programs of
conquest outlined by the pan-movements before and during the first World
War that totalitarian aims have frequently been mistaken for the pursuance
of some permanent German or Russian interests. While neither Hitler nor
Stalin has ever acknowledged his debt to imperialism in the development
of his methods of rule, neither has hesitated to admit his indebtedness to
the pan-movements' ideology or to imitate their slogans.[1]

The birth of the pan-movements did not coincide with the birth of imperialism; around 1870, Pan-Slavism had already outgrown the vague and
confused theories of the Slavophiles,[2] and Pan-German sentiment was current in Austria as early as the middle of the nineteenth century. They crys-
tallized into movements, however, and captured the imagination of broader
strata only with the triumphant imperialist expansion of the Western nations
in the eighties. The Central and Eastern European nations, which had no
colonial possessions and little hope for overseas expansion, now decided
that they "had the same right to expand as other great peoples and that if
[they were] not granted this possibility overseas, [they would] be forced

---

[1] Hitler wrote in *Mein Kampf* (New York, 1939): In Vienna, "I laid the foundations for a world concept in general and a way of political thinking in particular
which I had later only to complete in detail, but which never afterward forsook me"
(p. 129).—Stalin came back to Pan-Slav slogans during the last war. The 1945 Pan-
Slav Congress in Sofia, which had been called by the victorious Russians, adopted
a resolution pronouncing it "not only an international political necessity to declare
Russian its language of general communication and the official language of all Slav
countries, but a moral necessity." (See *Aufbau*, New York, April 6, 1945.) Shortly
before, the Bulgarian radio had broadcast a message by the Metropolitan Stefan,
vicar of the Holy Bulgarian Synod, in which he called upon the Russian people "to
remember their messianic mission" and prophesied the coming "unity of the Slav
people." (See *Politics*, January, 1945.)

[2] For an exhaustive presentation and discussion of the Slavophiles see Alexandre
Koyré, *La philosophie et le problème national en Russie au début du 19e siècle*
(Institut Français de Leningrad, Bibliothèque Vol. X, Paris, 1929).

to do it in Europe." [3] Pan-Germans and Pan-Slavs agreed that, living in "continental states" and being "continental peoples," they had to look for colonies on the continent,[4] to expand in geographic continuity from a center of power,[5] that against "the idea of England . . . expressed by the words: I want to rule the sea, [stands] the idea of Russia [expressed] by the words: I want to rule the land," [6] and that eventually the "tremendous superiority of the land to the sea . . ., the superior significance of land power to sea power . . .," would become apparent.[7]

The chief importance of continental, as distinguished from overseas, imperialism lies in the fact that its concept of cohesive expansion does not allow for any geographic distance between the methods and institutions of colony and of nation, so that it did not require boomerang effects in order to make itself and all its consequences felt in Europe. Continental imperialism truly begins at home.[8] If it shared with overseas imperialism the contempt for the narrowness of the nation-state, it opposed to it not so much economic arguments, which after all quite frequently expressed authentic national needs, as an "enlarged tribal consciousness" [9] which was supposed to unite all people of similar folk origin, independent of history and no matter where

---

[3] Ernst Hasse, *Deutsche Politik*. 4. Heft. *Die Zukunft des deutschen Volkstums*, 1907, p. 132.

[4] *Ibid.*, 3. Heft. *Deutsche Grenzpolitik*, pp. 167-168. Geopolitical theories of this kind were current among the Alldeutschen, the members of the Pan-German League. They always compared Germany's geopolitical needs with those of Russia. Austrian Pan-Germans characteristically never drew such a parallel.

[5] The Slavophile writer Danilewski, whose *Russia and Europe* (1871) became the standard work of Pan-Slavism, praised the Russians' "political capacity" because of their "tremendous thousand-year-old state that still grows and whose power does not expand like the European power in a colonial way but remains always concentrated around its nucleus, Moscow." See K. Staehlin, *Geschichte Russlands von den Anfängen bis zur Gegenwart*, 1923-1939, 5 vols., IV/1, 274.

[6] The quotation is from J. Slowacki, a Polish publicist who wrote in the forties. See N. O. Lossky, *Three Chapters from the History of Polish Messianism*, Prague, 1936, in International Philosophical Library, II, 9.

Pan-Slavism, the first of the pan-isms (see Hoetzsch, *Russland*, Berlin, 1913, p. 439), expressed these geopolitical theories almost forty years before Pan-Germanism began to "think in continents." The contrast between English sea power and continental land power was so conspicuous that it would be far-fetched to look for influences.

[7] Reismann-Grone, *Ueberseepolitik oder Festlandspolitik?*, 1905, in Alldeutsche Flugschriften, No. 22, p. 17.

[8] Ernst Hasse of the Pan-German League proposed to treat certain nationalities (Poles, Czechs, Jews, Italians, etc.) in the same way as overseas imperialism treated natives in non-European continents. See *Deutsche Politik*. 1. Heft: *Das Deutsche Reich als Nationalstaat*, 1905, p. 62. This is the chief difference between the Pan-German League, founded in 1886, and earlier colonial societies such as the Central-Verein für Handelsgeographie (founded in 1863). A very reliable description of the activities of the Pan-German League is given in Mildred S. Wertheimer, *The Pan-German League, 1890-1914*, 1924.

[9] Emil Deckert, *Panlatinismus, Panslawismus und Panteutonismus in ihrer Bedeutung für die politische Weltlage*, Frankfurt a/M, 1914, p. 4.

they happened to live.[10] Continental imperialism, therefore, started with a much closer affinity to race concepts, enthusiastically absorbed the tradition of race-thinking,[11] and relied very little on specific experiences. Its race concepts were completely ideological in basis and developed much more quickly into a convenient political weapon than similar theories expressed by overseas imperialists which could always claim a certain basis in authentic experience.

The pan-movements have generally been given scant attention in the discussion of imperialism. Their dreams of continental empires were overshadowed by the more tangible results of overseas expansion, and their lack of interest in economics [12] stood in ridiculous contrast to the tremendous profits of early imperialism. Moreover, in a period when almost everybody had come to believe that politics and economics were more or less the same thing, it was easy to overlook the similarities as well as the significant differences between the two brands of imperialism. The protagonists of the pan-movements share with Western imperialists that awareness of all foreign-policy issues which had been forgotten by the older ruling groups of the nation-state.[13] Their influence on intellectuals was even more pronounced— the Russian intelligentsia, with only a few exceptions, was Pan-Slavic, and Pan-Germanism started in Austria almost as a students' movement.[14] Their chief difference from the more respectable imperialism of the Western nations was the lack of capitalist support; their attempts to expand were not

[10] Pan-Germans already talked before the first World War of the distinction between "*Staatsfremde*," people of Germanic origin who happened to live under the authority of another country, and "*Volksfremde*," people of non-Germanic origin who happened to live in Germany. See Daniel Frymann (pseud. for Heinrich Class), *Wenn ich der Kaiser wär. Politische Wahrheiten und Notwendigkeiten*, 1912.

When Austria was incorporated into the Third Reich, Hitler addressed the German people of Austria with typically Pan-German slogans. "Wherever we may have been born," he told them, we are all "the sons of the German people." *Hitler's Speeches*, ed. by N. H. Baynes, 1942, II, 1408.

[11] Th. G. Masaryk, *Zur russischen Geschichts- und Religionsphilosophie* (1913), describes the "zoological nationalism" of the Slavophiles since Danilewski (p. 257). Otto Bonhard, official historian of the Pan-German League, stated the close relationship between its ideology and the racism of Gobineau and H. S. Chamberlain. See *Geschichte des alldeutschen Verbandes*, 1920, p. 95.

[12] An exception is Friedrich Naumann, *Central Europe* (London, 1916), who wanted to replace the many nationalities in Central Europe with one united "economic people" (*Wirtschaftsvolk*) under German leadership. Although his book was a best-seller throughout the first World War, it influenced only the Austrian Social Democratic Party; see Karl Renner, *Oesterreichs Erneuerung. Politisch-programmatische Aufsätze*, Vienna, 1916, pp. 37 ff.

[13] "At least before the war, the interest of the great parties in foreign affairs had been completely overshadowed by domestic issues. The Pan-German League's attitude is different and this is undoubtedly a propaganda asset" (Martin Wenck, *Alldeutsche Taktik*, 1917).

[14] See Paul Molisch, *Geschichte der deutschnationalen Bewegung in Oesterreich*, Jena, 1926, p. 90: It is a fact "that the student body does not at all simply mirror the general political constellation; on the contrary, strong Pan-German opinions have largely originated in the student body and thence found their way into general politics."

and could not be preceded by export of superfluous money and superfluous men, because Europe did not offer colonial opportunities for either. Among their leaders, we find therefore almost no businessmen and few adventurers, but many members of the free professions, teachers, and civil servants.[15]

While overseas imperialism, its antinational tendencies notwithstanding, succeeded in giving a new lease on life to the antiquated institutions of the nation-state, continental imperialism was and remained unequivocally hostile to all existing political bodies. Its general mood, therefore, was far more rebellious and its leaders far more adept at revolutionary rhetoric. While overseas imperialism had offered real enough panaceas for the residues of all classes, continental imperialism had nothing to offer except an ideology and a movement. Yet this was quite enough in a time which preferred a key to history to political action, when men in the midst of communal disintegration and social atomization wanted to belong at any price. Similarly, the visible distinction of a white skin, whose advantages in a black or brown environment are easily understood, could be matched successfully by a purely imaginary distinction between an Eastern and a Western, or an Aryan and a non-Aryan soul. The point is that a rather complicated ideology and an organization which furthered no immediate interest proved to be more attractive than tangible advantages and commonplace convictions.

Despite their lack of success, with its proverbial appeal to the mob, the pan-movements exerted from the beginning a much stronger attraction than overseas imperialism. This popular appeal, which withstood tangible failures and constant changes of program, foreshadowed later totalitarian groups which were similarly vague as to actual goals and subject to day-to-day changes of political lines. What held the pan-movements' membership together was much more a general mood than a clearly defined aim. It is true that overseas imperialism also placed expansion as such above any program of conquest and therefore took possession of every territory that offered itself as an easy opportunity. Yet, however capricious the export of superfluous money may have been, it served to delimit the ensuing expansion; the aims of the pan-movements lacked even this rather anarchic element of human planning and geographic restraint. Yet, though they had no specific programs for world conquest, they generated an all-embracing mood of total predominance, of touching and embracing all human issues, of "pan-humanism," as Dostoevski once put it.[16]

In the imperialist alliance between mob and capital, the initiative lay mostly with the representatives of business—except in the case of South Africa, where a clear-cut mob policy developed very early. In the pan-

---

[15] Useful information about the social composition of the membership of the Pan-German League, its local and executive officers, can be found in Wertheimer, *op. cit.* See also Lothar Werner, *Der alldeutsche Verband. 1890-1918.* Historische Studien. Heft 278, Berlin, 1935, and Gottfried Nippold, *Der deutsche Chauvinismus,* 1913, pp. 179 ff.

[16] Quoted from Hans Kohn, "The Permanent Mission" in *The Review of Politics,* July, 1948.

movements, on the other hand, the initiative always lay exclusively with
the mob, which was led then (as today) by a certain brand of intellectuals.
They still lacked the ambition to rule the globe, and they did not even
dream of the possibilities of total domination. But they did know how to organize the mob, and they were aware of the organizational, not merely
ideological or propaganda, uses to which race concepts can be put. Their
significance is only superficially grasped in the relatively modest theories of
foreign policy—a Germanized Central Europe or a Russianized Eastern
and Southern Europe—which served as starting points for the world-con-
quest programs of Nazism and Bolshevism.[17] The "Germanic peoples" outside the Reich and "our minor Slavonic brethren" outside Holy Russia
generated a comfortable smoke screen of national rights to self-determination, easy stepping-stones to further expansion. Yet, much more essential
was the fact that the totalitarian governments inherited an aura of holiness:
they had only to invoke the past of "Holy Russia" or "the Holy Roman Empire" to arouse all kinds of superstitions in Slav or German intellectuals.[18]
Pseudomystical nonsense, enriched by countless and arbitrary historical
memories, provided an emotional appeal that seemed to transcend, in depth
and breadth, the limitations of nationalism. Out of it, at any rate, grew that
new kind of nationalist feeling whose violence proved an excellent motor
to set mob masses in motion and quite adequate to replace the older national patriotism as an emotional center.

This new type of tribal nationalism, more or less characteristic of all
Central and Eastern European nations and nationalities, was quite different
in content and significance—though not in violence—from Western nationalist excesses. Chauvinism—now usually thought of in connection with the
"nationalisme intégral" of Maurras and Barrès around the turn of the century, with its romantic glorification of the past and its morbid cult of the
dead—even in its most wildly fantastic manifestations, did not hold that men
of French origin, born and raised in another country, without any knowledge
of French language or culture, would be "born Frenchmen" thanks to some
mysterious qualities of body or soul. Only with the "enlarged tribal consciousness" did that peculiar identification of nationality with one's own soul
emerge, that turned-inward pride that is no longer concerned only with
public affairs but pervades every phase of private life until, for example,
"the private life of each true Pole . . . is a public life of Polishness." [19]

In psychological terms, the chief difference between even the most violent

[17] Danilewski, op. cit., included in a future Russian empire all Balkan countries,
Turkey, Hungary, Czechoslovakia, Galicia, and Istria with Trieste.

[18] The Slavophile K. S. Aksakow, writing in the middle of the nineteenth century,
took the official name "Holy Russia" quite literally, as did later Pan-Slavs. See Th. G.
Masaryk, op. cit., pp. 234 ff.—Very characteristic of the vague nonsense of Pan-
Germanism is Moeller van den Bruck, Germany's Third Empire (New York, 1934),
in which he proclaims: "There is only One Empire, as there is only One Church. Anything else that claims the title may be a state or a community or a sect. There exists
only The Empire" (p. 263).

[19] George Cleinow, Die Zukunft Polens, Leipzig, 1914, II, 93 ff.

chauvinism and this tribal nationalism is that the one is extroverted, concerned with visible spiritual and material achievements of the nation, whereas the other, even in its mildest forms (for example, the German youth movement) is introverted, concentrates on the individual's own soul which is considered as the embodiment of general national qualities. Chauvinist mystique still points to something that really existed in the past (as in the case of the *nationalisme intégral*) and merely tries to elevate this into a realm beyond human control; tribalism, on the other hand, starts from nonexistent pseudomystical elements which it proposes to realize fully in the future. It can be easily recognized by the tremendous arrogance, inherent in its self-concentration, which dares to measure a people, its past and present, by the yardstick of exalted inner qualities and inevitably rejects its visible existence, tradition, institutions, and culture.

Politically speaking, tribal nationalism always insists that its own people is surrounded by "a world of enemies," "one against all," that a fundamental difference exists between this people and all others. It claims its people to be unique, individual, incompatible with all others, and denies theoretically the very possibility of a common mankind long before it is used to destroy the humanity of man.

I: *Tribal Nationalism*

JUST AS continental imperialism sprang from the frustrated ambitions of countries which did not get their share in the sudden expansion of the eighties, so tribalism appeared as the nationalism of those peoples who had not participated in national emancipation and had not achieved the sovereignty of a nation-state. Wherever the two frustrations were combined, as in multinational Austria-Hungary and Russia, the pan-movements naturally found their most fertile soil. Moreover, since the Dual Monarchy harbored both Slavic and German irredentist nationalities, Pan-Slavism and Pan-Germanism concentrated from the beginning on its destruction, and Austria-Hungary became the real center of pan-movements. Russian Pan-Slavs claimed as early as 1870 that the best possible starting point for a Pan-Slav empire would be the disintegration of Austria,[20] and Austrian Pan-Germans were so violently aggressive against their own government that even the Alldeutsche Verband in Germany complained frequently about the "exag-

---

[20] During the Crimean War (1853-1856) Michael Pagodin, a Russian folklorist and philologist, wrote a letter to the Czar in which he called the Slav peoples Russia's only reliable powerful allies (Staehlin, *op. cit.,* p. 35); shortly thereafter General Nikolai Muravyev-Amursky, "one of the great Russian empire-builders," hoped for "the liberation of the Slavs from Austria and Turkey" (Hans Kohn, *op. cit.*); and as early as 1870 a military pamphlet appeared which demanded the "destruction of Austria as a necessary condition for a Pan-Slav federation" (see Staehlin, *op. cit.,* p. 282).

gerations" of the Austrian brother movement.[21] The German-conceived blueprint for the economic union of Central Europe under German leadership, along with all similar continental-empire projects of the German Pan-Germans, changed at once, when Austrian Pan-Germans got hold of it, into a structure that would become "the center of German life all over the earth and be allied with all other Germanic states." [22]

It is self-evident that the expansionist tendencies of Pan-Slavism were as embarrassing to the Czar as the Austrian Pan-Germans' unsolicited professions of loyalty to the Reich and disloyalty to Austria were to Bismarck.[23] For no matter how high national feelings occasionally ran, or how ridiculous nationalistic claims might become in times of emergency, as long as they were bound to a defined national territory and controlled by pride in a limited nation-state they remained within limits which the tribalism of the pan-movements overstepped at once.

The modernity of the pan-movements may best be gauged from their entirely new position on antisemitism. Suppressed minorities like the Slavs in Austria and the Poles in Czarist Russia were more likely, because of their conflict with the government, to discover the hidden connections between the Jewish communities and the European nation-states, and this discovery could easily lead to more fundamental hostility. Wherever antagonism to the state was not identified with lack of patriotism, as in Poland, where it was a sign of Polish loyalty to be disloyal to the Czar, or in Austria, where Germans looked upon Bismarck as their great national figure, this antisemitism assumed more violent forms because the Jews then appeared as agents not only of an oppressive state machine but of a foreign oppressor. But the fundamental role of antisemitism in the pan-movements is explained as little by the position of minorities as by the specific experiences which Schoenerer, the protagonist of Austrian Pan-Germanism, had had in his earlier career when, still a member of the Liberal Party, he became aware of the connections between the Hapsburg monarchy and the Rothschilds' domination of Austria's railroad system.[24] This by itself would hardly have made him announce that "we Pan-Germans regard antisemitism as the mainstay of our

[21] See Otto Bonhard, *op. cit.,* pp. 58 ff., and Hugo Grell, *Der alldeutsche Verband, seine Geschichte, seine Bestrebungen, seine Erfolge,* 1898, in Alldeutsche Flugschriften, No. 8.

[22] According to the Austrian Pan-German program of 1913, quoted from Eduard Pichl (al. Herwig), *Georg Schoenerer,* 1938, 6 vols., VI, 375.

[23] When Schoenerer, with his admiration for Bismarck, declared in 1876 that "Austria as a great power must cease" (Pichl, *op. cit.,* I, 90), Bismarck thought and told his Austrian admirers that "a powerful Austria is a vital necessity to Germany." See F. A. Neuschaefer, *Georg Ritter von Schoenerer* (Dissertation), Hamburg, 1935. The Czars' attitude toward Pan-Slavism was much more equivocal because the Pan-Slav conception of the state included strong popular support for despotic government. Yet even under such tempting circumstances, the Czar refused to support the expansionist demand of the Slavophiles and their successors. See Staehlin, *op. cit.,* pp. 30 ff.

[24] See chapter ii.

national ideology," [25] nor could anything similar have induced the Pan-Slav Russian writer Rozanov to pretend that "there is no problem in Russian life in which like a 'comma' there is not also the question: How to cope with the Jew." [26]

The clue to the sudden emergence of antisemitism as the center of a whole outlook on life and the world—as distinguished from its mere political role in France during the Dreyfus Affair or its role as an instrument of propaganda in the German Stoecker movement—lies in the nature of tribalism rather than in political facts and circumstances. The true significance of the pan-movements' antisemitism is that hatred of the Jews was, for the first time, severed from all actual experience concerning the Jewish people, political, social, or economic, and followed only the peculiar logic of an ideology.

Tribal nationalism, the driving force behind continental imperialism, had little in common with the nationalism of the fully developed Western nation-state. The nation-state, with its claim to popular representation and national sovereignty, as it had developed since the French Revolution through the nineteenth century, was the result of a combination of two factors that were still separate in the eighteenth century and remained separate in Russia and Austria-Hungary: nationality and state. Nations entered the scene of history and were emancipated when peoples had acquired a consciousness of themselves as cultural and historical entities, and of their territory as a permanent home, where history had left its visible traces, whose cultivation was the product of the common labor of their ancestors and whose future would depend upon the course of a common civilization. Wherever nation-states came into being, migrations came to an end, while, on the other hand, in the Eastern and Southern European regions the establishment of nation-states failed because they could not fall back upon firmly rooted peasant classes.[27] Sociologically the nation-state was the body politic of the European emancipated peasant classes, and this is the reason why national armies could keep their permanent position within these states only up to the end of the last century, that is, only as long as they were truly representative of the rural class. "The Army," as Marx has pointed out, "was the 'point of honor' with the allotment farmers: it was themselves turned into masters, defending abroad their newly established property. . . . The uniform was their state costume, war was their poetry; the allotment was the fatherland, and patriotism became the ideal form of property." [28] The Western nationalism which

[25] Pichl, *op. cit.*, I, 26. The translation is quoted from the excellent article by Oscar Karbach, "The Founder of Modern Political Antisemitism: Georg von Schoenerer," in *Jewish Social Studies*, Vol. VII, No 1, January, 1945.

[26] Vassiliff Rozanov, *Fallen Leaves*, 1929, pp. 163-164.

[27] See C. A. Macartney, *National States and National Minorities*, London, 1934, pp. 432 ff.

[28] Karl Marx, *The Eighteenth Brumaire of Louis Bonaparte* English translation by De Leon, 1898.

culminated in general conscription was the product of firmly rooted *and* emancipated peasant classes.

While consciousness of nationality is a comparatively recent development, the structure of the state was derived from centuries of monarchy and enlightened despotism. Whether in the form of a new republic or of a reformed constitutional monarchy, the state inherited as its supreme function the protection of all inhabitants in its territory no matter what their nationality, and was supposed to act as a supreme legal institution. The tragedy of the nation-state was that the people's rising national consciousness interfered with these functions. In the name of the will of the people the state was forced to recognize only "nationals" as citizens, to grant full civil and political rights only to those who belonged to the national community by right of origin and fact of birth. This meant that the state was partly transformed from an instrument of the law into an instrument of the nation.

The conquest of the state by the nation [29] was greatly facilitated by the downfall of the absolute monarchy and the subsequent new development of classes. The absolute monarch was supposed to serve the interests of the nation as a whole, to be the visible exponent and proof of the existence of such a common interest. The enlightened despotism was based on Rohan's "kings command the peoples and interest commands the king"; [30] with the abolition of the king and sovereignty of the people, this common interest was in constant danger of being replaced by a permanent conflict among class interests and struggle for control of the state machinery, that is, by a permanent civil war. The only remaining bond between the citizens of a nation-state without a monarch to symbolize their essential community, seemed to be national, that is, common origin. So that in a century when every class and section in the population was dominated by class or group interest, the interest of the nation as a whole was supposedly guaranteed in a common origin, which sentimentally expressed itself in nationalism.

The secret conflict between state and nation came to light at the very birth of the modern nation-state, when the French Revolution combined the declaration of the Rights of Man with the demand for national sovereignty. The same essential rights were at once claimed as the inalienable heritage of all human beings *and* as the specific heritage of specific nations, the same nation was at once declared to be subject to laws, which supposedly would flow from the Rights of Man, *and* sovereign, that is, bound by no universal law and acknowledging nothing superior to itself.[31] The practical outcome of this contradiction was that from then on human rights were protected and enforced only as national rights and that the very institution of a state, whose supreme task was to protect and guarantee man his rights as man, as citizen

[29] See J. T. Delos, *La Nation,* Montreal, 1944, an outstanding study on the subject.

[30] See the Duc de Rohan, *De l'Intérêt des Princes et Etats de la Chrétienté,* 1638, dedicated to the Cardinal Richelieu.

[31] One of the most illuminating discussions of the principle of sovereignty is still Jean Bodin, *Six Livres de la République,* 1576. For a good report and discussion of Bodin's main theories, see George H. Sabine, *A History of Political Theory,* 1937.

and as national, lost its legal, rational appearance and could be interpreted by the romantics as the nebulous representative of a "national soul" which through the very fact of its existence was supposed to be beyond or above the law. National sovereignty, accordingly, lost its original connotation of freedom of the people and was being surrounded by a pseudomystical aura of lawless arbitrariness.

Nationalism is essentially the expression of this perversion of the state into an instrument of the nation and the identification of the citizen with the member of the nation. The relationship between state and society was determined by the fact of class struggle, which had supplanted the former feudal order. Society was pervaded by liberal individualism which wrongly believed that the state ruled over mere individuals, when in reality it ruled over classes, and which saw in the state a kind of supreme individual before which all others had to bow. It seemed to be the will of the nation that the state protect it from the consequences of its social atomization and, at the same time, guarantee its possibility of remaining in a state of atomization. To be equal to this task, the state had to enforce all earlier tendencies toward centralization; only a strongly centralized administration which monopolized all instruments of violence and power-possibilities could counterbalance the centrifugal forces constantly produced in a class-ridden society. Nationalism, then, became the precious cement for binding together a centralized state and an atomized society, and it actually proved to be the only working, live connection between the individuals of the nation-state.

Nationalism always preserved this initial intimate loyalty to the government and never quite lost its function of preserving a precarious balance between nation and state on one hand, between the nationals of an atomized society on the other. Native citizens of a nation-state frequently looked down upon naturalized citizens, those who had received their rights by law and not by birth, from the state and not from the nation; but they never went so far as to propose the Pan-German distinction between *"Staatsfremde,"* aliens of the state, and *"Volksfremde,"* aliens of the nation, which was later incorporated into Nazi legislation. Insofar as the state, even in its perverted form, remained a legal institution, nationalism was controlled by some law, and insofar as it had sprung from the identification of nationals with their territory, it was limited by definite boundaries.

Quite different was the first national reaction of peoples for whom nationality had not yet developed beyond the inarticulateness of ethnic consciousness, whose languages had not yet outgrown the dialect stage through which all European languages went before they became suited for literary purposes, whose peasant classes had not struck deep roots in the country and were not on the verge of emancipation, and to whom, consequently, their national quality appeared to be much more a portable private matter, inherent in their very personality, than a matter of public concern and civilization.[32] If

---

[32] Interesting in this context are the socialist propositions of Karl Renner and Otto Bauer in Austria to separate nationality entirely from its territorial basis and to make it a kind of personal status; this of course corresponded to a situation in which ethnic

they wanted to match the national pride of Western nations, they had no country, no state, no historic achievement to show but could only point to themselves, and that meant, at best, to their language—as though language by itself were already an achievement—at worst, to their Slavic, or Germanic, or God-knows-what soul. Yet in a century which naïvely assumed that all peoples were virtually nations there was hardly anything else left to the oppressed peoples of Austria-Hungary, Czarist Russia, or the Balkan countries, where no conditions existed for the realization of the Western national trinity of people-territory-state, where frontiers had changed constantly for many centuries and populations had been in a stage of more or less continuous migration. Here were masses who had not the slightest idea of the meaning of *patria* and patriotism, not the vaguest notion of responsibility for a common, limited community. This was the trouble with the "belt of mixed populations" (Macartney) that stretched from the Baltic to the Adriatic and found its most articulate expression in the Dual Monarchy.

Tribal nationalism grew out of this atmosphere of rootlessness. It spread widely not only among the peoples of Austria-Hungary but also, though on a higher level, among members of the unhappy intelligentsia of Czarist Russia. Rootlessness was the true source of that "enlarged tribal consciousness" which actually meant that members of these peoples had no definite home but felt at home wherever other members of their "tribe" happened to live. "It is our distinction," said Schoenerer, ". . . that we do not gravitate toward Vienna but gravitate to whatever place Germans may live in." [33] The hallmark of the pan-movements was that they never even tried to achieve national emancipation, but at once, in their dreams of expansion, transcended the narrow bounds of a national community and proclaimed a folk community that would remain a political factor even if its members were dispersed all over the earth. Similarly, and in contrast to the true national liberation movements of small peoples, which always began with an exploration of the national past, they did not stop to consider history but projected the basis of their community into a future toward which the movement was supposed to march.

Tribal nationalism, spreading through all oppressed nationalities in Eastern and Southern Europe, developed into a new form of organization, the pan-movements, among those peoples who combined some kind of national home country, Germany and Russia, with a large, dispersed irredenta, Germans and Slavs abroad. [34] In contrast to overseas imperialism, which was

---

groups were dispersed all over the empire without losing any of their national character. See Otto Bauer, *Die Nationalitätenfrage und die österreichische Sozialdemokratie*, Vienna, 1907, on the personal (as opposed to the territorial) principle, pp. 332 ff., 353 ff. "The personal principle wants to organize nations not as territorial bodies but as mere associations of persons."

[33] Pichl, *op. cit.*, I, 152.

[34] No full-fledged pan-movement ever developed except under these conditions. Pan-Latinism was a misnomer for a few abortive attempts of the Latin nations to make some kind of alliance against the German danger, and even Polish Messianism never claimed more than what at some time might conceivably have been Polish-

content with relative superiority, a national mission, or a white man's burden, the pan-movements started with absolute claims to chosenness. Nationalism has been frequently described as an emotional surrogate of religion, but only the tribalism of the pan-movements offered a new religious theory and a new concept of holiness. It was not the Czar's religious function and position in the Greek Church that led Russian Pan-Slavs to the affirmation of the Christian nature of the Russian people, of their being, according to Dostoevski, the "Christopher among the nations" who carry God directly into the affairs of this world.[35] It was because of claims to being "the true divine people of modern times"[36] that the Pan-Slavs abandoned their earlier liberal tendencies and, notwithstanding governmental opposition and occasionally even persecution, became staunch defenders of Holy Russia.

Austrian Pan-Germans laid similar claims to divine chosenness even though they, with a similar liberal past, remained anticlerical and became anti-Christians. When Hitler, a self-confessed disciple of Schoenerer, stated during the last war: "God the Almighty has made our nation. We are defending His work by defending its very existence,"[37] the reply from the other side, from a follower of Pan-Slavism, was equally true to type: "The German monsters are not only our foes, but God's foes."[38] These recent formulations were not born of propaganda needs of the moment, and this kind of fanaticism does not simply abuse religious language; behind it lies a veritable theology which gave the earlier pan-movements their momentum and retained a considerable influence on the development of modern totalitarian movements.

The pan-movements preached the divine origin of their own people as against the Jewish-Christian faith in the divine origin of Man. According to them, man, belonging inevitably to some people, received his divine origin only indirectly through membership in a people. The individual, therefore, has his divine value only as long as he belongs to the people singled out for divine origin. He forfeits this whenever he decides to change his nationality, in which case he severs all bonds through which he was endowed with

---

dominated territory. See also Deckert, *op. cit.*, who stated in 1914: "that Pan-Latinism has declined more and more, and that nationalism and state consciousness have become stronger and retained a greater potential there than anywhere else in Europe" (p. 7).

[35] Nicolas Berdyaev, *The Origin of Russian Communism*, 1937, p. 102.—K. S. Aksakow called the Russian people the "only Christian people on earth" in 1855 (see Hans Ehrenberg and N. V. Bubnoff, *Oestliches Christentum*, Bd. I, pp. 92 ff.), and the poet Tyutchev asserted at the same time that "the Russian people is Christian not only through the Orthodoxy of its faith but by something more intimate. It is Christian by that faculty of renunciation and sacrifice which is the foundation of its moral nature." Quoted from Hans Kohn, *op. cit.*

[36] According to Chaadayev whose *Philosophical Letters. 1829-1831* constituted the first systematic attempt to see world history centered around the Russian people. See Ehrenberg, *op. cit.*, I, 5 ff.

[37] Speech of January 30, 1945, as recorded in the New York *Times*, January 31.

[38] The words of Luke, the Archbishop of Tambov, as quoted in *The Journal of the Moscow Patriarchate*, No. 2, 1944.

divine origin and falls, as it were, into metaphysical homelessness. The political advantage of this concept was twofold. It made nationality a permanent quality which no longer could be touched by history, no matter what happened to a given people—emigration, conquest, dispersion. Of even more immediate impact, however, was that in the absolute contrast between the divine origin of one's own people and all other nondivine peoples all differences between the individual members of the people disappeared, whether social or economic or psychological. Divine origin changed the people into a uniform "chosen" mass of arrogant robots.[39]

The untruth of this theory is as conspicuous as its political usefulness. God created neither men—whose origin clearly is procreation—nor peoples —who came into being as the result of human organization. Men are unequal according to their natural origin, their different organization, and fate in history. Their equality is an equality of rights only, that is, an equality of human purpose; yet behind this equality of human purpose lies, according to Jewish-Christian tradition, another equality, expressed in the concept of one common origin beyond human history, human nature, and human purpose —the common origin in the mythical, unidentifiable Man who alone is God's creation. This divine origin is the metaphysical concept on which the political equality of purpose may be based, the purpose of establishing mankind on earth. Nineteenth-century positivism and progressivism perverted this purpose of human equality when they set out to demonstrate what cannot be demonstrated, namely, that men are equal by nature and different only by history and circumstances, so that they can be equalized not by rights, but by circumstances and education. Nationalism and its concept of a "national mission" perverted the national concept of mankind as a family of nations into a hierarchical structure where differences of history and organization were misinterpreted as differences between men, residing in natural origin. Racism, which denied the common origin of man and repudiated the common purpose of establishing humanity, introduced the concept of the divine origin of one people as contrasted with all others, thereby covering the temporary and changeable product of human endeavor with a pseudomystical cloud of divine eternity and finality.

This finality is what acts as the common denominator between the pan-movements' philosophy and race concepts, and explains their inherent affinity in theoretical terms. Politically, it is not important whether God or nature is thought to be the origin of a people; in both cases, no matter how exalted the claim for one's own people, peoples are transformed into animal species so that a Russian appears as different from a German as a wolf is from a fox. A "divine people" lives in a world in which it is the born perse-

---

[39] This was already recognized by the Russian Jesuit, Prince Ivan S. Gagarin, in his pamphlet *La Russie sera-t-elle catholique?* (1856) in which he attacked the Slavophiles because "they wish to establish the most complete religious, political, and national uniformity. In their foreign policy, they wish to fuse all Orthodox Christians of whatever nationality, and all Slavs of whatever religion, in a great Slav and Orthodox empire." (Quoted from Hans Kohn, *op. cit.*)

cutor of all other weaker species, or the born victim of all other stronger species. Only the rules of the animal kingdom can possibly apply to its political destinies.

The tribalism of the pan-movements with its concept of the "divine origin" of one people owed part of its great appeal to its contempt for liberal individualism,[40] the ideal of mankind and the dignity of man. No human dignity is left if the individual owes his value only to the fact that he happens to be born a German or a Russian; but there is, in its stead, a new coherence, a sense of mutual reliability among all members of the people which indeed was very apt to assuage the rightful apprehensions of modern men as to what might happen to them if, isolated individuals in an atomized society, they were not protected by sheer numbers and enforced uniform coherence. Similarly, the "belt of mixed populations," more exposed than other sections of Europe to the storms of history and less rooted in Western tradition, felt earlier than other European peoples the terror of the ideal of humanity and of the Judaeo-Christian faith in the common origin of man. They did not harbor any illusions about the "noble savage," because they knew something of the potentialities of evil without research into the habits of cannibals. The more peoples know about one another, the less they want to recognize other peoples as their equals, the more they recoil from the ideal of humanity.

The appeal of tribal isolation and master race ambitions was partly due to an instinctive feeling that mankind, whether a religious or humanistic ideal, implies a common sharing of responsibility.[41] The shrinking of geographic distances made this a political actuality of the first order.[42] It also made idealistic talk about mankind and the dignity of man an affair of the past simply because all these fine and dreamlike notions, with their time-honored traditions, suddenly assumed a terrifying timeliness. Even insistence on the sinfulness of all men, of course absent from the phraseology of the liberal protagonists of "mankind," by no means suffices for an understanding of the fact—which the people understood only too well—that the idea

[40] "People will recognize that man has no other destination in this world but to work for the destruction of his personality and its replacement through a social and unpersonal existence." Chaadayev, *op. cit.* Quoted from Ehrenberg, *op. cit.,* p. 60.

[41] The following passage in Frymann, *op. cit.,* p. 186, is characteristic: "We know our own people, its qualities and its shortcomings—mankind we do not know and we refuse to care or get enthusiastic about it. Where does it begin, where does it end, that we are supposed to love because it belongs to mankind . . . ? Are the decadent or half-bestial Russian peasant of the *mir,* the Negro of East-Africa, the half-breed of German South-West Africa, or the unbearable Jews of Galicia and Rumania all members of mankind? . . . One can believe in the solidarity of the Germanic peoples—whoever is outside this sphere does not matter to us."

[42] It was this shrinking of geographic distances that found an expression in Friedrich Naumann's *Central Europe:* "The day is still distant when there shall be 'one fold and one shepherd,' but the days are past when shepherds without number, lesser or greater, drove their flocks unrestrained over the pastures of Europe. The spirit of large-scale industry and of super-national organisation has seized politics. People think, as Cecil Rhodes once expressed it, 'in Continents.' " These few sentences were quoted in innumerable articles and pamphlets of the time.

of humanity, purged of all sentimentality, has the very serious consequence that in one form or another men must assume responsibility for all crimes committed by men, and that eventually all nations will be forced to answer for the evil committed by all others.

Tribalism and racism are the very realistic, if very destructive, ways of escaping this predicament of common responsibility. Their metaphysical rootlessness, which matched so well the territorial uprootedness of the nationalities it first seized, was equally well suited to the needs of the shifting masses of modern cities and was therefore grasped at once by totalitarianism; even the fanatical adoption by the Bolsheviks of the greatest antinational doctrine, Marxism, was counteracted and Pan-Slav propaganda reintroduced in Soviet Russia because of the tremendous isolating value of these theories in themselves.[43]

It is true that the system of rule in Austria-Hungary and Czarist Russia served as a veritable education in tribal nationalism, based as it was upon the oppression of nationalities. In Russia this oppression was the exclusive monopoly of the bureaucracy which also oppressed the Russian people with the result that only the Russian intelligentsia became Pan-Slav. The Dual Monarchy, on the contrary, dominated its troublesome nationalities by giving to them just enough freedom to oppress other nationalities, with the result that these became the real mass basis for the ideology of the pan-movements. The secret of the survival of the House of Hapsburg in the nineteenth century lay in careful balance and support of a supranational machinery by the mutual antagonism and exploitation of Czechs by Germans, of Slovaks by Hungarians, of Ruthenians by Poles, and so on. For all of them it became a matter of course that one might achieve nationhood at the expense of the others and that one would gladly be deprived of freedom if the oppression came from one's own national government.

The two pan-movements developed without any help from the Russian or German governments. This did not prevent their Austrian adherents from indulging in the delights of high treason against the Austrian government. It was this possibility of educating masses in the spirit of high treason which provided Austrian pan-movements with the sizable popular support they always lacked in Germany and Russia proper. It was as much easier to induce the German worker to attack the German bourgeoisie than the government, as it was easier in Russia "to arouse the peasants against squires than against the Czar."[44] The difference in the attitudes of German workers

[43] Very interesting in this respect are the new theories of Soviet Russian genetics. Inheritance of acquired characteristics clearly means that populations living under unfavorable conditions pass on poorer hereditary endowment and *vice versa.* "In a word, we should have innate master and subject races." See H. S. Muller, "The Soviet Master Race Theory," in *New Leader,* July 30, 1949.

[44] G. Fedotov's "Russia and Freedom," in *The Review of Politics,* Vol. VIII, No. 1, January, 1946, is a veritable masterpiece of historical writing; it gives the gist of the whole of Russian history.

and Russian peasants were surely tremendous; the former looked upon a not too beloved monarch as the symbol of national unity, and the latter considered the head of their government to be the true representative of God on earth. These differences, however, mattered less than the fact that neither in Russia nor in Germany was the government so weak as in Austria, nor had its authority fallen into such disrepute that the pan-movements could make political capital out of revolutionary unrest. Only in Austria did the revolutionary impetus find its natural outlet in the pan-movements. The (not very ably carried out) device of *divide et impera* did little to diminish the centrifugal tendencies of national sentiments, but it succeeded quite well in inducing superiority complexes and a general mood of disloyalty.

Hostility to the state as an institution runs through the theories of all pan-movements. The Slavophiles' opposition to the state has been rightly described as "entirely different from anything to be found in the system of official nationalism"; [45] the state by its very nature was held to be alien to the people. Slav superiority was felt to lie in the Russian people's indifference to the state, in their keeping themselves as a *corpus separatum* from their own government. This is what the Slavophiles meant when they called the Russians a "stateless people" and this made it possible for these "liberals" to reconcile themselves to despotism; it was in accord with the demand of despotism that the people not "interfere with state power," that is, with the absoluteness of that power. [46] The Pan-Germans, who were more articulate politically, always insisted on the priority of national over state interest [47] and usually argued that "world politics transcends the framework of the state," that the only permanent factor in the course of history was the people and not states; and that therefore national needs, changing with circumstances, should determine, at all times, the political acts of the state. [48] But what in Germany and Russia remained only high-sounding phrases up to the end of the first World War, had a real enough aspect in the Dual Monarchy whose decay generated a permanent spiteful contempt for the government.

It would be a serious error to assume that the leaders of the pan-movements were reactionaries or "counter-revolutionaries." Though as a rule not too interested in social questions, they never made the mistake of siding with capitalist exploitation and most of them had belonged, and quite a few continued to belong, to liberal, progressive parties. It is quite true, in a

[45] N. Berdyaev, *op. cit.*, p. 29.

[46] K. S. Aksakov in Ehrenberg, *op. cit.*, p. 97.

[47] See for instance Schoenerer's complaint that the Austrian *"Verfassungspartei"* still subordinated national interests to state interests (Pichl, *op. cit.*, I, 151). See also the characteristic passages in the Pan-German Graf E. Reventlow's *Judas Kampf und Niederlage in Deutschland*, 1937, pp. 39 ff. Reventlow saw National Socialism as the realization of Pan-Germanism because of its refusal to "idolize" the state which is only one of the functions of folk life.

[48] Ernst Hasse, *Deutsche Weltpolitik*, 1897, in Alldeutsche Flugschriften, No. 5, and *Deutsche Politik*, 1. Heft: *Das deutsche Reich als Nationalstaat*, 1905, p. 50.

sense, that the Pan-German League "embodied a real attempt at popular
control in foreign affairs. It believed firmly in the efficiency of a strong nationally minded public opinion . . . and initiating national policies through
force of popular demand." [49] Except that the mob, organized in the pan-
movements and inspired by race ideologies, was not at all the same people
whose revolutionary actions had led to constitutional government and whose
true representatives at that time could be found only in the workers' movements, but with its "enlarged tribal consciousness" and its conspicuous lack
of patriotism resembled much rather a "race."

   Pan-Slavism, in contrast to Pan-Germanism, was formed by and perme-
ated the whole Russian intelligentsia. Much less developed in organizational
form and much less consistent in political programs, it maintained for a
remarkably long time a very high level of literary sophistication and philosophical speculation. While Rozanov speculated about the mysterious differences between Jewish and Christian sex power and came to the surprising conclusion that the Jews are "united with that power, Christians being
separated from it," [50] the leader of Austria's Pan-Germans cheerfully discovered devices to "attract the interest of the little man by propaganda songs,
post cards, Schoenerer beer mugs, walking sticks and matches.[51] Yet eventually "Schelling and Hegel were discarded and natural science was called upon
to furnish the theoretical ammunition" by the Pan-Slavs as well.[52]

   Pan-Germanism, founded by a single man, Georg von Schoenerer, and
chiefly supported by German-Austrian students, spoke from the beginning a
strikingly vulgar language, destined to appeal to much larger and different
social strata. Schoenerer was consequently also "the first to perceive the
possibilities of antisemitism as an instrument for forcing the direction of
foreign policy and disrupting . . . the internal structure of the state." [53]
Some of the reasons for the suitability of the Jewish people for this purpose
are obvious: their very prominent position with respect to the Hapsburg
monarchy together with the fact that in a multinational country they were
more easily recognized as a separate nationality than in nation-states whose
citizens, at least in theory, were of homogeneous stock. This, however, while
it certainly explains the violence of the Austrian brand of antisemitism and
shows how shrewd a politician Schoenerer was when he exploited the issue,
does not help us understand the central ideological role of antisemitism in
both pan-movements.

   "Enlarged tribal consciousness" as the emotional motor of the pan-movements was fully developed before antisemitism became their central and cen-
tralizing issue. Pan-Slavism, with its longer and more respectable history of

[49] Wertheimer, *op. cit.*, p. 209.
[50] Rozanov, *op. cit.*, pp. 56-57.
[51] Oscar Karbach, *op. cit.*
[52] Louis Levine, *Pan-Slavism and European Politics*, New York, 1914, describes this
change from the older Slavophile generation to the new Pan-Slav movement.
[53] Oscar Karbach, *op. cit.*

philosophic speculation and a more conspicuous political ineffectiveness, turned antisemitic only in the last decades of the nineteenth century; Schoenerer the Pan-German had already openly announced his hostility to state institutions when many Jews were still members of his party.[54] In Germany, where the Stoecker movement had demonstrated the usefulness of antisemitism as a political propaganda weapon, the Pan-German League started with a certain antisemitic tendency, but before 1918 it never went so far as to exclude Jews from membership.[55] The Slavophiles' occasional antipathy to Jews turned into antisemitism in the whole Russian intelligentsia when, after the assassination of the Czar in 1881, a wave of pogroms organized by the government brought the Jewish question into the focus of public attention.

Schoenerer, who discovered antisemitism at the same time, probably became aware of its possibilities almost by accident: since he wanted above all to destroy the Hapsburg empire, it was not difficult to calculate the effect of the exclusion of one nationality on a state structure that rested on a multitude of nationalities. The whole fabric of this peculiar constitution, the precarious balance of its bureaucracy could be shattered if the moderate oppression, under which all nationalities enjoyed a certain amount of equality, was undermined by popular movements. Yet, this purpose could have been equally well served by the Pan-Germans' furious hatred of the Slav nationalities, a hatred which had been well established long before the movement turned antisemitic and which had been approved by its Jewish members.

What made the antisemitism of the pan-movements so effective that it could survive the general decline of antisemitic propaganda during the deceptive quiet that preceded the outbreak of the first World War was its merger with the tribal nationalism of Eastern Europe. For there existed an inherent affinity between the pan-movements' theories about peoples and the rootless existence of the Jewish people. It seemed the Jews were the one perfect example of a people in the tribal sense, their organization the model the pan-movements were striving to emulate, their survival and their supposed power the best proof of the correctness of racial theories.

If other nationalities in the Dual Monarchy were but weakly rooted in the soil and had little sense of the meaning of a common territory, the Jews were the example of a people who without any home at all had been able to keep their identity through the centuries and could therefore be cited as proof that no territory was needed to constitute a nationality.[56] If the pan-movements insisted on the secondary importance of the state and the paramount importance of the people, organized throughout countries and not necessarily represented in visible institutions, the Jews were a perfect model

---

[54] The Linz Program, which remained the Pan-Germans' program in Austria, was originally phrased without its Jew paragraph; there were even three Jews on the drafting committee in 1882. The Jew paragraph was added in 1885. See Oscar Karbach, *op. cit.*

[55] Otto Bonhard, *op. cit.*, p. 45.

[56] So by the certainly not antisemitic Socialist Otto Bauer, *op. cit.*, p. 373.

of a nation without a state and without visible institutions.[57] If tribal nationalities pointed to themselves as the center of their national pride, regardless of historical achievements and partnership in recorded events, if they believed that some mysterious inherent psychological or physical quality made them the incarnation not of Germany but Germanism, not of Russia, but the Russian soul, they somehow knew, even if they did not know how to express it, that the Jewishness of assimilated Jews was exactly the same kind of personal individual embodiment of Judaism and that the peculiar pride of secularized Jews, who had not given up the claim to chosenness, really meant that they believed they were different and better simply because they happend to be born as Jews, regardless of Jewish achievements and tradition.

It is true enough that this Jewish attitude, this, as it were, Jewish brand of tribal nationalism, had been the result of the abnormal position of the Jews in modern states, outside the pale of society and nation. But the position of these shifting ethnic groups, who became conscious of their nationality only through the example of other—Western—nations, and later the position of the uprooted masses of the big cities, which racism mobilized so efficiently, was in many ways very similar. They too were outside the pale of society, and they too were outside the political body of the nation-state which seemed to be the only satisfactory political organization of peoples. In the Jews they recognized at once their happier, luckier competitors because, as they saw it, the Jews had found a way of constituting a society of their own which, precisely because it had no visible representation and no normal political outlet, could become a substitute for the nation.

But what drove the Jews into the center of these racial ideologies more than anything else was the even more obvious fact that the pan-movements' claim to chosenness could clash seriously only with the Jewish claim. It did not matter that the Jewish concept had nothing in common with the tribal theories about the divine origin of one's own people. The mob was not much concerned with such niceties of historical correctness and was hardly aware of the difference between a Jewish mission in history to achieve the establishment of mankind and its own "mission" to dominate all other peoples on earth. But the leaders of the pan-movements knew quite well that the Jews had divided the world, exactly as they had, into two halves—themselves and all the others.[58] In this dichotomy the Jews again appeared

[57] Very instructive for Jewish self-interpretation is A. S. Steinberg's essay "Die weltanschaulichen Voraussetzungen der jüdischen Geschichtsschreibung," in *Dubnov Festschrift*, 1930: "If one . . . is convinced of the concept of life as expressed in Jewish history . . . then the state question loses its importance, no matter how one may answer it."

[58] The closeness of these concepts to each other may be seen in the following coincidence to which many other examples could be added: Steinberg, *op. cit.*, says of the Jews: their history takes place outside all usual historical laws; Chaadayev calls the Russians an exception people. Berdyayev stated bluntly (*op. cit.*, p. 135): "Russian Messianism is akin to Jewish Messianism."

to be the luckier competitors who had inherited something, were recognized for something which Gentiles had to build from scratch.[59]

It is a "truism" that has not been made truer by repetition that antisemitism is only a form of envy. But in relation to Jewish chosenness it is true enough. Whenever peoples have been separated from action and achievements, when these natural ties with the common world have broken or do not exist for one reason or another, they have been inclined to turn upon themselves in their naked natural givenness and to claim divinity and a mission to redeem the whole world. When this happens in Western civilization, such peoples will invariably find the age-old claim of the Jews in their way. This is what the spokesmen of pan-movements sensed, and this is why they remained so untroubled by the realistic question of whether the Jewish problem in terms of numbers and power was important enough to make hatred of Jews the mainstay of their ideology. As their own national pride was independent of all achievements, so their hatred of the Jews had emancipated itself from all specific Jewish deeds and misdeeds. In this the pan-movements were in complete agreement, although neither knew how to utilize this ideological mainstay for purposes of political organization.

The time-lag between the formulation of the pan-movements' ideology and the possibility of its serious political application is demonstrated by the fact that the "Protocols of the Elders of Zion"—forged around 1900 by agents of the Russian secret police in Paris upon the suggestion of Pobyedonostzev, the political adviser of Nicholas II, and the only Pan-Slav ever in an influential position—remained a half-forgotten pamphlet until 1919, when it began its veritably triumphal procession through all European countries and languages;[60] its circulation some thirty years later was second only to Hitler's *Mein Kampf*. Neither the forger nor his employer knew that a time would come when the police would be the central institution of a society and the whole power of a country organized according to the supposedly Jewish principles laid down in the Protocols. Perhaps it was Stalin who was the first to discover all the potentialities for rule that the police possessed; it certainly was Hitler who, shrewder than Schoenerer his spiritual father, knew how to use the hierarchical principle of racism, how to exploit the antisemitic assertion of the existence of a "worst" people in order properly to organize the "best" and all the conquered and oppressed in between, how to generalize the superiority complex of the pan-movements so that each people, with the necessary exception of the Jews, could look down upon one that was even worse off than itself.

Apparently a few more decades of hidden chaos and open despair were necessary before large strata of people happily admitted that they were going

[59] See the antisemite E. Reventlow, *op. cit.*, but also the philosemite Russian philosopher Vladimir Solovyov, *Judaism and the Christian Question* (1884): Between the two religious nations, the Russians and the Poles, history has introduced a third religious people, the Jews. See Ehrenberg, *op. cit.*, p. 314 ff. See also Cleinow, *op. cit.*, pp. 44 ff.
[60] See John S. Curtiss, *The Protocols of Zion*, New York, 1942.

to achieve what, as they believed, only Jews in their innate devilishness had been able to achieve thus far. The leaders of the pan-movements, at any rate, though already vaguely aware of the social question, were very one-sided in their insistence on foreign policy. They therefore were unable to see that antisemitism could form the necessary link connecting domestic with external methods; they did not know yet how to establish their "folk community," that is, the completely uprooted, racially indoctrinated horde.

That the pan-movements' fanaticism hit upon the Jews as the ideological center, which was the beginning of the end of European Jewry, constitutes one of the most logical and most bitter revenges history has ever taken. For of course there is some truth in "enlightened" assertions from Voltaire to Renan and Taine that the Jews' concept of chosenness, their identification of religion and nationality, their claim to an absolute position in history and a singled-out relationship with God, brought into Western civilization an otherwise unknown element of fanaticism (inherited by Christianity with its claim to exclusive possession of Truth) on one side, and on the other an element of pride that was dangerously close to its racial perversion.[61] Politically, it was of no consequence that Judaism and an intact Jewish piety always were notably free of, and even hostile to, the heretical immanence of the Divine.

For tribal nationalism is the precise perversion of a religion which made God choose one nation, one's own nation; only because this ancient myth, together with the only people surviving from antiquity, had struck deep roots in Western civilization could the modern mob leader, with a certain amount of plausibility, summon up the impudence to drag God into the petty conflicts between peoples and to ask His consent to an election which the leader had already happily manipulated.[62] The hatred of the racists against the Jews sprang from a superstitious apprehension that it actually might be the Jews, and not themselves, whom God had chosen, to whom success was granted by divine providence. There was an element of feeble-minded resentment against a people who, it was feared, had received a rationally incomprehensible guarantee that they would emerge eventually, and in spite of appearances, as the final victors in world history.

For to the mentality of the mob the Jewish concept of a divine mission to

[61] See Berdyaev, *op. cit.*, p. 5: "Religion and nationality in the Muscovite kingdom grew up together, as they did also in the consciousness of the ancient Hebrew people. And in the same way as Messianic consciousness was an attribute of Judaism, it was an attribute of Russian Orthodoxy also."

[62] A fantastic example of the madness in the whole business is the following passage in Léon Bloy—which fortunately is not characteristic of French nationalism: "France is so much the first of the nations that all others, no matter who they are, must be honored if they are permitted to eat the bread of her dogs. If only France is happy, then the rest of the world can be satisfied even though they have to pay for France's happiness with slavery or destruction. But if France suffers, then God Himself suffers, the terrible God. . . . This is as absolute and as inevitable as the secret of predestination." Quoted from R. Nadolny, *Germanisierung oder Slavisierung?*, 1928, p. 55.

bring about the kingdom of God could only appear in the vulgar terms of success and failure. Fear and hatred were nourished and somewhat rationalized by the fact that Christianity, a religion of Jewish origin, had already conquered Western mankind. Guided by their own ridiculous superstition, the leaders of the pan-movements found that little hidden cog in the mechanics of Jewish piety that made a complete reversion and perversion possible, so that chosenness was no longer the myth for an ultimate realization of the ideal of a common humanity—but for its final destruction.

ii: *The Inheritance of Lawlessness*

OPEN DISREGARD for law and legal institutions and ideological justification of lawlessness has been much more characteristic of continental than of overseas imperialism. This is partly due to the fact that continental imperialists lacked the geographical distance to separate the illegality of their rule on foreign continents from the legality of their home countries' institutions. Of equal importance is the fact that the pan-movements originated in countries which had never known constitutional government, so that their leaders naturally conceived of government and power in terms of arbitrary decisions from above.

Contempt for law became characteristic of all movements. Though more fully articulated in Pan-Slavism than in Pan-Germanism it reflected the actual conditions of rule in both Russia and Austria-Hungary. To describe these two despotisms, the only ones left in Europe at the outbreak of the first World War, in terms of multinational states gives only one part of the picture. As much as for their rule over multinational territories they were distinguished from other governments in that they governed the peoples directly (and not only exploited them) by a bureaucracy; parties played insignificant roles, and parliaments had no legislative functions; the state ruled through an administration that applied decrees. The significance of Parliament for the Dual Monarchy was little more than that of a not too bright debating society. In Russia as well as pre-war Austria serious opposition could hardly be found there but was exerted by outside groups who knew that their entering the parliamentary system would only detract popular attention and support from them.

Legally, government by bureaucracy is government by decree, and this means that power, which in constitutional government only enforces the law, becomes the direct source of all legislation. Decrees moreover remain anonymous (while laws can always be traced to specific men or assemblies), and therefore seem to flow from some over-all ruling power that needs no justification. Pobyedonostzev's contempt for the "snares" of the law was the eternal contempt of the administrator for the supposed lack of freedom of the legislator, who is hemmed in by principles, and for the inaction of the executors of law, who are restricted by its interpretation. The bureaucrat, who by merely administering decrees has the illusion of constant action, feels tremendously superior to these "impractical" people who are forever entangled in "legal niceties" and therefore stay outside the sphere of power which to him is the source of everything.

The administrator considers the law to be powerless because it is by definition separated from its application. The decree, on the other hand, does not exist at all except if and when it is applied; it needs no justification except applicability. It is true that decrees are used by all governments in times of emergency, but then the emergency itself is a clear justification and automatic limitation. In governments by bureaucracy decrees appear in their naked purity as though they were no longer issued by powerful men, but were the incarnation of power itself and the administrator only its accidental agent. There are no general principles which simple reason can understand behind the decree, but ever-changing circumstances which only an expert can know in detail. People ruled by decree never know what rules them because of the impossibility of understanding decrees in themselves and the carefully organized ignorance of specific circumstances and their practical significance in which all administrators keep their subjects. Colonial imperialism, which also ruled by decree and was sometimes even defined as the "*régime des décrets*," [62a] was dangerous enough; yet the very fact that the administrators over native populations were imported and felt to be usurpers, mitigated its influence on the subject peoples. Only where, as in Russia and Austria, native rulers and a native bureaucracy were accepted as the legitimate government, could rule by decree create the atmosphere of arbitrariness and secretiveness which effectively hid its mere expediency.

Rule by decree has conspicuous advantages for the domination of far-flung territories with heterogeneous populations and for a policy of oppression. Its efficiency is superior simply because it ignores all intermediary stages between issuance and application, and because it prevents political reasoning by the people through the withholding of information. It can easily overcome the variety of local customs and need not rely on the necessarily slow process of development of general law. It is most helpful for the establishment of a centralized administration because it overrides automatically all matters of local autonomy. If rule by good laws has sometimes been called the rule of wisdom, rule by appropriate decrees may rightly be called the rule of cleverness. For it is clever to reckon with ulterior motives and aims, and it is wise to understand and create by deduction from generally accepted principles.

Government by bureaucracy has to be distinguished from the mere outgrowth and deformation of civil services which frequently accompanied the decline of the nation-state—as, notably, in France. There the administration has survived all changes in regime since the Revolution, entrenched itself like a parasite in the body politic, developed its own class interests, and become a useless organism whose only purpose appears to be chicanery and prevention of normal economic and political development. There are of

[62a] See M. Larcher, *Traité Elémentaire de Législation Algérienne*, 1903, Vol. II, pp. 150-152: "The *régime des decrets* is the government of all French colonies."

course many superficial similarities between the two types of bureaucracy, especially if one pays too much attention to the striking psychological similarity of petty officials. But if the French people have made the very serious mistake of accepting their administration as a necessary evil, they have never committed the fatal error of allowing it to rule the country—even though the consequence has been that nobody rules it. The French atmosphere of government has become one of inefficiency and vexations; but it has not created an aura of pseudomysticism.

And it is this pseudomysticism that is the stamp of bureaucracy when it becomes a form of government. Since the people it dominates never really know why something is happening, and a rational interpretation of laws does not exist, there remains only one thing that counts, the brutal naked event itself. What happens to one then becomes subject to an interpretation whose possibilities are endless, unlimited by reason and unhampered by knowledge. Within the framework of such endless interpretative speculation, so characteristic of all branches of Russian pre-revolutionary literature, the whole texture of life and world assume a mysterious secrecy and depth. There is a dangerous charm in this aura because of its seemingly inexhaustible richness; interpretation of suffering has a much larger range than that of action for the former goes on in the inwardness of the soul and releases all the possibilities of human imagination, whereas the latter is constantly checked, and possibly led into absurdity, by outward consequence and controllable experience.

One of the most glaring differences between the old-fashioned rule by bureaucracy and the up-to-date totalitarian brand is that Russia's and Austria's pre-war rulers were content with an idle radiance of power and, satisfied to control its outward destinies, left the whole inner life of the soul intact. Totalitarian bureaucracy, with a more complete understanding of the meaning of absolute power, intruded upon the private individual and his inner life with equal brutality. The result of this radical efficiency has been that the inner spontaneity of people under its rule was killed along with their social and political activities, so that the merely political sterility under the older bureaucracies was followed by total sterility under totalitarian rule.

The age which saw the rise of the pan-movements, however, was still happily ignorant of total sterilization. On the contrary, to an innocent observer (as most Westerners were) the so-called Eastern soul appeared to be incomparably richer, its psychology more profound, its literature more meaningful than that of the "shallow" Western democracies. This psychological and literary adventure into the "depths" of suffering did not come to pass in Austria-Hungary because its literature was mainly German-language literature, which after all was and remained part and parcel of German literature in general. Instead of inspiring profound humbug, Austrian bureaucracy rather caused its greatest modern writer to become the humorist and critic of the whole matter. Franz Kafka knew well enough the superstition of fate which possesses people who live under the perpetual rule of accidents, the inevitable tendency to read a special superhuman meaning into happenings whose rational significance is beyond the knowledge and understanding of the concerned. He was well aware of the weird attractiveness of such peoples, their melancholy and beautifully sad folk tales which seemed so superior to the lighter and brighter literature of more fortunate peoples. He exposed the pride in necessity as such, even the necessity of evil, and the nauseating conceit which identifies evil and misfortune with destiny. The miracle is only that he could do this in a world in which the main elements of this atmosphere were not fully articulated; he trusted his great powers of imagination to draw all the necessary conclusions and, as it were, to complete what reality had somehow neglected to bring into full focus.[63]

Only the Russian Empire of that time offered a complete picture of rule by bureaucracy. The chaotic conditions of the country—too vast to be ruled, populated by primitive peoples without experience in political organization of any kind, who vegetated under the incomprehensible overlordship of the Russian bureaucracy—conjured up an atmosphere of anarchy and hazard in which the conflicting whims of petty officials and the daily accidents of incompetence and inconsistency inspired a philosophy that saw in the Accident the true Lord of Life, something like the apparition of Divine Providence.[64] To the Pan-Slav who always insisted on the so much more "interesting" conditions in Russia against the shallow boredom of civilized countries, it looked as though the Divine had found an intimate immanence in the soul of the unhappy Russian people, matched nowhere else on earth. In an unending stream of literary variations the Pan-Slavs opposed the profundity and violence of Russia to the superficial banality of the West, which did not know suffering or the meaning of sacrifice, and behind whose sterile civilized surface were hidden frivolity and triteness.[65] The totalitarian movements still owed much of their appeal to this vague and embittered anti-

[63] See especially the magnificent story in *The Castle* (1930) of the Barnabases, which reads like a weird travesty of a piece of Russian literature. The family is living under a curse, treated as lepers till they feel themselves such, merely because one of their pretty daughters once dared to reject the indecent advances of an important official. The plain villagers, controlled to the last detail by a bureaucracy, and slaves even in their thoughts to the whims of their all-powerful officials, had long since come to realize that to be in the right or to be in the wrong was for them a matter of pure "fate" which they could not alter. It is not, as K. naïvely assumes, the sender of an obscene letter who is exposed, but the recipient who becomes branded and tainted. This is what the villagers mean when they speak of their "fate." In K.'s view, "it's unjust and monstrous, but [he is] the only one in the village of that opinion."

[64] Deification of accidents serves of course as rationalization for every people that is not master of its own destiny. See for instance Steinberg, *op. cit.*: "For it is Accident that has become decisive for the structure of Jewish history. And Accident . . . , in the language of religion is called Providence" (p. 34).

[65] A Russian writer once said that Pan-Slavism "engenders an implacable hatred of the West, a morbid cult of everything Russian; . . . the salvation of the universe is still possible, but it can come about only through Russia. . . . The Pan-Slavists, seeing enemies of their idea everywhere, persecute everybody who does not agree with them . . ." (Victor Bérard, *L'Empire russe et le tsarisme*, 1905.) See also N. V. Bubnoff, *Kultur und Geschichte im russischen Denken der Gegenwart*, 1927, in Osteuropa: Quellen und Studien. Heft 2. Chapter v.

Western mood that was especially in vogue in pre-Hitler Germany and Austria, but had seized the general European intelligentsia of the twenties as well. Up to the moment of actual seizure of power, they could use this passion for the profound and rich "irrational," and during the crucial years when the exiled Russian intelligentsia exerted a not negligible influence upon the spiritual mood of an entirely disturbed Europe, this purely literary attitude proved to be a strong emotional factor in preparing the ground for totalitarianism.[66]

Movements, as contrasted to parties, did not simply degenerate into bureaucratic machines,[67] but saw in bureaucratic regimes possible models of organization. The admiration which inspired the Pan-Slav Pogodin's description of the machine of Czarist Russian bureaucracy would have been shared by them all: "A tremendous machine, constructed after the simplest principles, guided by the hand of *one* man . . . which sets it in motion at every moment with a single movement, no matter which direction and speed he may choose. And this is not merely a mechanical motion, the machine is entirely animated by inherited emotions, which are subordination, limitless confidence and devotion to the Czar who is their God on earth. Who would dare to attack us and whom could we not force into obedience?" [68]

Pan-Slavists were less opposed to the state than their Pan-Germanist colleagues. They sometimes even tried to convince the Czar to become the head of the movement. The reason for this tendency is of course that the Czar's position differed considerably from that of any European monarch, the Emperor of Austria-Hungary not excluded, and that the Russian despotism never developed into a rational state in the Western sense but remained fluid, anarchic, and unorganized. Czarism, therefore, sometimes appeared to the Pan-Slavists as the symbol of a gigantic moving force surrounded by a halo of unique holiness.[69] Pan-Slavism, in contrast to Pan-Germanism, did not have to invent a new ideology to suit the needs of the

[66] Ehrenberg, *op. cit.*, stresses this in his epilogue: The ideas of a Kirejewski, Chomjakow, Leontjew "may have died out in Russia after the Revolution. But now they have spread all over Europe and live today in Sofia, Constantinople, Berlin, Paris, London. Russians, and precisely the disciples of these authors, . . . publish books and edit magazines that are read in all European countries; through them, these ideas—the ideas of their spiritual fathers—are represented. The Russian spirit has become European" (p. 334).

[67] For the bureaucratization of party machines, Robert Michels, *Political Parties; a sociological study of the oligarchical tendencies of modern democracy* (English translation Glencoe, 1949, from the German edition of 1911), is still the standard work.

[68] K. Staehlin, "Die Entstehung des Panslawismus," in *Germano-Slavica*, 1936, Heft 4.

[69] M. N. Katkov: "All power has its derivation from God; the Russian Czar, however, was granted a special significance distinguishing him from the rest of the world's rulers. . . . He is a successor of the Caesars of the Eastern Empire, . . . the founders of the very creed of the Faith of Christ. . . . Herein lies the mystery of the deep distinction between Russia and all the nations of the world." Quoted from Salo W. Baron, *Modern Nationalism and Religion*, 1947.

Slavic soul and its movement, but could interpret—and make a mystery of—Czarism as the anti-Western, anticonstitutional, antistate expression of the movement itself. This mystification of anarchic power inspired Pan-Slavism with its most pernicious theories about the transcendent nature and inherent goodness of all power. Power was conceived as a divine emanation pervading all natural and human activity. It was no longer a means to achieve something: it simply existed, men were dedicated to its service for the love of God, and any law that might regulate or restrain its "limitless and terrible strength" was clearly sacrilege. In its complete arbitrariness, power as such was held to be holy, whether it was the power of the Czar or the power of sex. Laws were not only incompatible with it, they were sinful, manmade "snares" that prevented the full development of the "divine." [70] The government, no matter what it did, was still the "Supreme Power in action," [71] and the Pan-Slav movement only had to adhere to this power and to organize its popular support, which eventually would permeate and therefore sanctify the whole people—a colossal herd, obedient to the arbitrary will of one man, ruled neither by law nor interest, but kept together solely by the cohesive force of their numbers and the conviction of their own holiness.

From the beginning, the movements lacking the "strength of inherited emotions" had to differ from the model of the already existing Russian despotism in two respects. They had to make propaganda which the established bureaucracy hardly needed, and did this by introducing an element of violence; [72] and they found a substitute for the role of "inherited emo-

[70] Pobyedonostzev in his *Reflections of a Russian Statesman,* London, 1898: "Power exists not for itself alone but for the love of God. It is a service to which men are dedicated. Thence comes the limitless, terrible strength of power and its limitless and terrible burden" (p. 254). Or: "The law becomes a snare not only to the people, but . . . to the very authorities engaged in its administration . . . if at every step the executor of the law finds in the law itself restrictive prescriptions . . . then all authority is lost in doubt, weakened by the law . . . and crushed by the fear of responsibility" (p. 88).

[71] According to Katkov "government in Russia means a thing totally different from what is understood by this term in other countries. . . . In Russia the government in the highest sense of the word, is the Supreme Power in action. . . ." Moissaye J. Olgin, *The Soul of the Russian Revolution,* New York, 1917, p. 57.—In a more rationalized form, we find the theory that "legal guarantees were needed in states founded upon conquest and threatened by the conflict of classes and races; they were superfluous in a Russia with harmony of classes and friendship of races" (Hans Kohn, *op. cit.*). Although idolization of power played a less articulate role in Pan-Germanism, there was always a certain antilegal tendency which for instance comes out clearly in Frymann, *op. cit.,* who as early as 1912 proposed the introduction of that "protective custody" (*Sicherheitshaft*), that is, arrest without any legal reason, which the Nazis then used to fill concentration camps.

[72] There is of course a patent similarity between the French mob organization during the Dreyfus Affair (see p. 111) and Russian pogrom groups such as the "Black Hundreds" in which the "wildest and the least cultivated dregs of old Russia [were gathered and which] kept contact with the majority of the Orthodox episcopate" (Fedotow, *op. cit.*)—or the "League of the Russian People" with its secret Fighting Squadrons recruited from the lower agents of the police, paid by the government, and led by intellectuals. See E. Cherikover, "New Materials on the Pogroms in Russia

tions" in the ideologies which Continental parties had already developed to a considerable extent. The difference in their use of ideology was that they not only added ideological justification to interest representation, but used ideologies as organizational principles. If the parties had been bodies for the organization of class interests, the movements became embodiments of ideologies. In other words, movements were "charged with philosophy" and claimed they had set into motion "the individualization of the moral universal within a collective." [73]

It is true that concretization of ideas had first been conceived in Hegel's theory of state and history and had been further developed in Marx's theory of the proletariat as the protagonist of mankind. It is of course not accidental that Russian Pan-Slavism was as much influenced by Hegel as Bolshevism was influenced by Marx. Yet neither Marx nor Hegel assumed actual human beings and actual parties or countries to be ideas in the flesh; both believed in the process of history in which ideas could be concretized only in a complicated dialectical movement. It needed the vulgarity of mob leaders to hit upon the tremendous possibilities of such concretization for the organization of masses. These men began to tell the mob that each of its members could become such a lofty all-important walking embodiment of something ideal if he would only join the movement. Then he no longer had to be loyal or generous or courageous, he would automatically be the very incarnation of Loyalty, Generosity, Courage. Pan-Germanism showed itself somewhat superior in organizational theory, insofar as it shrewdly deprived the individual German of all these wondrous qualities if he did not adhere to the movement (thereby foreshadowing the spiteful contempt which Nazism later expressed for the non-Party members of the German people), whereas Pan-Slavism, absorbed deeply in its limitless speculations about the Slav soul, assumed that every Slav consciously or unconsciously possessed such a soul no matter whether he was properly organized or not. It needed Stalin's ruthlessness to introduce into Bolshevism the same contempt for the Russian people that the Nazis showed toward the Germans.

It is this absoluteness of movements which more than anything else separates them from party structures and their partiality, and serves to justify their claim to overrule all objections of individual conscience. The particular reality of the individual person appears against the background of a spurious reality of the general and universal, shrinks into a negligible quantity or is submerged in the stream of dynamic movement of the universal itself. In this stream the difference between ends and means evaporates together with the personality, and the result is the monstrous immorality of ideological politics. All that matters is embodied in the moving movement itself; every idea, every value has vanished into a welter of superstitious pseudoscientific immanence.

+

at the Beginning of the Eighties" in *Historishe Shriftn* (Vilna), II, 463; and N. M. Gelber, "The Russian Pogroms in the Early Eighties in the Light of the Austrian Diplomatic Correspondence," *ibid.*

[73] Delos, *op. cit.*

III: *Party and Movement*

THE STRIKING and fateful difference between continental and overseas imperialism has been that their initial successes and failures were in exact opposition. While continental imperialism, even in its beginnings, succeeded in realizing the imperialist hostility against the nation-state by organizing large strata of people outside the party system, and always failed to get results in tangible expansion, overseas imperialism, in its mad and successful rushes to annex more and more far-flung territories, was never very successful when it attempted to change the home countries' political structure. The nation-state system's ruin, having been prepared by its own overseas imperialism, was eventually carried out by those movements which had originated outside its own realm. And when it came to pass that movements began successfully to compete with the nation-state's party system, it was also seen that they could undermine only countries with a multiparty system, that mere imperialist tradition was not sufficient to give them mass appeal, and that Great Britain, the classic country of two-party rule, did not produce a movement of either Fascist or Communist orientation of any consequence outside her party system.

The slogan "above the parties," the appeal to "men of all parties," and the boast that they would "stand far removed from the strife of parties and represent only a national purpose" was equally characteristic of all imperialist groups,[74] where it appeared as a natural consequence of their exclusive interest in foreign policy in which the nation was supposed to act as a whole in any event, independent of classes and parties.[75] Since, moreover, in the Continental systems this representation of the nation as a whole had

[74] As the President of the German Kolonialverein put it in 1884. See Mary E. Townsend, *Origin of Modern German Colonialism: 1871-1885*, New York, 1921. The Pan-German League always insisted on its being "above the parties; this was and is a vital condition for the League" (Otto Bonhard, *op. cit.*). The first real party that claimed to be more than a party, namely an "imperial party," was the National-Liberal Party in Germany under the leadership of Ernst Bassermann (Frymann, *op. cit.*).

In Russia, the Pan-Slavs needed only to pretend to be nothing more than popular support for the government, in order to be removed from all competition with parties; for the government as "the Supreme Power in action . . . cannot be understood as related to parties." Thus M. N. Katkov, close journalistic collaborator of Pobyedonostzev. See Olgin, *op. cit.*, p. 57.

[75] This clearly was still the purpose of the early "beyond party" groups among which up to 1918 the Pan-German League must still be counted. "Standing outside of all organized political parties, we may go our purely national way. We do not ask: Are you conservative? Are you liberal? . . . The German nation is the meeting point upon which all parties can make common cause." Lehr, *Zwecke und Ziele des alldeutschen Verbandes*. Flugschriften, No. 14. Translation quoted from Wertheimer, *op. cit.*, p. 110.

been the "monopoly" of the state,[76] it could even seem that the imperialists put the state's interests above everything else, or that the interest of the nation as a whole had found in them its long-sought popular support. Yet despite all such claims to true popularity the "parties above parties" remained small societies of intellectuals and well-to-do people who, like the Pan-German League, could hope to find a larger appeal only in times of national emergency.[77]

The decisive invention of the pan-movements, therefore, was not that they too claimed to be outside and above the party system, but that they called themselves "movements," their very name alluding to the profound distrust for all parties that was already widespread in Europe at the turn of the century and finally became so decisive that in the days of the Weimar Republic, for instance, "each new group believed it could find no better legitimization and no better appeal to the masses than a clear insistence that it was not a 'party' but a 'movement.' "[78]

It is true that the actual disintegration of the European party system was brought about, not by the pan- but by the totalitarian movements. The pan-movements, however, which found their place somewhere between the small and comparatively harmless imperialist societies and the totalitarian movements, were forerunners of the totalitarians, insofar as they had already discarded the element of snobbery so conspicuous in all imperialist leagues, whether the snobbery of wealth and birth in England or of education in Germany, and therefore could take advantage of the deep popular hatred for those institutions which were supposed to represent the people.[79]

It is not surprising that the appeal of movements in Europe has not been hurt much by the defeat of Nazism and the growing fear of Bolshevism. As matters stand now, the only country in Europe where Parliament is not despised and the party system not hated is Great Britain.[80]

[76] Carl Schmitt, *Staat, Bewegung, Volk* (1934), speaks of the "monopoly of politics which the state had acquired during the seventeenth and eighteenth centuries."

[77] Wertheimer, *op. cit.*, depicts the situation quite correctly when she says: "That there was any vital connection before the war between the Pan-German League and the imperial government is entirely preposterous." On the other hand, it was perfectly true that German policy during the first World War was decisively influenced by Pan-Germans because the higher officer corps had become Pan-German. See Hans Delbrück, *Ludendorffs Selbstportrait*, Berlin, 1922. Compare also his earlier article on the subject, "Die Alldeutschen," in *Preussische Jahrbücher*, 154, December, 1913.

[78] Sigmund Neumann, *Die deutschen Parteien*, 1932, p. 99.

[79] Moeller van den Bruck, *Das dritte Reich*, 1923, pp. vii-viii, describes the situation: "When the World War ended in defeat . . . we met Germans everywhere who said they were outside all parties, who talked about 'freedom from parties,' who tried to find a point of view 'above parties.' . . . A complete lack of respect for Parliaments . . . which at no time have the faintest idea of what is really going on in the country . . . is very widespread among the people."

[80] British dissatisfaction with the Front Bench system has nothing to do with this anti-Parliamentarian sentiment, the British in this instance being opposed to something that prevents Parliament from functioning properly.

Faced with the stability of political institutions in the British Isles and the simultaneous decline of all nation-states on the Continent, one can hardly avoid concluding that the difference between the Anglo-Saxon and the Continental party system must be an important factor. For the merely material differences between a greatly impoverished England and an undestroyed France were not great after the close of this war; unemployment, the greatest revolutionizing factor in prewar Europe, had hit England even harder than many Continental countries; and the shock to which England's political stability was being exposed right after the war through the Labor Government's liquidation of imperialist government in India and its tentative efforts to rebuild an English world policy along nonimperialist lines must have been tremendous. Nor does mere difference in social structure account for the relative strength of Great Britain; for the economic basis of her social system has been severely changed by the socialist Government without any decisive change in political institutions.

Behind the external difference between the Anglo-Saxon two-party and the Continental multiparty system lies a fundamental distinction between the party's function within the body politic, which has great consequences for the party's attitude to power, and the citizen's position in his state. In the two-party system one party always represents the government and actually rules the country, so that, temporarily, the party in power becomes identical with the state. The state, as a permanent guarantee of the country's unity, is represented only in the permanence of the office of the King [81] (for the permanent Undersecretaryship of the Foreign Office is only a matter of continuity). As the two parties are planned and organized for alternate rule,[82] all branches of the administration are planned and organized for alternation. Since the rule of each party is limited in time, the opposition party exerts a control whose efficiency is strengthened by the certainty that it is the ruler of tomorrow. In fact, it is the opposition rather than the symbolic position of the King that guarantees the integrity of the whole against one-party dictatorship. The obvious advantages of this system are that there is no essential difference between government and state, that power as well as the state remain within the grasp of the citizens organized in the party, which represents the power and the state either of today or of tomorrow, and that consequently there is no occasion for indulgence in lofty speculations about Power and State as though they were something beyond human reach, metaphysical entities independent of the will and action of the citizens.

[81] The British party system, the oldest of all, "began to take shape . . . only when the affairs of state ceased to be exclusively the prerogative of the crown . . . ," that is, after 1688. "The King's role has been historically to represent the nation as a unity as against the factional strife of parties." See article "Political Parties" 3, "Great Britain" by W. A. Rudlin in *Encyclopedia of the Social Sciences.*

[82] In what seems to be the earliest history of the "party," George W. Cooke, *The History of Party,* London, 1836, in the preface defines the subject as a system by which "two classes of statesmen . . . alternately govern a mighty empire."

The Continental party system supposes that each party defines itself consciously as a part of the whole, which in turn is represented by a state above parties.[83] A one-party rule therefore can only signify the dictatorial domination of one part over all others. Governments formed by alliances between party leaders are always only party governments, clearly distinguished from the state which rests above and beyond them. One of the minor shortcomings of this system is that cabinet members cannot be chosen according to competence, for too many parties are represented, and ministers are necessarily chosen according to party alliances;[84] the British system, on the other hand, permits a choice of the best men from the large ranks of one party. Much more relevant, however, is the fact that the multiparty system never allows any one man or any one party to assume full responsibility, with the natural consequence that no government, formed by party alliances, ever feels fully responsible. Even if the improbable happens and an absolute majority of one party dominates Parliament and results in one-party rule, this can only end either in dictatorship, because the system is not prepared for such government, or in the bad conscience of a still truly democratic leadership which, accustomed to thinking of itself only as part of the whole, will naturally be afraid of using its power. This bad conscience functioned in a well-nigh exemplary fashion when, after the first World War, the German and Austrian Social Democratic parties emerged for a short moment as absolute majority parties, yet repudiated the power which went with this position.[85]

Since the rise of the party systems it has been a matter of course to identify parties with particular interests, economic or others,[86] and all Con-

[83] The best account of the essence of the Continental party system is given by the Swiss jurist Johann Caspar Bluntschli, *Charakter und Geist der politischen Parteien,* 1869. He states: "It is true that a party is only part of a greater whole, never this whole itself. . . . It must never identify itself with the whole, the people or the state . . . ; therefore a party may fight against other parties, but it must never ignore them and usually must not want to destroy them. No party can exist all by itself" (p. 3). The same idea is expressed by Karl Rosenkranz, a German Hegelian philosopher, whose book on political parties appeared before parties existed in Germany: *Ueber den Begriff der politischen Partei* (1843): "Party is conscious partiality" (p. 9).

[84] See John Gilbert Heinberg, *Comparative Major European Governments,* New York, 1937, chapters vii and viii. "In England one political party usually has a majority in the House of Commons, and the leaders of the party are members of the Cabinet. . . . In France, no political party in practice ever has a majority of the members of the Chamber of Deputies, and, consequently, the Council of Ministers is composed of the leaders of a number of party groups" (p. 158).

[85] See *Demokratie und Partei,* ed. by Peter R. Rohden, Vienna, 1932, Introduction: "The distinguishing characteristic of German parties is . . . that all parliamentary groups are resigned not to represent the *volonté générale.* . . . That is why the parties were so embarrassed when the November Revolution brought them to power. Each of them was so organized that it could only make a relative claim, *i.e.,* it always reckoned with the existence of other parties representing other partial interests and thus naurally limited its own ambitions" (pp. 13-14).

[86] The Continental party system is of very recent date. With the exception of the French parties which date back to the French Revolution, no European country knew party representation prior to 1848. Parties came into being through formation of

tinental parties, not only the labor groups, have been very frank in admit-
ting this as long as they could be sure that a state above parties exerts its
power more or less in the interest of all. The Anglo-Saxon party, on the
contrary, founded on some "particular principle" for the service of the
"national interest," [87] is itself the actual or future state of the country;
particular interests are represented in the party itself, as its right and left
wing, and held in check by the very necessities of government. And since
in the two-party system a party cannot exist for any length of time if it
does not win enough strength to assume power, no theoretical justification
is needed, no ideologies are developed, and the peculiar fanaticism of Continental party strife, which springs not so much from conflicting interests
as from antagonistic ideologies, is completely absent.[88]

The trouble with the Continental parties, separated on principle from
government and power, was not so much that they were trapped in the narrowness of particular interests as that they were ashamed of these interests
and therefore developed those justifications which led each one into an
ideology claiming that its particular interests coincided with the most general interests of humanity. The conservative party was not content to defend
the interests of landed property but needed a philosophy according to which
God had created man to till the soil by the sweat of his brow. The same
is true for the progress ideology of the middle-class parties and for the
labor parties' claim that the proletariat is the leader of mankind. This
strange combination of lofty philosophy and down-to-earth interests is paradoxical only at first glance. Since these parties did not organize their
members (or educate their leaders) for the purpose of handling public
affairs, but represented them only as private individuals with private interests, they had to cater to all private needs, spiritual as well as material.
In other words, the chief difference between the Anglo-Saxon and the
Continental party is that the former is a political organization of citizens
who need to "act in concert" in order to act at all,[89] while the latter is

---

factions in Parliament. In Sweden, the Social Democratic Party was the first party
(in 1889) with a fully formulated program (*Encyclopedia of Social Sciences, loc. cit.*).
For Germany, see Ludwig Bergstraesser, *Geschichte der politischen Parteien,* 1921.
All parties were frankly based upon protection of interests; the German Conservative
Party for instance developed from the "Association to protect the interests of big
landed property" founded in 1848. Interests were not necessarily economic, however.
The Dutch parties, for instance, were formed "over the two questions that so largely
dominate Dutch politics—the broadening of the franchise and the subsidizing of
private [mainly denominational] education" (*Encyclopedia of the Social Sciences,
loc. cit.*).

[87] Edmund Burke's definition of party: "Party is a body of men united for promot-
ing, by their joint endeavor, the national interest, upon some particular principle in
which they are all agreed" (*Upon Party,* 2nd edition, London, 1850).

[88] Arthur N. Holcombe (*Encyclopedia of the Social Sciences, loc. cit.*) rightly
stressed that in the double party system the principles of the two parties "have tended
to be the same. If they had not been substantially the same, submission to the victor
would have been intolerable to the vanquished."

[89] Burke, *op. cit.:* "They believed that no men could act with effect, who did not
act in concert; that no men could act in concert, who did not act with confidence; that

the organization of private individuals who want their interests to be protected against interference from public affairs.

It is consistent with this system that the Continental state philosophy recognized men to be citizens only insofar as they were not party members, *i.e.,* in their individual unorganized relationship to the state (*Staatsbürger*) or in their patriotic enthusiasm in times of emergency (*citoyens*).[90] This was the unfortunate result of the transformation of the *citoyen* of the French Revolution into the *bourgeois* of the nineteenth century on one hand, and of the antagonism between state and society on the other. The Germans tended to consider patriotism an obedient self-oblivion before the authorities and the French an enthusiastic loyalty to the phantom of "eternal France." In both cases, patriotism meant an abandonment of one's party and partial interests in favor of the government and the national interest. The point is that such nationalistic deformation was almost inevitable in a system that created political parties out of private interests, so that the public good had to depend upon force from above and a vague generous self-sacrifice from below which could be achieved only by arousing nationalistic passions. In England, on the contrary, antagonism between private and national interest never played a decisive role in politics. The more, therefore, the party system on the Continent corresponded to class interests, the more urgent was the need of the nation for nationalism, for some popular expression and support of national interests, a support which England with its direct government by party and opposition never needed so much.

If we consider the difference between the Continental multiparty and the British two-party system with regard to their predisposition to the rise of movements, it seems plausible that it should be easier for a one-party dictatorship to seize the state machinery in countries where the state is above the parties, and thereby above the citizens, than in those where the citizens by acting "in concert," *i.e.,* through party organization, can win power legally and feel themselves to be the proprietors of the state either of today or of tomorrow. It appears even more plausible that the mystifica-

---

no men could act with confidence, who were not bound together by common opinions, common affections, and common interests."

[90] For the Central European concept of citizen (the *Staatsbürger*) as opposed to party member, see Bluntschli, *op. cit.:* "Parties are not state institutions, . . . not members of the state organism, but free social associations whose formations depend upon a changing membership united for common political action by a definite conviction." The difference between state and party interest is stressed time and again: "The party must never put itself above the state, must never put its party interest above the state interest" (pp. 9 and 10).

Burke, on the contrary, argues against the concept according to which party interests or party membership make a man a worse citizen. "Commonwealths are made of families, free commonwealths of parties also; and we may as well affirm that our natural regards and ties of blood tend inevitably to make men bad citizens, as that the bonds of our party weaken those by which we are held to our country" (*op. cit.*). Lord John Russell, *On Party* (1850), even goes one step further when he asserts that the chief of the good effects of parties is "that it gives a substance to the shadowy opinions of politicians, and attaches them to steady and lasting principles."

tion of power inherent in the movements should be more easily achieved the farther removed the citizens are from the sources of power—easier in bureaucratically ruled countries where power positively transcends the capacity to understand on the part of the ruled, than in constitutionally governed countries where the law is above power and power is only a means of its enforcement; and easier yet in countries where the state power is beyond the reach of the parties and therefore, even if it remains within the reach of the citizen's intelligence, is removed beyond the reach of his practical experience and action.

The alienation of the masses from government, which was the beginning of their eventual hatred of and disgust with Parliament, was different in France and other Western democracies on one hand, and in the Central European countries, Germany chiefly, on the other. In Germany, where the state was by definition above the parties, party leaders as a rule surrendered their party allegiance the moment they became ministers and were charged with official duties. Disloyalty to one's own party was the duty of everyone in public office.[91] In France, ruled by party alliances, no real government has been possible since the establishment of the Third Republic and its fantastic record of cabinets. Her weakness was the opposite of the German one; she had liquidated the state which was above the parties and above Parliament without reorganizing her party system into a body capable of governing. The government necessarily became a ridiculous exponent of the ever-changing moods of Parliament and public opinion. The German system, on the other hand, made Parliament a more or less useful battlefield for conflicting interests and opinions whose main function was to influence the government but whose practical necessity in the handling of state affairs was, to say the least, debatable. In France, the parties suffocated the government; in Germany, the state emasculated the parties.

Since the end of the last century, the repute of these Constitutional parliaments and parties has constantly declined; to the people at large they looked like expensive and unnecessary institutions. For this reason alone each group that claimed to present something above party and class interests and started outside of Parliament had a great chance for popularity. Such groups seemed more competent, more sincere, and more concerned with public affairs. This, however, was so in appearance only, for the true goal of every "party above parties" was to promote one particular interest until it had devoured all others, and to make one particular group the master of the state machine. This is what finally happened in Italy under

[91] Compare with this attitude the telling fact that in Great Britain Ramsay MacDonald was never able to live down his "betrayal" of the Labor Party. In Germany the spirit of civil service asked of those in public office to be "above the parties." Against this spirit of the old Prussian civil service the Nazis asserted the priority of the Party, because they wanted dictatorship. Goebbels demanded explicitly: "Each party member who becomes a state functionary has to remain a National Socialist first . . . and to co-operate closely with the party administration" (quoted from Gottfried Neesse, *Partei und Staat,* 1939, p. 28).

Mussolini's Fascism, which up to 1938 was not totalitarian but just an ordinary nationalist dictatorship developed logically from a multiparty democracy. For there is indeed some truth in the old truism about the affinity between majority rule and dictatorship, but this affinity has nothing whatever to do with totalitarianism. It is obvious that, after many decades of inefficient and muddled multiparty rule, the seizure of the state for the advantage of one party can come as a great relief because it assures at least, though only for a limited time, some consistency, some permanence, and a little less contradiction.

The fact that the seizure of power by the Nazis was usually identified with such a one-party dictatorship merely showed how much political thinking was still rooted in the old established patterns, and how little the people were prepared for what really was to come. The only typically modern aspect of the Fascist party dictatorship is that here, too, the party insisted that it was a movement; that it was nothing of the kind, but merely usurped the slogan "movement" in order to attract the masses, became evident as soon as it seized the state machine without drastically changing the power structure of the country, being content to fill all government positions with party members. It was precisely through the identification of the party with the state, which both the Nazis and the Bolsheviks have always carefully avoided, that the party ceased to be a "movement" and became tied to the basically stable structure of the state.

Even though the totalitarian movements and their predecessors, the pan-movements, were not "parties above parties" aspiring to seize the state machine but movements aiming at the destruction of the state, the Nazis found it very convenient to pose as such, that is, to pretend to follow faithfully the Italian model of Fascism. Thus they could win the help of those upper-class and business elite who mistook the Nazis for the older groups they had themselves frequently initiated and which had made only the rather modest pretense of conquering the state machine for one party.[92] The businessmen who helped Hitler into power naïvely believed that they were only supporting a dictator, and one of their own making, who would naturally rule to the advantage of their own class and the disadvantage of all others.

The imperialist-inspired "parties above parties" had never known how to profit from popular hatred of the party system as such; Germany's frustrated pre-war imperialism, in spite of its dreams of continental expansion and its violent denunciation of the nation-state's democratic institutions, never reached the scope of a movement. It certainly was not sufficient to haughtily discard class interests, the very foundation of the nation's party system, for this left them less appeal than even the ordinary parties still

[92] Such as the Kolonialverein, the Centralverein für Handelsgeographie, the Flottenverein, or even the Pan-German League, which however prior to the first World War had no connection whatsoever with big business. See Wertheimer, *op. cit.*, p. 73. Typical of this "above parties" of the bourgeoisie were of course the Nationalliberalen; see note 74.

enjoyed. What they conspicuously lacked, despite all high-sounding nationalist phrases, was a real nationalist or other ideology. After the first World War, when the German Pan-Germans, especially Ludendorff and his wife, recognized this error and tried to make up for it, they failed despite their remarkable ability to appeal to the most superstitious beliefs of the masses because they clung to an outdated nontotalitarian state worship and could not understand that the masses' furious interest in the so-called "suprastate powers" (*überstaatliche Mächte*)—i.e., the Jesuits, the Jews, and the Freemasons—did not spring from nation or state worship but, on the contrary, from envy and the desire also to become a "suprastate power."[93]

The only countries where to all appearances state idolatry and nation worship were not yet outmoded and where nationalist slogans against the "suprastate" forces were still a serious concern of the people were those Latin-European countries like Italy and, to a lesser degree, Spain and Portugal, which had actually suffered a definite hindrance to their full national development through the power of the Church. It was partly due to this authentic element of belated national development and partly to the wisdom of the Church, which very sagely recognized that Fascism was neither anti-Christian nor totalitarian in principle and only established a separation of Church and State which already existed in other countries, that the initial anticlerical flavor of Fascist nationalism subsided rather quickly and gave way to a *modus vivendi* as in Italy, or to a positive alliance, as in Spain and Portugal.

Mussolini's interpretation of the corporate state idea was an attempt to overcome the notorious national dangers in a class-ridden society with a new integrated social organization[94] and to solve the antagonism between state and society, on which the nation-state had rested, by the incorporation of the society into the state.[95] The Fascist movement, a "party above parties," because it claimed to represent the interest of the nation as a whole, seized the state machine, identified itself with the highest national

[93] Erich Ludendorff, *Die überstaatlichen Mächte im letzten Jahre des Weltkrieges,* Leipzig, 1927. See also *Feldherrnworte,* 1938, 2 vols.; I, 43, 55; II, 80.

[94] The main purpose of the corporate state was "that of correcting and neutralizing a condition brought about by the industrial revolution of the nineteenth century which dissociated capital and labor in industry, giving rise on the one hand to a capitalist class of employers of labor and on the other to a great propertyless class, the industrial proletariat. The juxtaposition of these classes inevitably led to the clash of their opposing interests" (*The Fascist Era,* published by the Fascist Confederation of Industrialists, Rome, 1939, Chapter iii).

[95] "If the State is truly to represent the nation, then the people composing the nation must be part of the State.

"How is this to be secured?

"The Fascist answer is by organizing the people in groups according to their respective activities, groups which through their leaders . . . rise by stages as in a pyramid, at the base of which are the masses and at the apex the State.

"No group outside the State, no group against the State, all groups within the State . . . which . . . is the nation itself rendered articulate." (*Ibid.*)

authority, and tried to make the whole people "part of the state." It did not, however, think itself "above the state," and its leaders did not conceive of themselves as "above the nation."[96] As regards the Fascists, their movement had come to an end with the seizure of power, at least with respect to domestic policies; the movement could now maintain its motion only in matters of foreign policy, in the sense of imperialist expansion and typically imperialist adventures. Even before the seizure of power, the Nazis clearly kept aloof from this Fascist form of dictatorship, in which the "movement" merely serves to bring the party to power, and consciously used the party "to drive on the movement," which, contrary to the party, must not have any "definite, closely determined goals."[97]

The difference between the Fascist and the totalitarian movements is best illustrated by their attitude toward the army, that is, toward the national institution *par excellence*. In contrast to the Nazis and the Bolsheviks, who destroyed the spirit of the army by subordinating it to the political commissars or totalitarian elite formations, the Fascists could use such intensely nationalist instruments as the army, with which they identified themselves as they had identified themselves with the state. They wanted a Fascist state and a Fascist army, but still an army and a state; only in Nazi Germany and Soviet Russia army and state became subordinated functions of the movement. The Fascist dictator—but neither Hitler nor Stalin—was the only true usurper in the sense of classical political theory, and his one-party rule was in a sense the only one still intimately connected with the multiparty system. He carried out what the imperialist-minded leagues, societies, and "parties above parties" had aimed at, so that it is particularly Italian Fascism that has become the only example of a modern mass movement organized within the framework of an existing state, inspired solely by extreme nationalism, and which transformed the people permanently into such *Staatsbürger* or *patriotes* as the nation-state had mobilized only in times of emergency and *union sacrée*.[98]

There are no movements without hatred of the state, and this was virtually unknown to the German Pan-Germans in the relative stability of pre-war Germany. The movements originated in Austria-Hungary, where hatred of the state was an expression of patriotism for the oppressed nationalities and where the parties—with the exception of the Social Demo-

---

[96] For the relationship between party and state in totalitarian countries and especially the incorporation of the Fascist party into the state of Italy, see Franz Neumann, *Behemoth*, 1942, chapter 1.

[97] See the extremely interesting presentation of the relationship between party and movement in the "Dienstvorschrift für die Parteiorganisation der NSDAP," 1932, p. II ff., and the presentation by Werner Best in *Die deutsche Polizei*, 1941, p. 107, which has the same orientation: "It is the task of the Party . . . to hold the movement together and give it support and direction."

[98] Mussolini, in his speech of November 14, 1933, defends his one-party rule with arguments current in all nation-states during a war: A single political party is needed so "that political discipline may exist . . . and that the bond of a common fate may unite everyone above contrasting interests" (Benito Mussolini, *Four Speeches on the Corporate State*, Rome, 1935).

cratic Party (next to the Christian-Social Party the only one sincerely loyal to Austria)—were formed along national, and not along class lines. This was possible because economic and national interests were almost identical here and because economic and social status depended largely on nationality; nationalism, therefore, which had been a unifying force in the nation-states, here became at once a principle of internal disruption, which resulted in a decisive difference in the structure of the parties as compared with those of nation-states. What held together the members of the parties in multinational Austria-Hungary was not a particular interest, as in the other Continental party systems, or a particular principle for organized action as in the Anglo-Saxon, but chiefly the sentiment of belonging to the same nationality. Strictly speaking, this should have been and was a great weakness in the Austrian parties, because no definite goals or programs could be deduced from the sentiment of tribal belonging. The pan-movements made a virtue of this shortcoming by transforming parties into movements and by discovering that form of organization which, in contrast to all others, would never need a goal or program but could change its policy from day to day without harm to its membership. Long before Nazism proudly pronounced that though it had a program it did not need one, Pan-Germanism discovered how much more important for mass appeal a general mood was than laid-down outlines and platforms. For the only thing that counts in a movement is precisely that it keeps itself in constant movement.[99] The Nazis, therefore, used to refer to the fourteen years of the Weimar Republic as the "time of the System"—*Systemzeit*—the implication being that this time was sterile, lacked dynamism, did not "move," and was followed by their "era of the movement."

The state, even as a one-party dictatorship, was felt to be in the way of the ever-changing needs of an ever-growing movement. There was no more characteristic difference between the imperialist "above party group" of the Pan-German League in Germany itself and the Pan-German movement in Austria than their attitudes toward the state:[100] while the "party above parties" wanted only to seize the state machine, the true movement aimed at its destruction; while the former still recognized the state as highest authority once its representation had fallen into the hands of the members of one party (as in Mussolini's Italy), the latter recognized the movement as independent of and superior in authority to the state.

The pan-movements' hostility to the party system acquired practical significance when, after the first World War, the party system ceased to be

[99] The following anecdote recorded by Berdyaev is noteworthy: "A Soviet young man went to France . . . [and] was asked what impression France left upon him. He answered: 'There is no freedom in this country.' . . . The young man expounded his idea of freedom: . . . The so-called [French] freedom was of the kind which leaves everything unchanged; every day was like its predecessors; . . . and so the young man who came from Russia was bored in France" (*op. cit.,* pp. 182-183).

[100] The Austrian state hostility sometimes occurred also among German Pan-Germans, especially if these were *Auslandsdeutsche,* like Moeller van den Bruck.

a working device and the class system of European society broke down under the weight of growing masses entirely declassed by events. What came to the fore then were no longer mere pan-movements but their totalitarian successors, which in a few years determined the politics of all other parties to such a degree that they became either anti-Fascist or anti-Bolshevik or both.[101] By this negative approach seemingly forced upon them from the outside, the older parties showed clearly that they too were no longer able to function as representatives of specific class interests but had become mere defenders of the status quo. The speed with which the German and Austrian Pan-Germans rallied to Nazism has a parallel in the much slower and more complicated course through which Pan-Slavs finally found out that the liquidation of Lenin's Russian Revolution had been thorough enough to make it possible for them to support Stalin wholeheartedly. That Bolshevism and Nazism at the height of their power outgrew mere tribal nationalism and had little use for those who were still actually convinced of it in principle, rather than as mere propaganda material, was neither the Pan-Germans' nor the Pan-Slavs' fault and hardly checked their enthusiasm.

The decay of the Continental party system went hand in hand with a decline of the prestige of the nation-state. National homogeneity was severely disturbed by migrations and France, the *nation par excellence,* became in a matter of years utterly dependent on foreign labor; a restrictive immigration policy, inadequate to new needs, was still truly "national," but made it all the more obvious that the nation-state was no longer capable of facing the major political issues of the time.[102] Even more serious was the ill-fated effort of the peace treaties of 1919 to introduce national state organizations into Eastern and Southern Europe where the state people frequently had only a relative majority and were outnumbered by the combined "minorities." This new situation would have been sufficient in itself to undermine seriously the class basis of the party system; everywhere parties were now organized along national lines as though the liquidation of the Dual Monarchy had served only to enable a host of similar experiments to start on a dwarfed scale.[103] In other countries, where the nation-state and the class basis of its parties were not touched by migrations and heterogeneity of population, inflation and unemployment caused a similar breakdown; and it is obvious that the more rigid the country's

[101] Hitler described the situation correctly when he said during the elections of 1932: "Against National Socialism there are only negative majorities in Germany" (quoted from Konrad Heiden, *Der Führer,* 1944, p. 564).

[102] At the outbreak of the second World War, at least 10 per cent of France's population was foreign and not naturalized. Her mines in the north were chiefly worked by Poles and Belgians, her agriculture in the south by Spaniards and Italians. See Carr-Saunders, *World Population,* Oxford, 1936, pp. 145-158.

[103] "Since 1918 none of the [succession states] has produced . . . a party which might embrace more than one race, one religion, one social class or one region. The only exception is the Communist Party of Czechoslovakia" (*Encyclopedia of the Social Sciences, loc. cit.*).

class system, the more class-conscious its people had been, the more dramatic and dangerous was this breakdown.

This was the situation between the two wars when every movement had a greater chance than any party because the movement attacked the institution of the state and did not appeal to classes. Fascism and Nazism always boasted that their hatred was directed not against individual classes, but the class system as such, which they denounced as an invention of Marxism. Even more significant was the fact that the Communists also, notwithstanding their Marxist ideology, had to abandon the rigidity of their class appeal when, after 1935, under the pretext of enlarging their mass base, they formed Popular Fronts everywhere and began to appeal to the same growing masses outside all class strata which up to then had been the natural prey to Fascist movements. None of the old parties was prepared to receive these masses, nor did they gauge correctly the growing importance of their numbers and the growing political influence of their leaders. This error in judgment by the older parties can be explained by the fact that their secure position in Parliament and safe representation in the offices and institutions of the state made them feel much closer to the sources of power than to the masses; they thought the state would remain forever the undisputed master of all instruments of violence, and that the army, that supreme institution of the nation-state, would remain the decisive element in all domestic crises. They therefore felt free to ridicule the numerous paramilitary formations which had sprung up without any officially recognized help. For the weaker the party system grew under the pressure of movements outside of Parliament and classes, the more rapidly all former antagonism of the parties to the state disappeared. The parties, laboring under the illusion of a "state above parties," misinterpreted this harmony as a source of strength, as a wondrous relationship to something of a higher order. But the state was as threatened as the party system by the pressure of revolutionary movements, and it could no longer afford to keep its lofty and necessarily unpopular position above internal domestic strife. The army had long since ceased to be a reliable bulwark against revolutionary unrest, not because it was in sympathy with the revolution but because it had lost its position. Twice in modern times, and both times in France, the *nation par excellence,* the army had already proved its essential unwillingness or incapacity to help those in power or to seize power by itself: in 1850, when it permitted the mob of the "Society of December 10" to carry Napoleon III to power,[104] and again at the end of the nineteenth century, during the Dreyfus Affair, when nothing would have been easier than the establishment of a military dictatorship. The neutrality of the army, its willingness to serve every master, eventually left the state in a position of "mediation between the organized party interests. It was no longer *above* but *between* the classes of society."[105] In other words, the state and the parties together defended

---

[104] See Karl Marx, *op. cit.*
[105] Carl Schmitt, *op. cit.*, p. 31.

the status quo without realizing that this very alliance served as much as anything else to change the status quo.

The breakdown of the European party system occurred in a spectacular way with Hitler's rise to power. It is now often conveniently forgotten that at the moment of the outbreak of the second World War, the majority of European countries had already adopted some form of dictatorship and discarded the party system, and that this revolutionary change in government had been effected in most countries without revolutionary upheaval. Revolutionary action more often than not was a theatrical concession to the desires of violently discontented masses rather than an actual battle for power. After all, it did not make much difference if a few thousand almost unarmed people staged a march on Rome and took over the government in Italy, or whether in Poland (in 1934) a so-called "partyless bloc," with a program of support for a semifascist government and a membership drawn from the nobility and the poorest peasantry, workers and businessmen, Catholics and orthodox Jews, legally won two-thirds of the seats in Parliament.[106]

In France, Hitler's rise to power, accompanied by a growth of Communism and Fascism, quickly cancelled the other parties' original relationships to each other and changed time-honored party lines overnight. The French Right, up to then strongly anti-German and pro-war, after 1933 became the vanguard of pacifism and understanding with Germany. The Left switched with equal speed from pacifism at any price to a firm stand against Germany and was soon accused of being a party of warmongers by the same parties which only a few years before had denounced its pacifism as national treachery.[107] The years that followed Hitler's rise to power proved even more disastrous to the integrity of the French party system. In the Munich crisis each party, from Right to Left, split internally on the only relevant political issue: who was for, who was against war with Germany.[108] Each party harbored a peace faction and a war faction; none of them could remain united on major political decisions and none stood the test of Fascism and Nazism without splitting into anti-Fascist on one side, Nazi fellow-travelers on the other. That Hitler could choose freely from all parties for the erection of puppet regimes was the consequence of this pre-war situation, and not of an especially shrewd Nazi maneuver. There was not a single party in Europe that did not produce collaborators.

Against the disintegration of the older parties stood the clear-cut unity of the Fascist and Communist movements everywhere—the former, outside of Germany and Italy, loyally advocating peace even at the price of foreign domination, and the latter for a long while preaching war even at the price

[106] Vaclav Fiala, "Les Partis politiques polonais," in *Monde Slave*, Février, 1935.

[107] See the careful analysis by Charles A. Micaud, *The French Right and Nazi Germany. 1933-1939*, 1943.

[108] The most famous instance was the split in the French socialist party in 1938 when Blum's faction remained in a minority against Déat's pro-Munich group during the party Congress of the Seine Department.

of national ruin. The point, however, is not so much that the extreme Right everywhere had abandoned its traditional nationalism in favor of Hitler's Europe and that the extreme Left had forgotten its traditional pacifism in favor of old nationalist slogans, but rather that both movements could count on the loyalty of a membership and leadership which would not be disturbed by a sudden switch in policy. This was dramatically exposed in the German-Russian nonaggression pact, when the Nazis had to drop their chief slogan against Bolshevism and the Communists had to return to a pacifism which they always had denounced as petty-bourgeois. Such sudden turns did not hurt them in the least. It is still well remembered how strong the Communists remained after their second *volte-face* less than two years later when the Soviet Union was attacked by Nazi Germany, and this in spite of the fact that both political lines had involved the rank and file in serious and dangerous political activities which demanded real sacrifices and constant action.

Different in appearance but much more violent in reality was the breakdown of the party system in pre-Hitler Germany. This came into the open during the last presidential elections in 1932 when entirely new and complicated forms of mass propaganda were adopted by all parties.

The choice of candidates was itself peculiar. While it was a matter of course that the two movements, which stood outside of and fought the parliamentary system from opposite sides, would present their own candidates (Hitler for the Nazis, and Thälmann for the Communists), it was rather surprising to see that all other parties could suddenly agree upon one candidate. That this candidate happened to be old Hindenburg who enjoyed the matchless popularity which, since the time of MacMahon, awaits the defeated general at home, was not just a joke; it showed how much the old parties wanted merely to identify themselves with the old-time state, the state above the parties whose most potent symbol had been the national army, to what an extent, in other words, they had already given up the party system itself. For in the face of the movements, the differences between the parties had indeed become quite meaningless; the existence of all of them was at stake and consequently they banded together and hoped to maintain a status quo that guaranteed their existence. Hindenburg became the symbol of the nation-state and the party system, while Hitler and Thälmann competed with each other to become the true symbol of the people.

As significant as the choice of candidates were the electoral posters. None of them praised its candidate for his own merits; the posters for Hindenburg claimed merely that "a vote for Thälmann is a vote for Hitler"—warning the workers not to waste their votes on a candidate sure to be beaten (Thälmann) and thus put Hitler in the saddle. This was how the Social Democrats reconciled themselves to Hindenburg., who was not even mentioned. The parties of the Right played the same game and emphasized that "a vote for Hitler is a vote for Thälmann." Both, in addition, alluded quite clearly to the instances in which the Nazis and Communists had made common cause, in order to convince all loyal party members, whether

Right or Left, that the preservation of the status quo demanded Hindenburg. In contrast to the propaganda for Hindenburg that appealed to those who wanted the status quo at any price—and in 1932 that meant unemployment for almost half the German people—the candidates of the movements had to reckon with those who wanted change at any price (even at the price of destruction of all legal institutions), and these were at least as numerous as the ever-growing millions of unemployed and their families. The Nazis therefore did not wince at the absurdity that "a vote for Thälmann is a vote for Hindenburg," the Communists did not hesitate to reply that "a vote for Hitler is a vote for Hindenburg," both threatening their voters with the menace of the status quo in exactly the same way their opponents had threatened their members with the specter of the revolution.

Behind the curious uniformity of method used by the supporters of all the candidates lay the tacit assumption that the electorate would go to the polls because it was frightened—afraid of the Communists, afraid of the Nazis, or afraid of the status quo. In this general fear all class divisions disappeared from the political scene; while the party alliance for the defense of the status quo blurred the older class structure maintained in the separate parties, the rank and file of the movements was completely heterogeneous and as dynamic and fluctuating as unemployment itself.[109] While within the framework of the national institutions the parliamentary Left had joined the parliamentary Right, the two movements were busy organizing together the famous transportation strike on the streets of Berlin in November, 1932.

When one considers the extraordinarily rapid decline of the Continental party system, one should bear in mind the very short life span of the whole institution. It existed nowhere before the nineteenth century, and in most European countries the formation of political parties took place only after 1848, so that its reign as an unchallenged institution in national politics lasted hardly four decades. During the last two decades of the nineteenth century, all the significant political developments in France, as well as in Austria-Hungary, already took place outside of and in opposition to parliamentary parties, while everywhere smaller imperialist "parties above parties" challenged the institution for the sake of popular support for an aggressive, expansionist foreign policy.

While the imperialist leagues set themselves above parties for the sake of identification with the nation-state, the pan-movements attacked these same parties as part and parcel of a general system which included the nation-state; they were not so much "above parties" as "above the state" for the sake of a direct identification with the people. The totalitarian

---

[109] The German socialist party underwent a typical change from the beginning of the century to 1933. Prior to the first World War only 10 per cent of its members did not belong to the working class whereas about 25 per cent of its votes came from the middle classes. In 1930, however, only 60 per cent of its members were workers and at least 40 per cent of its votes were middle-class votes. See Sigmund Neumann, *op. cit.*, pp. 28 ff.

movements eventually were led to discard the people also, whom, however, following closely in the footsteps of the pan-movements they used
for propaganda purposes. The "totalitarian state" is a state in appearance
only, and the movement no longer truly identifies itself even with the
needs of the people. The Movement by now is above state and people,
ready to sacrifice both for the sake of its ideology: "The Movement . . . is
State as well as People, and neither the present state . . . nor the present
German people can even be conceived without the Movement." [110]

Nothing proves better the irreparable decay of the party system than the
great efforts after this war to revive it on the Continent, their pitiful results,
the enhanced appeal of movements after the defeat of Nazism, and the
obvious threat of Bolshevism to national independence. The result of all
efforts to restore the status quo has been only the restoration of a political
situation in which the destructive movements are the only "parties" that
function properly. Their leadership has maintained authority under the
most trying circumstances and in spite of constantly changing party lines.
In order to gauge correctly the chances for survival of the European nation-
state, it would be wise not to pay too much attention to nationalist slogans
which the movements occasionally adopt for purposes of hiding their
true intentions, but rather to consider that by now everybody knows that
they are regional branches of international organizations, that the rank
and file is not disturbed in the least when it becomes obvious that their
policy serves foreign-policy interests of another and even hostile power,
and that denunciations of their leaders as fifth columnists, traitors to the
country, etc., do not impress their members to any considerable degree. In
contrast to the old parties, the movements have survived the last war and
are today the only "parties" which have remained alive and meaningful
to their adherents.

[110] Schmitt, *op. cit.*

CHAPTER FIVE

The Decline of the Nation-State and the End of the Rights of Man

I T IS ALMOST impossible even now to describe what actually happened in Europe on August 4, 1914. The days before and the days after the first World War are separated not like the end of an old and the beginning of a new period, but like the day before and the day after an explosion. Yet this figure of speech is as inaccurate as are all others, because the quiet of sorrow which settles down after a catastrophe has never come to pass. The first explosion seems to have touched off a chain reaction in which we have been caught ever since and which nobody seems to be able to stop. The first World War exploded the European comity of nations beyond repair, something which no other war had ever done. Inflation destroyed the whole class of small property owners beyond hope for recovery or new formation, something which no monetary crisis had ever done so radically before. Unemployment, when it came, reached fabulous proportions, was no longer restricted to the working class but seized with insignificant exceptions whole nations. Civil wars which ushered in and spread over the twenty years of uneasy peace were not only bloodier and more cruel than all their predecessors; they were followed by migrations of groups who, unlike their happier predecessors in the religious wars, were welcomed nowhere and could be assimilated nowhere. Once they had left their homeland they remained homeless, once they had left their state they became stateless; once they had been deprived of their human rights they were rightless, the scum of the earth. Nothing which was being done, no matter how stupid, no matter how many people knew and foretold the consequences, could be undone or prevented. Every event had the finality of a last judgment, a judgment that was passed neither by God nor by the devil, but looked rather like the expression of some unredeemably stupid fatality.

Before totalitarian politics consciously attacked and partially destroyed the very structure of European civilization, the explosion of 1914 and its severe consequences of instability had sufficiently shattered the façade of Europe's political system to lay bare its hidden frame. Such visible exposures were the sufferings of more and more groups of people to whom suddenly the rules of the world around them had ceased to apply. It was precisely the seeming stability of the surrounding world that made each group forced out of its protective boundaries look like an unfortunate exception to an otherwise sane and normal rule, and which filled with equal cynicism victims and observers of an apparently unjust and abnormal fate. Both mistook this cynicism for growing wisdom in the ways of the world, while actually they were more baffled and therefore became more stupid than they ever had been before. Hatred, certainly not lacking in the pre-war world, began to play a central role in public affairs everywhere, so that the political scene in the deceptively quiet years of the twenties assumed the sordid and weird atmosphere of a Strindbergian family quarrel. Nothing perhaps illustrates the general disintegration of political life better than this vague, pervasive hatred of everybody and everything, without a focus for its passionate attention, with nobody to make responsible for the state of affairs—neither the government nor the bourgeoisie nor an outside power. It consequently turned in all directions, haphazardly and unpredictably, incapable of assuming an air of healthy indifference toward anything under the sun.

This atmosphere of disintegration, though characteristic of the whole of Europe between the two wars, was more visible in the defeated than in the victorious countries, and it developed fully in the states newly established after the liquidation of the Dual Monarchy and the Czarist Empire. The last remnants of solidarity between the nonemancipated nationalities in the "belt of mixed populations" evaporated with the disappearance of a central despotic bureaucracy which had also served to gather together and divert from each other the diffuse hatreds and conflicting national claims. Now everybody was against everybody else, and most of all against his closest neighbors—the Slovaks against the Czechs, the Croats against the Serbs, the Ukrainians against the Poles. And this was not the result of the conflict between nationalities and the state peoples (or minorities and majorities); the Slovaks not only constantly sabotaged the democratic Czech government in Prague, but at the same time persecuted the Hungarian minority on their own soil, while a similar hostility against the state people on one hand, and among themselves on the other, existed among the dissatisfied minorities in Poland.

At first glance these troubles in the old European trouble spot looked like petty nationalist quarrels without any consequence for the political destinies of Europe. Yet in these regions and out of the liquidation of the two multinational states of pre-war Europe, Russia and Austria-Hungary, two victim groups emerged whose sufferings were different from those of all others in the era between the wars; they were worse off than the dispossessed middle classes, the unemployed, the small *rentiers,* the pensioners whom events had deprived of social status, the possibility to work, and the right to hold property: they had lost those rights which had been thought of and even defined as inalienable, namely the Rights of Man. The stateless and the minorities, rightly termed "cousins-germane," [1] had no

[1] By S. Lawford Childs, "Refugees—a Permanent Problem in International Organization" in *War is not Inevitable. Problems of Peace.* 13th Series, London, 1938, published by the International Labor Office.

governments to represent and to protect them and therefore were forced to live either under the law of exception of the Minority Treaties, which all governments (except Czechoslovakia) had signed under protest and never recognized as law, or under conditions of absolute lawlessness. With the emergence of the minorities in Eastern and Southern Europe and with the stateless people driven into Central and Western Europe, a completely new element of disintegration was introduced into postwar Europe. Denationalization became a powerful weapon of totalitarian politics, and the constitutional inability of European nation-states to guarantee human rights to those who had lost nationally guaranteed rights, made it possible for the persecuting governments to impose their standard of values even upon their opponents. Those whom the persecutor had singled out as scum of the earth—Jews, Trotskyites, etc.—actually were received as scum of the earth everywhere; those whom persecution had called undesirable became the *indésirables* of Europe. The official SS newspaper, the *Schwarze Korps*, stated explicitly in 1938 that if the world was not yet convinced that the Jews were the scum of the earth, it soon would be when unidentifiable beggars, without nationality, without money, and without passports crossed their frontiers.[2] And it is true that this kind of factual propaganda worked better than Goebbels' rhetoric, not only because it established the Jews as scum of the earth, but also because the incredible plight of an ever-growing group of innocent people was like a practical demonstration of the totalitarian movements' cynical claims that no such thing as inalienable human rights existed and that the affirmations of the democracies to the contrary were mere prejudice, hypocrisy, and cowardice in the face of the cruel majesty of a new world. The very phrase "human rights" became for all concerned—victims, persecutors, and onlookers alike—the evidence of hopeless idealism or fumbling feeble-minded hypocrisy.

I: *The "Nation of Minorities" and the Stateless People*

MODERN POWER CONDITIONS which make national sovereignty a mockery except for giant states, the rise of imperialism, and the pan-movements un-

---

[2] The early persecution of German Jews by the Nazis must be considered as an attempt to spread antisemitism among "those peoples who are friendlily disposed to Jews, above all the Western democracies" rather than as an effort to get rid of the Jews. A circular letter from the Ministry of Foreign Affairs to all German authorities abroad shortly after the November pogroms of 1938, stated: "The emigration movement of only about 100,000 Jews has already sufficed to awaken the interest of many countries in the Jewish danger. . . . Germany is very interested in maintaining the dispersal of Jewry . . . the influx of Jews in all parts of the world invokes the opposition of the native population and thereby forms the best propaganda for the German Jewish policy. . . . The poorer and therefore more burdensome the immigrating Jew is to the country absorbing him, the stronger the country will react." See *Nazi Conspiracy and Aggression,* Washington, 1946, published by the U. S. Government, VI, 87 ff.

dermined the stability of Europe's nation-state system from the outside. None of these factors, however, had sprung directly from the tradition and the institutions of nation-states themselves. Their internal disintegration began only after the first World War, with the appearance of minorities created by the Peace Treaties and of a constantly growing refugee movement, the consequence of revolutions.

The inadequacy of the Peace Treaties has often been explained by the fact that the peacemakers belonged to a generation formed by experiences in the pre-war era, so that they never quite realized the full impact of the war whose peace they had to conclude. There is no better proof of this than their attempt to regulate the nationality problem in Eastern and Southern Europe through the establishment of nation-states and the introduction of minority treaties. If the wisdom of the extension of a form of government which even in countries with old and settled national tradition could not handle the new problems of world politics had become questionable, it was even more doubtful whether it could be imported into an area which lacked the very conditions for the rise of nation-states: homogeneity of population and rootedness in the soil. But to assume that nation-states could be established by the methods of the Peace Treaties was simply preposterous. Indeed: "One glance at the demographic map of Europe should be sufficient to show that the nation-state principle cannot be introduced into Eastern Europe."[3] The Treaties lumped together many peoples in single states, called some of them "state people" and entrusted them with the government, silently assumed that others (such as the Slovaks in Czechoslovakia, or the Croats and Slovenes in Yugoslavia) were equal partners in the government, which of course they were not,[4] and with equal arbitrariness created out of the remnant a third group of nationalities called "minorities," thereby adding to the many burdens of the new states the trouble of observing special regulations for part of the population.[5] The result was that those peoples to whom states were not conceded, no matter whether they were official minorities or only nationalities, considered the Treaties an arbitrary game which handed out rule to some and servitude to others. The newly created states, on the other hand, which were promised equal status in national sovereignty with the Western nations, regarded the Minority Treaties as an open breach of promise and discrimination

---

[3] Kurt Tramples, "Völkerbund und Völkerfreiheit," in *Süddeutsche Monatshefte,* 26. Jahrgang, Juli 1929.

[4] The struggle of the Slovaks against the "Czech" government in Prague ended with the Hitler-supported independence of Slovakia; the Yugoslav constitution of 1921 was "accepted" in Parliament against the votes of all Croat and Slovene representatives. For a good summary of Yugoslav history between the two wars, see *Propyläen Weltgeschichte. Das Zeitalter des Imperialismus,* 1933, Band 10, 471 ff.

[5] Mussolini was quite right when he wrote after the Munich crisis: "If Czechoslovakia finds herself today in what might be called a 'delicate situation,' it is because she was not just Czechoslovakia, but Czech-Germano-Polono-Magyaro-Rutheno-Rumano-Slovakia. . . ." (Quoted from Hubert Ripka, *Munich: Before and After,* London, 1939, p. 117.)

because only new states, and not even defeated Germany, were bound to them.

The perplexing power vacuum resulting from the dissolution of the Dual Monarchy and the liberation of Poland and the Baltic countries from Czarist despotism was not the only factor that had tempted the statesmen into this disastrous experiment. Much stronger was the impossibility of arguing away any longer the more than 100 million Europeans who had never reached the stage of national freedom and self-determination to which colonial peoples already aspired and which was being held out to them. It was indeed true that the role of the Western and Central European proletariat, the oppressed history-suffering group whose emancipation was a matter of life and death for the whole European social system, was played in the East by "peoples without a history." [6] The national liberation movements of the East were revolutionary in much the same way as the workers' movements in the West; both represented the "unhistorical" strata of Europe's population and both strove to secure recognition and participation in public affairs. Since the object was to conserve the European status quo, the granting of national self-determination and sovereignty to all European peoples seemed indeed inevitable; the alternative would have been to condemn them ruthlessly to the status of colonial peoples (something the pan-movements had always proposed) and to introduce colonial methods into European affairs.[7]

The point, of course, is that the European status quo could not be preserved and that it became clear only after the downfall of the last remnants of European autocracy that Europe had been ruled by a system which had never taken into account or responded to the needs of at least 25 per cent of her population. This evil, however, was not cured with the establishment of the succession states, because about 30 per cent of their roughly 100 million inhabitants were officially recognized as exceptions who had to be specially protected by minority treaties. This figure, moreover, by no

---

[6] This term was first coined by Otto Bauer, *Die Nationalitätenfrage und die österreichische Sozialdemokratie*, Vienna, 1907.

Historical consciousness played a great role in the formation of national consciousness. The emancipation of nations from dynastic rule and the overlordship of an international aristocracy was accompanied by the emancipation of literature from the "international" language of the learned (Latin first and later French) and the growth of national languages out of the popular vernacular. It seemed that peoples whose language was fit for literature had reached national maturity *per definitionem*. The liberation movements of Eastern European nationalities, therefore, started with a kind of philological revival (the results were sometimes grotesque and sometimes very fruitful) whose political function it was to prove that the people who possessed a literature and a history of their own, had the right to national sovereignty.

[7] Of course this was not always a clear-cut alternative. So far nobody has bothered to find out the characteristic similarities between colonial and minority exploitation. Only Jacob Robinson, "Staatsbürgerliche und wirtschaftliche Gleichberechtigung" in *Süddeutsche Monatshefte*, 26: Jahrgang, July, 1929, remarks in passing: "A peculiar economic protectionism appeared, not directed against other countries but against certain groups of the population. Surprisingly, certain methods of colonial exploitation could be observed in Central Europe."

means tells the whole story; it only indicates the difference between peoples with a government of their own and those who supposedly were too small and too scattered to reach full nationhood. The Minority Treaties covered only those nationalities of whom there were considerable numbers in at least two of the succession states, but omitted from consideration all the other nationalities without a government of their own, so that in some of the succession states the nationally frustrated peoples constituted 50 per cent of the total population.[8] The worst factor in this situation was not even that it became a matter of course for the nationalities to be disloyal to their imposed government and for the governments to oppress their nationalities as efficiently as possible, but that the nationally frustrated population was firmly convinced—as was everybody else—that true freedom, true emancipation, and true popular sovereignty could be attained only with full national emancipation, that people without their own national government were deprived of human rights. In this conviction, which could base itself on the fact that the French Revolution had combined the declaration of the Rights of Man with national sovereignty, they were supported by the Minority Treaties themselves, which did not entrust the governments with the protection of different nationalities but charged the League of Nations with the safeguarding of the rights of those who, for reasons of territorial settlement, had been left without national states of their own.

Not that the minorities would trust the League of Nations any more than they had trusted the state peoples. The League, after all, was composed of national statesmen whose sympathies could not but be with the unhappy new governments which were hampered and opposed on principle by between 25 and 50 per cent of their inhabitants. Therefore the creators of the Minority Treaties were soon forced to interpret their real intentions more strictly and to point out the "duties" the minorities owed to the new states;[9] it now developed that the Treaties had been conceived merely as a painless and humane method of assimilation, an interpretation which naturally enraged the minorities.[10] But nothing else could have been ex-

[8] It has been estimated that prior to 1914 there were about 100 million people whose national aspirations had not been fulfilled. (See Charles Kingsley Webster, "Minorities: History," in *Encyclopedia Britannica*, 1929.) The population of minorities was estimated approximately between 25 and 30 millions. (P. de Azcarate, "Minorities: League of Nations," *ibid.*). The actual situation in Czechoslovakia and Yugoslavia was much worse. In the former, the Czech "state people" constituted, with 7,200,000, about 50 per cent of the population, and in the latter 5,000,000 Serbs formed only 42 per cent of the total. See W. Winkler, *Statistisches Handbuch der europäischen Nationalitäten*, Vienna, 1931; Otto Junghann, *National Minorities in Europe*, 1932. Slightly different figures are given by Tramples, *op. cit.*

[9] P. de Azcarate, *op. cit.*: "The Treaties contain no stipulations regarding the 'duties' of minorities towards the States of which they are a part. The Third Ordinary Assembly of the League, however, in 1922, . . . adopted . . . resolutions regarding the 'duties of minorities.'. . . ."

[10] The French and the British delegates were most outspoken in this respect. Said Briand: "The process at which we should aim is not the disappearance of the minorities, but a kind of assimilation. . . ." And Sir Austen Chamberlain, British representative,

pected within a system of sovereign nation-states; if the Minority Treaties had been intended to be more than a temporary remedy for a topsy-turvy situation, then their implied restriction on national sovereignty would have affected the national sovereignty of the older European powers. The representatives of the great nations knew only too well that minorities within nation-states must sooner or later be either assimilated or liquidated. And it did not matter whether they were moved by humanitarian considerations to protect splinter nationalities from persecution, or whether political considerations led them to oppose bilateral treaties between the concerned states and the majority countries of the minorities (after all, the Germans were the strongest of all the officially recognized minorities, both in numbers and economic position); they were neither willing nor able to overthrow the laws by which nation-states exist.[11]

Neither the League of Nations nor the Minority Treaties would have prevented the newly established states from more or less forcefully assimilating their minorities. The strongest factor against assimilation was the numerical and cultural weakness of the so-called state peoples. The Russian or the Jewish minority in Poland did not feel Polish culture to be superior to its own and neither was particularly impressed by the fact that Poles formed roughly 60 per cent of Poland's population.

The embittered nationalities, completely disregarding the League of Nations, soon decided to take matters into their own hands. They banded together in a minority congress which was remarkable in more than one respect. It contradicted the very idea behind the League treaties by calling itself officially the "Congress of Organized National Groups in European States," thereby nullifying the great labor spent during the peace negotiations to avoid the ominous word "national."[12] This had the important consequence that all "nationalities," and not just "minorities," would join and that the number of the "nation of minorities" grew so considerably that

even claimed that "the object of the Minority Treaties [is] . . . to secure . . . that measure of protection and justice which would gradually prepare them to be merged in the national community to which they belonged" (C. A. Macartney, *National States and National Minorities,* London, 1934, pp. 276, 277).

[11] It is true that some Czech statesmen, the most liberal and democratic of the leaders of national movements, once dreamed of making the Czechoslovak republic a kind of Switzerland. The reason why even Beneš never serious attempted to effectuate such a solution to his harassing nationality problems was that Switzerland was not a model that could be imitated, but rather a particularly fortunate exception that proved an otherwise established rule. The newly established states did not feel secure enough to abandon a centralized state apparatus and could not create overnight those small self-administrative bodies of communes and cantons upon whose very extensive powers the Swiss system of federation is based.

[12] Wilson notably, who had been a fervent advocate of granting "racial, religious, and linguistic rights to the minorities," "feared that 'national rights' would prove harmful inasmuch as minority groups thus marked as separate corporate bodies would be rendered thereby 'liable to jealousy and attack'" (Oscar J. Janowsky, *The Jews and Minority Rights,* New York, 1933, p. 351). Macartney, *op. cit.,* p. 4, describes the situation and the "prudent work of the Joint Foreign Committee" that labored to avoid the term "national."

the combined nationalities in the succession states outnumbered the state peoples. But in still another way the "Congress of National Groups" dealt a decisive blow to the League treaties. One of the most baffling aspects of the Eastern European nationality problem (more baffling than the small size and great number of peoples involved, or the "belt of mixed populations"[13]) was the interregional character of the nationalities which, in case they put their national interests above the interests of their respective governments, made them an obvious risk to the security of their countries.[14] The League treaties had attempted to ignore the interregional character of the minorities by concluding a separate treaty with each country, as though there were no Jewish or German minority beyond the borders of the respective states. The "Congress of National Groups" not only sidestepped the territorial principle of the League; it was naturally dominated by the two nationalities which were represented in all succession states and were therefore in a position, if they wished, to make their weight felt all over Eastern and Southern Europe. These two groups were the Germans and the Jews. The German minorities in Rumania and Czechoslovakia voted of course with the German minorities in Poland and Hungary, and nobody could have expected the Polish Jews, for instance, to remain indifferent to discriminatory practices of the Rumanian government. In other words, national interests and not common interests of minorities as such formed the true basis of membership in the Congress,[15] and only the harmonious relationship between the Jews and the Germans (the Weimar Republic had successfully played the role of special protector of minorities) kept it together. Therefore, in 1933 when the Jewish delegation demanded a protest against the treatment of Jews in the Third Reich (a move which they had no right to make, strictly speaking, because German Jews were no minority) and the Germans announced their solidarity with Germany and were supported by a majority (antisemitism was ripe in all succession states), the Congress, after the Jewish delegation had left forever, sank into complete insignificance.

The real significance of the Minority Treaties lies not in their practical application but in the fact that they were guaranteed by an international body, the League of Nations. Minorities had existed before,[16] but the

[13] The term is Macartney's, *op. cit., passim.*

[14] "The result of the Peace settlement was that every State in the belt of mixed population . . . now looked upon itself as a national state. But the facts were against them. . . . Not one of these states was in fact uni-national, just as there was not, on the other hand, one nation all of whose members lived in a single state" (Macartney, *op. cit.,* p. 210).

[15] In 1933 the chairman of the Congress expressly emphasized: "One thing is certain: we do not meet in our congresses merely as members of abstract minorities; each of us belongs body and soul to a specific people, his own, and feels himself tied to the fate of that people for better or worse. Consequently, each of us stands here, if I may say so, as a full-blooded German or full-blooded Jew, as a full-blooded Hungarian or full-blooded Ukrainian." See *Sitzungsbericht des Kongresses der organisierten nationalen Gruppen in den Staaten Europas,* 1933, p. 8.

[16] The first minorities arose when the Protestant principle of freedom of conscience

minority as a permanent institution, the recognition that millions of people lived outside normal legal protection and needed an additional guarantee of their elementary rights from an outside body, and the assumption that this state of affairs was not temporary but that the Treaties were needed in order to establish a lasting *modus vivendi*—all this was something new, certainly on such a scale, in European history. The Minority Treaties said in plain language what until then had been only implied in the working system of nation-states, namely, that only nationals could be citizens, only people of the same national origin could enjoy the full protection of legal institutions, that persons of different nationality needed some law of exception until or unless they were completely assimilated and divorced from their origin. The interpretative speeches on the League treaties by statesmen of countries without minority obligations spoke an even plainer language: they took it for granted that the law of a country could not be responsible for persons insisting on a different nationality.[17] They thereby admitted—and were quickly given the opportunity to prove it practically with the rise of stateless people—that the transformation of the state from an instrument of the law into an instrument of the nation had been completed; the nation had conquered the state, national interest had priority over law long before Hitler could pronounce "right is what is good for the German people." Here again the language of the mob was only the language of public opinion cleansed of hypocrisy and restraint.

Certainly the danger of this development had been inherent in the structure of the nation-state since the beginning. But insofar as the establishment of nation-states coincided with the establishment of constitutional government, they always had represented and been based upon the rule of law as against the rule of arbitrary administration and despotism. So that when the precarious balance between nation and state, between national interest and legal institutions broke down, the disintegration of this form of government and of organization of peoples came about with terrifying swiftness. Its disintegration, curiously enough, started at precisely the moment when the right to national self-determination was recognized for all of Europe and when its essential conviction, the supremacy of the will of the nation over all legal and "abstract" institutions, was universally accepted.

---

accomplished the suppression of the principle *cuius regio eius religio.* The Congress of Vienna in 1815 had already taken steps to secure certain rights to the Polish populations in Russia, Prussia, and Austria, rights that certainly were not merely "religious"; it is, however, characteristic that all later treaties—the protocol guaranteeing the independence of Greece in 1830, the one guaranteeing the independence of Moldavia and Wallachia in 1856, and the Congress of Berlin in 1878 concerned with Rumania—speak of "religious," and not "national" minorities, which were granted "civil" but not "political" rights.

[17] De Mello Franco, representative of Brazil on the Council of the League of Nations, put the problem very clearly: "It seems to me obvious that those who conceived this system of protection did not dream of creating within certain States a group of inhabitants who would regard themselves as permanently foreign to the general organization of the country" (Macartney, *op. cit.,* p. 277).

At the time of the Minority Treaties it could be, and was, argued in their favor, as it were as their excuse, that the older nations enjoyed constitutions which implicitly or explicitly (as in the case of France, the *nation par excellence*) were founded upon the Rights of Man, that even if there were other nationalities within their borders they needed no additional law for them, and that only in the newly established succession states was a temporary enforcement of human rights necessary as a compromise and exception.[18] The arrival of the stateless people brought an end to this illusion.

The minorities were only half stateless; *de jure* they belonged to some political body even though they needed additional protection in the form of special treaties and guarantees; some secondary rights, such as speaking one's own language and staying in one's own cultural and social milieu, were in jeopardy and were halfheartedly protected by an outside body; but other more elementary rights, such as the right to residence and to work, were never touched. The framers of the Minority Treaties did not foresee the possibility of wholesale population transfers or the problem of people who had become "undeportable" because there was no country on earth in which they enjoyed the right to residence. The minorities could still be regarded as an exceptional phenomenon, peculiar to certain territories that deviated from the norm. This argument was always tempting because it left the system itself untouched; it has in a way survived the second World War whose peacemakers, convinced of the impracticability of minority treaties, began to "repatriate" nationalities as much as possible in an effort to unscramble "the belt of mixed populations."[19] And this attempted large-scale repatriation was not the direct result of the catastrophic experiences following in the wake of the Minority Treaties; rather, it was hoped that such a step would finally solve a problem which, in the preceding decades, had assumed ever larger proportions and for which an internationally recognized and accepted procedure simply did not exist—the problem of the stateless people.

Much more stubborn in fact and much more far-reaching in consequence

[18] "The regime for the protection of minorities was designed to provide a remedy in cases where a territorial settlement was inevitably imperfect from the point of view of nationality" (Joseph Roucek, *The Minority Principle as a Problem of Political Science,* Prague, 1928, p. 29). The trouble was that imperfection of territorial settlement was the fault not only in the minority settlements but in the establishment of the succession states themselves, since there was no territory in this region to which several nationalities could not lay claim.

[19] An almost symbolic evidence of this change of mind can be found in statements of President Eduard Beneš of Czechoslovakia, the only country that after the first World War had submitted with good grace to the obligations of the Minority Treaties. Shortly after the outbreak of World War II Beneš began to lend his support to the principle of transfer of populations, which finally led to the expulsion of the German minority and the addition of another category to the growing mass of Displaced Persons. For Beneš' stand, see Oscar I. Janowsky, *Nationalities and National Minorities,* New York, 1945, pp. 136 ff.

has been statelessness, the newest mass phenomenon in contemporary history, and the existence of an ever-growing new people comprised of stateless persons, the most symptomatic group in contemporary politics.[20] Their existence can hardly be blamed on one factor alone, but if we consider the different groups among the stateless it appears that every political event since the end of the first World War inevitably added a new category to those who lived outside the pale of the law, while none of the categories, no matter how the original constellation changed, could ever be renormalized.[21]

Among them, we still find that oldest group of stateless people, the *Heimatlosen* produced by the Peace Treaties of 1919, the dissolution of Austria-Hungary, and the establishment of the Baltic states. Sometimes their real origin could not be determined, especially if at the end of the war they happened not to reside in the city of their birth,[22] sometimes their place of

[20] "The problem of statelessness became prominent after the Great War. Before the war, provisions existed in some countries, notably in the United States, under which naturalization could be revoked in those cases in which the naturalized person ceased to maintain a genuine attachment to his adopted country. A person so denaturalized became stateless. During the war, the principal European States found it necessary to amend their laws of nationality so as to take power to cancel naturalization" (John Hope Simpson, *The Refugee Problem*, Institute of International Affairs, Oxford, 1939, p. 231). The class of stateless persons created through revocation of naturalization was very small; they established, however, an easy precedent so that, in the interwar period, naturalized citizens were as a rule the first section of a population that became stateless. Mass cancellation of naturalizations, such as the one introduced by Nazi Germany in 1933 against all naturalized Germans of Jewish origin, usually preceded denationalization of citizens by birth in similar categories, and the introduction of laws that made denaturalization possible through simple decree, like the ones in Belgium and other Western democracies in the thirties, usually preceded actual mass denaturalization; a good instance is the practice of the Greek government with respect to the Armenian refugees: of 45,000 Armenian refugees 1,000 were naturalized between 1923 and 1928. After 1928, a law which would have naturalized all refugees under twenty-two years of age was suspended, and in 1936, all naturalizations were canceled by the government. (See Simpson, *op. cit.*, p. 41.)

[21] Twenty-five years after the Soviet regime had disowned one and a half million Russians, it was estimated that at least 350,000 to 450,000 were still stateless—which is a tremendous percentage if one considers that a whole generation had passed since the initial flight, that a considerable portion had gone overseas, and that another large part had acquired citizenship in different countries through marriage. (See Simpson, *op. cit.*, p. 559; Eugene M. Kulischer, *The Displacement of Population in Europe*, Montreal, 1943; Winifred N. Hadsel, "Can Europe's Refugees Find New Homes?" in *Foreign Policy Reports*, August, 1943, Vol. X, no. 10.)

It is true that the United States has placed stateless immigrants on a footing of complete equality with other foreigners, but this has been possible only because this, the country *par excellence* of immigration, has always considered newcomers as prospective citizens of its own, regardless of their former national allegiances.

[22] The *American Friends Service Bulletin* (General Relief Bulletin, March, 1943) prints the perplexed report of one of their field workers in Spain who had been confronted with the problem of "a man who was born in Berlin, Germany, but who is of Polish origin because of his Polish parents and who is therefore . . . Apatride, but is claiming Ukrainian nationality and has been claimed by the Russian government for repatriation and service in the Red Army."

origin changed hands so many times in the turmoil of postwar disputes
that the nationality of its inhabitants changed from year to year (as in Vilna
which a French official once termed *la capitale des apatrides*); more often
than one would imagine, people took refuge in statelessness after the first
World War in order to remain where they were and avoid being deported
to a "homeland" where they would be strangers (as in the case of many
Polish and Rumanian Jews in France and Germany, mercifully helped by
the antisemitic attitude of their respective consulates).

Unimportant in himself, apparently just a legal freak, the *apatride*
received belated attention and consideration when he was joined in his
legal status by the postwar refugees who had been forced out of their countries by revolutions, and were promptly denationalized by the victorious
governments at home. To this group belong, in chronological order, millions of Russians, hundreds of thousands of Armenians, thousands of Hungarians, hundreds of thousands of Germans, and more than half a million
Spaniards—to enumerate only the more important categories. The behavior
of these governments may appear today to be the natural consequence of
civil war; but at the time mass denationalizations were something entirely
new and unforeseen. They presupposed a state structure which, if it was
not yet fully totalitarian, at least would not tolerate any opposition and
would rather lose its citizens than harbor people with different views. They
revealed, moreover, what had been hidden throughout the history of national sovereignty, that sovereignties of neighboring countries could come
into deadly conflict not only in the extreme case of war but in peace. It now
became clear that full national sovereignty was possible only as long as the
comity of European nations existed; for it was this spirit of unorganized
solidarity and agreement that prevented any government's exercise of its
full sovereign power. Theoretically, in the sphere of international law, it
had always been true that sovereignty is nowhere more absolute than in
matters of "emigration, naturalization, nationality, and expulsion"; [23] the
point, however, is that practical consideration and the silent acknowledg-
ment of common interests restrained national sovereignty until the rise of
totalitarian regimes. One is almost tempted to measure the degree of totalitarian infection by the extent to which the concerned governments use
their sovereign right of denationalization (and it would be quite interesting
then to discover that Mussolini's Italy was rather reluctant to treat its
refugees this way [24]). But one should bear in mind at the same time that
there was hardly a country left on the Continent that did not pass between
the two wars some new legislation which, even if it did not use this right

[23] Lawrence Preuss, "La Dénationalisation imposée pour des motifs politiques," in
Revue Internationale Française du Droit des Gens, 1937, Vol. IV, Nos. 1, 2, 5.

[24] An Italian law of 1926 against "abusive emigration" seemed to foreshadow denaturalization measures against anti-Fascist refugees; however, after 1929 the denaturalization policy was abandoned and Fascist organizations abroad were introduced. Of the 40,000 members of the Unione Popolare Italiana in France, at least
10,000 were authentic anti-Fascist refugees, but only 3,000 were without passports.
See Simpson, *op. cit.,* pp. 122 ff.

extensively, was always phrased to allow for getting rid of a great number of its inhabitants at any opportune moment.[25]

No paradox of contemporary politics is filled with a more poignant irony than the discrepancy between the efforts of well-meaning idealists who stubbornly insist on regarding as "inalienable" those human rights, which are enjoyed only by citizens of the most prosperous and civilized countries, and the situation of the rightless themselves. Their situation has deteriorated just as stubbornly, until the internment camp—prior to the second World War the exception rather than the rule for the stateless—has become the routine solution for the problem of domicile of the "displaced persons."

Even the terminology applied to the stateless has deteriorated. The term "stateless" at least acknowledged the fact that these persons had lost the protection of their government and required international agreements for safeguarding their legal status. The postwar term "displaced persons" was invented during the war for the express purpose of liquidating statelessness once and for all by ignoring its existence. Nonrecognition of statelessness always means repatriation, *i.e.,* deportation to a country of origin, which either refuses to recognize the prospective repatriate as a citizen, or, on the contrary, urgently wants him back for punishment. Since non-totalitarian countries, in spite of their bad intentions inspired by the climate of war, generally have shied away from mass repatriations, the number of stateless people—twelve years after the end of the war—is larger than ever. The decision of the statesmen to solve the problem of statelessness by ignoring it is further revealed by the lack of any reliable statistics on the subject. This much is known, however: while there are one million "recognized" stateless, there are more than ten million so-called *"de facto"* stateless; and whereas the relatively innocuous problem of the *"de jure"* stateless occasionally comes up at international conferences, the core of statelessness, which is identical with the refugee question, is simply not mentioned. Worse still, the number of potentially stateless people is continually on the increase. Prior to the last war, only totalitarian or half-totalitarian dictatorships resorted to the weapon of denaturalization with

<hr>

[25] The first law of this type was a French war measure in 1915 which concerned only naturalized citizens of enemy origin who had retained their original nationality; Portugal went much farther in a decree of 1916 which automatically denaturalized all persons born of a German father. Belgium issued a law in 1922 which canceled naturalization of persons who had committed antinational acts during the war, and reaffirmed it by a new decree in 1934 which in the characteristically vague manner of the time spoke of persons *"manquant gravement à leurs devoirs de citoyen belge."* In Italy, since 1926, all persons could be denaturalized who were not "worthy of Italian citizenship" or a menace to the public order. Egypt and Turkey in 1926 and 1928 respectively issued laws according to which people could be denaturalized who were a threat to the social order. France threatened with denaturalization those of its new citizens who committed acts contrary to the interests of France (1927). Austria in 1933 could deprive of Austrian nationality any of her citizens who served or participated abroad in an action hostile to Austria. Germany, finally, in 1933 followed closely the various Russian nationality decrees since 1921 by stating that all persons "residing abroad" could at will be deprived of German nationality.

regard to those who were citizens by birth; now we have reached the point where even free democracies, as, for instance, the United States, were seriously considering depriving native Americans who are Communists of their citizenship. The sinister aspect of these measures is that they are being considered in all innocence. Yet, one need only remember the extreme care of the Nazis, who insisted that all Jews of non-German nationality "should be deprived of their citizenship either prior to, or, at the latest, on the day of deportation"[25a] (for German Jews such a decree was not needed, because in the Third Reich there existed a law according to which all Jews who had left the territory—including, of course, those deported to a Polish camp—automatically lost their citizenship) in order to realize the true implications of statelessness.

The first great damage done to the nation-states as a result of the arrival of hundreds of thousands of stateless people was that the right of asylum, the only right that had ever figured as a symbol of the Rights of Man in the sphere of international relationships, was being abolished. Its long and sacred history dates back to the very beginnings of regulated political life. Since ancient times it has protected both the refugee and the land of refuge from situations in which people were forced to become outlaws through circumstances beyond their control. It was the only modern remnant of the medieval principle that *quid quid est in territorio est de territorio*, for in all other cases the modern state tended to protect its citizens beyond its own borders and to make sure, by means of reciprocal treaties, that they remained subject to the laws of their country. But though the right of asylum continued to function in a world organized into nation-states and, in individual instances, even survived both World Wars, it was felt to be an anachronism and in conflict with the international rights of the state. Therefore it cannot be found in written law, in no constitution or international agreement, and the Covenant of the League of Nations never even so much as mentioned it.[26] It shares, in this respect, the fate of the Rights of Man, which also never became law but led a somewhat shadowy

[25a] The quotation is taken from an order of Hauptsturmführer Dannecker, dated March 10, 1943, and referring to the "deportation of 5,000 Jews from France, quota 1942." The document (photostat in the Centre de Documentation Juive in Paris) is part of the Nuremberg Documents No. RF 1216 Identical arrangements were made for the Bulgarian Jews. Cf. *ibidem* the relevant memorandum by L. R. Wagner, dated April 3, 1943, Document NG 4180.

[26] S. Lawford Childs (*op. cit.*) deplores the fact that the Covenant of the League contained "no charter for political refugees, no solace for exiles." The most recent attempt of the United Nations to obtain, at least for a small group of stateless—the so-called "*de jure* stateless"—an improvement of their legal status was no more than a mere gesture: namely, to gather the representatives of at least twenty states, but with the explicit assurance that participation in such a conference would entail no obligations whatsoever. Even under these circumstances it remained extremely doubtful whether the conference could be called. See the news item in the New York *Times*, October 17, 1954, p. 9.

existence as an appeal in individual exceptional cases for which normal legal institutions did not suffice.[27]

The second great shock that the European world suffered through the arrival of the refugees[28] was the realization that it was impossible to get rid of them or transform them into nationals of the country of refuge. From the beginning everybody had agreed that there were only two ways to solve the problem: repatriation or naturalization.[29] When the example of the first Russian and Armenian waves proved that neither way gave any tangible results, the countries of refuge simply refused to recognize statelessness in all later arrivals, thereby making the situation of the refugees even more intolerable.[30] From the point of view of the governments concerned it was understandable enough that they should keep reminding the League of Nations "that [its] Refugee work must be liquidated with the utmost rapidity";[31] they had many reasons to fear that those who had been ejected

[27] The only guardians of the right of asylum were the few societies whose special aim was the protection of human rights. The most important of them, the French-sponsored Ligue des Droits de l'Homme with branches in all democratic European countries, behaved as though the question were still merely the saving of individuals persecuted for their political convictions and activities. This assumption, pointless already in the case of millions of Russian refugees, became simply absurd for Jews and Armenians. The Ligue was neither ideologically nor administratively equipped to handle the new problems. Since it did not want to face the new situation, it stumbled into functions which were much better fulfilled by any of the many charity agencies which the refugees had built up themselves with the help of their compatriots. When the Rights of Man became the object of an especially inefficient charity organization, the concept of human rights naturally was discredited a little more.

[28] The many and varied efforts of the legal profession to simplify the problem by stating a difference between the stateless person and the refugee—such as maintaining "that the status of a stateless person is characterized by the fact of his having no nationality, whereas that of a refugee is determined by his having lost diplomatic protection" (Simpson, *op. cit.*, p. 232)—were always defeated by the fact that "all refugees are for practical purposes stateless" (Simpson, *op. cit.*, p. 4).

[29] The most ironical formulation of this general expectation was made by R. Yewdall Jermings, "Some International Aspects of the Refugee Question" in *British Yearbook of International Law*, 1939: "The status of a refugee is not, of course, a permanent one. The aim is that he should rid himself of that status as soon as possible, either by repatriation or by naturalization in the country of refuge."

[30] Only the Russians, in every respect the aristocracy of the stateless people, and the Armenians, who were assimilated to the Russian status, were ever officially recognized as "stateless," placed under the protection of the League of Nations' Nansen Office, and given traveling papers.

[31] Childs, *op. cit.* The reason for this desperate attempt at promptness was the fear of all governments that even the smallest positive gesture "might encourage countries to get rid of their unwanted people and that many might emigrate who would otherwise remain in their countries even under serious disabilities" (Louise W. Holborn, "The Legal Status of Political Refugees, 1920-38," in *American Journal of International Law*, 1938).

See also Georges Mauco (in *Esprit,* 7e année, No. 82, July, 1939, p. 590): "An assimilation of the German refugees to the status of other refugees who were taken care of by the Nansen office would naturally have been the simplest and best solution

from the old trinity of state-people-territory, which still formed the basis of European organization and political civilization, formed only the beginning of an increasing movement, were only the first trickle from an ever-growing reservoir. It was obvious, and even the Evian Conference recognized it in 1938, that all German and Austrian Jews were potentially stateless; and it was only natural that the minority countries should be encouraged by Germany's example to try to use the same methods for getting rid of some of their minority populations.[32] Among the minorities the Jews and the Armenians ran the greatest risks and soon showed the highest proportion of statelessness; but they proved also that minority treaties did not necessarily offer protection but could also serve as an instrument to single out certain groups for eventual expulsion.

Almost as frightening as these new dangers arising from the old trouble spots of Europe was the entirely new kind of behavior of all European nationals in "ideological" struggles. Not only were people expelled from country and citizenship, but more and more persons of all countries, including the Western democracies, volunteered to fight in civil wars abroad (something which up to then only a few idealists or adventurers had done) even when this meant cutting themselves off from their national communities. This was the lesson of the Spanish Civil War and one of the reasons why the governments were so frightened by the International Brigade. Matters would not have been quite so bad if this had meant that people no longer clung so closely to their nationality and were ready eventually to be assimilated into another national community. But this was not at all the case. The stateless people had already shown a surprising stubbornness in retaining their nationality; in every sense the refugees represented separate foreign minorities who frequently did not care to be naturalized, and they never banded together, as the minorities had done temporarily, to defend common interests.[33] The International Brigade was organized into national

for the German refugees themselves. But the governments did not want to extend the privileges already granted to a new category of refugees who, moreover, threatened to increase their number indefinitely."

[32] To the 600,000 Jews in Germany and Austria who were potentially stateless in 1938, must be added the Jews of Rumania (the president of the Rumanian Federal Commission for Minorities, Professor Dragomir, having just announced to the world the impending revision of the citizenship of all Rumanian Jews) and Poland (whose foreign minister Beck had officially declared that Poland had one million Jews too many). See Simpson, *op. cit.,* p. 235.

[33] It is difficult to decide what came first, the nation-states' reluctance to naturalize refugees (the practice of naturalization became increasingly restricted and the practice of denaturalization increasingly common with the arrival of refugees) or the refugees' reluctance to accept another citizenship. In countries with minority populations like Poland, the refugees (Russians and Ukrainians) had a definite tendency to assimilate to the minorities without however demanding Polish citizenship. (See Simpson, *op. cit.,* p. 364.)

The behavior of Russian refugees is quite characteristic. The Nansen passport described its bearer as *"personne d'origine russe,"* because "one would not have dared to tell the Russian émigré that he was without nationality or of doubtful nationality." (See Marc Vichniac, "Le Statut International des Apatrides," in *Recueil des Cours de*

battalions in which the Germans felt they fought against Hitler and the Italians against Mussolini, just as a few years later, in the Resistance, the Spanish refugees felt they fought against Franco when they helped the French against Vichy. What the European governments were so afraid of in this process was that the new stateless people could no longer be said to be of dubious or doubtful nationality (*de nationalité indéterminée*). Even though they had renounced their citizenship, no longer had any connection with or loyalty to their country of origin, and did not identify their nationality with a visible, fully recognized government, they retained a strong attachment to their nationality. National splinter groups and minorities, without deep roots in their territory and with no loyalty or relationship to the state, had ceased to be characteristic only of the East. They had by now infiltrated, as refugees and stateless persons, the older nation-states of the West.

The real trouble started as soon as the two recognized remedies, repatriation and naturalization, were tried. Repatriation measures naturally failed when there was no country to which these people could be deported. They failed not because of consideration for the stateless person (as it may appear today when Soviet Russia claims its former citizens and the democratic countries must protect them from a repatriation they do not want); and not because of humanitarian sentiments on the part of the countries that were swamped with refugees; but because neither the country of origin nor any other agreed to accept the stateless person. It would seem that the very undeportability of the stateless person should have prevented a government's expelling him; but since the man without a state was "an anomaly for whom there is no appropriate niche in the framework of the general law" [34]—an outlaw by definition—he was completely at the mercy of the police, which itself did not worry too much about committing a few illegal acts in order to diminish the country's burden of *indésirables*.[35] In other words, the state, insisting on its sovereign right of expulsion, was forced by

l'Académie de Droit International, Vol. XXXIII, 1933.) An attempt to provide all stateless persons with uniform identity cards was bitterly contested by the holders of Nansen passports, who claimed that their passport was "a sign of legal recognition of their peculiar status." (See Jermings, *op. cit.*) Before the outbreak of the war even refugees from Germany were far from eager to be merged with the mass of the stateless, but preferred the description *"réfugié provenant d'Allemagne"* with its remnant of nationality.

More convincing than the complaints of European countries about the difficulties of assimilating refugees are statements from overseas which agree with the former that "of all classes of European immigrants the least easy to assimilate are the South, Eastern, and Central Europeans." (See "Canada and the Doctrine of Peaceful Changes," edited by H. F. Angus in *International Studies Conference: Demographic Questions: Peaceful Changes,* 1937, pp. 75-76.)

[34] Jermings, *op. cit.*

[35] A circular letter of the Dutch authorities (May 7, 1938) expressly considered each refugee as an "undesirable alien," and defined a refugee as an "alien who left his country under the pressure of circumstances." See "L'Emigration, Problème Révolutionnaire," in *Esprit,* 7e année, No. 82, July, 1939, p. 602.

the illegal nature of statelessness into admittedly illegal acts.[36] It smuggled its expelled stateless into the neighboring countries, with the result that the latter retaliated in kind. The ideal solution of repatriation, to smuggle the refugee back into his country of origin, succeeded only in a few prominent instances, partly because a nontotalitarian police was still restrained by a few rudimentary ethical considerations, partly because the stateless person was as likely to be smuggled back from his home country as from any other, and last but not least because the whole traffic could go on only with neighboring countries. The consequences of this smuggling were petty wars between the police at the frontiers, which did not exactly contribute to good international relations, and an accumulation of jail sentences for the stateless who, with the help of the police of one country, had passed "illegally" into the territory of another.

Every attempt by international conferences to establish some legal status for stateless people failed because no agreement could possibly replace the territory to which an alien, within the framework of existing law, must be deportable. All discussions about the refugee problems revolved around this one question: How can the refugee be made deportable again? The second World War and the DP camps were not necessary to show that the only practical substitute for a nonexistent homeland was an internment camp. Indeed, as early as the thirties this was the only "country" the world had to offer the stateless.[37]

Naturalization, on the other hand, also proved to be a failure. The whole naturalization system of European countries fell apart when it was confronted with stateless people, and this for the same reasons that the right of asylum had been set aside. Essentially naturalization was an appendage to the nation-state's legislation that reckoned only with "nationals," people born in its territory and citizens by birth. Naturalization was needed in exceptional cases, for single individuals whom circumstances might have driven into a foreign territory. The whole process broke down when it be-

---

[36] Lawrence Preuss, *op. cit.*, describes the spread of illegality as follows: "The initial illegal act of the denationalizing government . . . puts the expelling country in the position of an offender of international law, because its authorities violate the law of the country to which the stateless person is expelled. The latter country, in turn, cannot get rid of him . . . except by violating . . . the law of a third country. . . . [The stateless person finds himself before the following alternative]: either he violates the law of the country where he resides . . . or he violates the law of the country to which he is expelled."

Sir John Fischer Williams ("Denationalisation," in *British Year Book of International Law*, VII, 1927) concludes from this situation that denationalization is contrary to international law; yet at the Conférence pour la Codification du Droit International at the Hague in 1930, it was only the Finnish government which maintained that "loss of nationality . . . should never constitute a punishment . . . nor be pronounced in order to get rid of an undesirable person through expulsion."

[37] Childs, *op. cit.*, after having come to the sad conclusion that "the real difficulty about receiving a refugee is that if he turns out badly . . . there is no way of getting rid of him," proposed "transitional centers" to which the refugee could be returned even from abroad, which, in other words, should replace a homeland for deportation purposes.

came a question of handling mass applications for naturalization:[38] even from the purely administrative point of view, no European civil service could possibly have dealt with the problem. Instead of naturalizing at least a small portion of the new arrivals, the countries began to cancel earlier naturalizations, partly because of general panic and partly because the arrival of great masses of newcomers actually changed the always precarious position of naturalized citizens of the same origin.[39] Cancellation of naturalization or the introduction of new laws which obviously paved the way for mass denaturalization [40] shattered what little confidence the refugees might have retained in the possibility of adjusting themselves to a new normal life; if assimilation to the new country once looked a little shabby or disloyal, it was now simply ridiculous. The difference between a naturalized citizen and a stateless resident was not great enough to justify taking any trouble, the former being frequently deprived of important civil rights and threatened at any moment with the fate of the latter. Naturalized persons were largely assimilated to the status of ordinary aliens, and since the naturalized had already lost their previous citizenship, these measures simply threatened another considerable group with statelessness.

It was almost pathetic to see how helpless the European governments were, despite their consciousness of the danger of statelessness to their established legal and political institutions and despite all their efforts to stem the tide. Explosive events were no longer necessary. Once a number of stateless people were admitted to an otherwise normal country, statelessness spread like a contagious disease. Not only were naturalized citizens in danger of reverting to the status of statelessness, but living conditions for all aliens markedly deteriorated. In the thirties it became increasingly diffi-

[38] Two instances of mass naturalization in the Near East were clearly exceptional: one involved Greek refugees from Turkey whom the Greek government naturalized en bloc in 1922 because it was actually a matter of repatriation of a Greek minority and not of foreign citizens; the other benefited Armenian refugees from Turkey in Syria, Lebanon, and other formerly Turkish countries, that is, a population with which the Near East had shared common citizenship only a few years ago.

[39] Where a wave of refugees found members of their own nationality already settled in the country to which they immigrated—as was the case with the Armenians and Italians in France, for example, and with Jews everywhere—a certain retrogression set in in the assimilation of those who had been there longer. For their help and solidarity could be mobilized only by appealing to the original nationality they had in common with the newcomers. This point was of immediate interest to countries flooded by refugees but unable or unwilling to give them direct help or the right to work. In all these cases, national feelings of the older group proved to be "one of the main factors in the successful establishment of the refugees" (Simpson, *op. cit.,* pp. 45-46), but by appealing to such national conscience and solidarity, the receiving countries naturally increased the number of unassimilated aliens. To take one particularly interesting instance, 10,000 Italian refugees were enough to postpone indefinitely the assimilation of almost one million Italian immigrants in France.

[40] The French government, followed by other Western countries, introduced during the thirties an increasing number of restrictions for naturalized citizens: they were eliminated from certain professions for up to ten years after their naturalization, they had no political rights, etc.

cult to distinguish clearly between stateless refugees and normal resident aliens. Once the government tried to use its right and repatriate a resident alien against his will, he would do his utmost to find refuge in statelessness. During the first World War enemy aliens had already discovered the great advantages of statelessness. But what then had been the cunning of individuals who found a loophole in the law had now become the instinctive reaction of masses. France, Europe's greatest immigrant-reception area,[41] because she had regulated the chaotic labor market by calling in alien workers in times of need and deporting them in times of unemployment and crisis, taught her aliens a lesson about the advantages of statelessness which they did not readily forget. After 1935, the year of mass repatriation by the Laval government from which only the stateless were saved, so-called "economic immigrants" and other groups of earlier origin—Balkans, Italians, Poles, and Spaniards—mixed with the waves of refugees into a tangle that never again could be unraveled.

Much worse than what statelessness did to the time-honored and necessary distinctions between nationals and foreigners, and to the sovereign right of states in matters of nationality and expulsion, was the damage suffered by the very structure of legal national institutions when a growing number of residents had to live outside the jurisdiction of these laws and without being protected by any other. The stateless person, without right to residence and without the right to work, had of course constantly to transgress the law. He was liable to jail sentences without ever committing a crime. More than that, the entire hierarchy of values which pertain in civilized countries was reversed in his case. Since he was the anomaly for whom the general law did not provide, it was better for him to become an anomaly for which it did provide, that of the criminal.

The best criterion by which to decide whether someone has been forced outside the pale of the law is to ask if he would benefit by committing a crime. If a small burglary is likely to improve his legal position, at least temporarily, one may be sure he has been deprived of human rights. For then a criminal offense becomes the best opportunity to regain some kind of human equality, even if it be as a recognized exception to the norm. The one important fact is that this exception is provided for by law. As a criminal even a stateless person will not be treated worse than another criminal, that is, he will be treated like everybody else. Only as an offender against the law can he gain protection from it. As long as his trial and his sentence last, he will be safe from that arbitrary police rule against which there are no lawyers and no appeals. The same man who was in jail yesterday because of his mere presence in this world, who had no rights whatever and lived under threat of deportation, or who was dispatched without sentence and without trial to some kind of internment because he had tried to work and make a living, may become almost a full-fledged citizen because of a little theft. Even if he is penniless he can now get a lawyer, complain about his jailers, and he will be listened to respectfully. He is no

[41] Simpson, *op. cit.,* p. 289.

longer the scum of the earth but important enough to be informed of all the details of the law under which he will be tried. He has become a respectable person.[42]

A much less reliable and much more difficult way to rise from an unrecognized anomaly to the status of recognized exception would be to become a genius. Just as the law knows only one difference between human beings, the difference between the normal noncriminal and the anomalous criminal, so a conformist society has recognized only one form of determined individualism, the genius. European bourgeois society wanted the genius to stay outside of human laws, to be a kind of monster whose chief social function was to create excitement, and it did not matter if he actually was an outlaw. Moreover, the loss of citizenship deprived people not only of protection, but also of all clearly established, officially recognized identity, a fact for which their eternal feverish efforts to obtain at least birth certificates from the country that denationalized them was a very exact symbol; one of their problems was solved when they achieved the degree of distinction that will rescue a man from the huge and nameless crowd. Only fame will eventually answer the repeated complaint of refugees of all social strata that "nobody here knows who I am"; and it is true that the chances of the famous refugee are improved just as a dog with a name has a better chance to survive than a stray dog who is just a dog in general.[43]

The nation-state, incapable of providing a law for those who had lost the protection of a national government, transferred the whole matter to the police. This was the first time the police in Western Europe had received authority to act on its own, to rule directly over people; in one sphere of public life it was no longer an instrument to carry out and enforce the law, but had become a ruling authority independent of government and ministries.[44] Its strength and its emancipation from law and government grew in direct proportion to the influx of refugees. The greater the ratio of state-

---

[42] In practical terms, any sentence meted out to him will be of small consequence compared with an expulsion order, cancellation of a work permit, or a decree sending him into an internment camp. A West Coast Japanese-American who was in jail when the army ordered the internment of all Americans of Japanese ancestry would not have been forced to liquidate his property at too low a price; he would have remained right where he was, armed with a lawyer to look after his interests; and if he was so lucky as to receive a long sentence, he might have returned righteously and peacefully to his former business and profession, even that of a professional thief. His jail sentence guaranteed him the constitutional rights that nothing else—no protests of loyalty and no appeals—could have obtained for him once his citizenship had become doubtful.

[43] The fact that the same principle of formation of an elite frequently worked in totalitarian concentration camps where the "aristocracy" was composed of a majority of criminals and a few "geniuses," that is entertainers and artists, shows how closely related the social positions of these groups are.

[44] In France, for instance, it was a matter of record that an order of expulsion emanating from the police was much more serious than one which was issued "only" by the Ministry of Interior and that the Minister of Interior could only in rare cases cancel a police expulsion, while the opposite procedure was often merely a question of bribery. Constitutionally, the police is under the authority of the Ministry of Interior.

less and potentially stateless to the population at large—in prewar France it had reached 10 per cent of the total—the greater the danger of a gradual transformation into a police state.

It goes without saying that the totalitarian regimes, where the police had risen to the peak of power, were especially eager to consolidate this power through the domination over vast groups of people, who, regardless of any offenses committed by individuals, found themselves anyway beyond the pale of the law. In Nazi Germany, the Nuremberg Laws with their distinction between Reich citizens (full citizens) and nationals (second-class citizens without political rights) had paved the way for a development in which eventually all nationals of "alien blood" could lose their nationality by official decree; only the outbreak of the war prevented a corresponding legislation, which had been prepared in detail.[44a] On the other hand, the increasing groups of stateless in the nontotalitarian countries led to a form of lawlessness, organized by the police, which practically resulted in a co-ordination of the free world with the legislation of the totalitarian countries. That concentration camps were ultimately provided for the same groups in all countries, even though there were considerable differences in the treatment of their inmates, was all the more characteristic as the selection of the groups was left exclusively to the initiative of the totalitarian regimes: if the Nazis put a person in a concentration camp and if he made a successful escape, say, to Holland, the Dutch would put him in an internment camp. Thus, long before the outbreak of the war the police in a number of Western countries, under the pretext of "national security," had on their own initiative established close connections with the Gestapo and the GPU, so that one might say there existed an independent foreign policy of the police. This police-directed foreign policy functioned quite independently of the official governments; the relations between the Gestapo and the French police were never more cordial than at the

[44a] In February, 1938, the Reich and Prussian Ministry of Interior presented the "draft of a law concerning the acquisition and loss of German nationality" which went far beyond the Nuremberg legislation. It provided that all children of "Jews, Jews of mixed blood or persons of otherwise alien blood" (who could never become Reich citizens anyway) were also no longer entitled to the nationality, "even if the father possesses German nationality by birth." That these measures were no longer merely concerned with anti-Jewish legislation is evident from an opinion expressed July 19, 1939, by the Minister of Justice, who suggests that "the words Jew and Jew of mixed blood should if possible be avoided in the law, to be replaced by 'persons of alien blood,' or 'persons of non-German or non-Germanic [*nicht artverwandt*] blood.'" An interesting feature in planning this extraordinary expansion of the stateless population in Nazi Germany concerns the foundlings, who are explicitly regarded as stateless, until "an investigation of their racial characteristics can be made." Here the principle that every individual is born with inalienable rights guaranteed by his nationality has been deliberately reversed: every individual is born rightless, namely stateless, unless subsequently other conclusions are reached.

The original dossier concerning the draft of this legislation, including the opinions of all Ministries and the *Wehrmacht* High Command, can be found in the archives of the Yiddish Scientific Institute in New York (G-75).

time of Leon Blum's popular-front government, which was guided by a decidedly anti-German policy. Contrary to the governments, the various police organizations were never overburdened with "prejudices" against any totalitarian regime; the information and denunciations received from GPU agents were just as welcome to them as those from Fascist or Gestapo agents. They knew about the eminent role of the police apparatus in all totalitarian regimes, they knew about its elevated social status and political importance, and they never bothered to conceal their sympathies. That the Nazis eventually met with so disgracefully little resistance from the police in the countries they occupied, and that they were able to organize terror as much as they did with the assistance of these local police forces, was due at least in part to the powerful position which the police had achieved over the years in their unrestricted and arbitrary domination of stateless and refugees.

Both in the history of the "nation of minorities" and in the formation of a stateless people, Jews have played a significant role. They were at the head of the so-called minority movement because of their great need for protection (matched only by the need of the Armenians) and their excellent international connections, but above all because they formed a majority in no country and therefore could be regarded as the *minorité par excellence, i.e.,* the only minority whose interests could be defended only by internationally guaranteed protection.[45]

The special needs of the Jewish people were the best possible pretext for denying that the Treaties were a compromise between the new nations' tendency forcefully to assimilate alien peoples *and* nationalities who for reasons of expediency could not be granted the right to national self-determination.

A similar incident made the Jews prominent in the discussion of the refugee and statelessness problem. The first *Heimatlose* or *apatrides,* as they were created by the Peace Treaties, were for the most part Jews who came from the succession states and were unable or unwilling to place themselves under the new minority protection of their homelands. Not until Germany forced German Jewry into emigration and statelessness did they form a very considerable portion of the stateless people. But in the years following Hitler's successful persecution of German Jews all the minority countries began to think in terms of expatriating their minorities, and it was only natural that they should start with the *minorité par excellence,* the only nationality that actually had no other protection than a minority system which by now had become a mockery.

The notion that statelessness is primarily a Jewish problem[46] was a pre-

---

[45] On the role of the Jews in formulating the Minority Treaties, see Macartney, *op. cit.,* pp. 4, 213, 281 and *passim;* David Erdstein, *Le Statut juridique des Minorités en Europe,* Paris, 1932, pp. 11 ff.; Oscar J. Janowsky, *op. cit.*

[46] This was by no means only a notion of Nazi Germany, though only a Nazi author dared to express it: "It is true that a refugee question will continue to exist even

text used by all governments who tried to settle the problem by ignoring it. None of the statesmen was aware that Hitler's solution of the Jewish problem, first to reduce the German Jews to a nonrecognized minority in Germany, then to drive them as stateless people across the borders, and finally to gather them back from everywhere in order to ship them to extermination camps, was an eloquent demonstration to the rest of the world how really to "liquidate" all problems concerning minorities and stateless. After the war it turned out that the Jewish question, which was considered the only insoluble one, was indeed solved—namely, by means of a colonized and then conquered territory—but this solved neither the problem of the minorities nor the stateless. On the contrary, like virtually all other events of our century, the solution of the Jewish question merely produced a new category of refugees, the Arabs, thereby increasing the number of the stateless and rightless by another 700,000 to 800,000 people. And what happened in Palestine within the smallest territory and in terms of hundreds of thousands was then repeated in India on a large scale involving many millions of people. Since the Peace Treaties of 1919 and 1920 the refugees and the stateless have attached themselves like a curse to all the newly established states on earth which were created in the image of the nation-state.

For these new states this curse bears the germs of a deadly sickness. For the nation-state cannot exist once its principle of equality before the law has broken down. Without this legal equality, which originally was destined to replace the older laws and orders of the feudal society, the nation dissolves into an anarchic mass of over- and underprivileged individuals. Laws that are not equal for all revert to rights and privileges, something contradictory to the very nature of nation-states. The clearer the proof of their inability to treat stateless people as legal persons and the greater the extension of arbitrary rule by police decree, the more difficult it is for states to resist the temptation to deprive all citizens of legal status and rule them with an omnipotent police.

II: *The Perplexities of the Rights of Man*

THE DECLARATION of the Rights of Man at the end of the eighteenth century was a turning point in history. It meant nothing more nor less than that from then on Man, and not God's command or the customs of history, should be the source of Law. Independent of the privileges which history had bestowed upon certain strata of society or certain nations, the declaration indicated man's emancipation from all tutelage and announced that he had now come of age.

---

when there is no longer a Jewish question; but since Jews form such a high percentage of the refugees, the refugee question will be much simplified" (Kabermann, "Das internationale Flüchtlingsproblem," in *Zeitschrift für Politik*, Bd. 29, Heft 3, 1939).

Beyond this, there was another implication of which the framers of the declaration were only half aware. The proclamation of human rights was also meant to be a much-needed protection in the new era where individuals were no longer secure in the estates to which they were born or sure of their equality before God as Christians. In other words, in the new secularized and emancipated society, men were no longer sure of these social and human rights which until then had been outside the political order and guaranteed not by government and constitution, but by social, spiritual, and religious forces. Therefore throughout the nineteenth century, the consensus of opinion was that human rights had to be invoked whenever individuals needed protection against the new sovereignty of the state and the new arbitrariness of society.

Since the Rights of Man were proclaimed to be "inalienable," irreducible to and undeducible from other rights or laws, no authority was invoked for their establishment; Man himself was their source as well as their ultimate goal. No special law, moreover, was deemed necessary to protect them because all laws were supposed to rest upon them. Man appeared as the only sovereign in matters of law as the people was proclaimed the only sovereign in matters of government. The people's sovereignty (different from that of the prince) was not proclaimed by the grace of God but in the name of Man, so that it seemed only natural that the "inalienable" rights of man would find their guarantee and become an inalienable part of the right of the people to sovereign self-government.

In other words, man had hardly appeared as a completely emancipated, completely isolated being who carried his dignity within himself without reference to some larger encompassing order, when he disappeared again into a member of a people. From the beginning the paradox involved in the declaration of inalienable human rights was that it reckoned with an "abstract" human being who seemed to exist nowhere, for even savages lived in some kind of a social order. If a tribal or other "backward" community did not enjoy human rights, it was obviously because as a whole it had not yet reached that stage of civilization, the stage of popular and national sovereignty, but was oppressed by foreign or native despots. The whole question of human rights, therefore, was quickly and inextricably blended with the question of national emancipation; only the emancipated sovereignty of the people, of one's own people, seemed to be able to insure them. As mankind, since the French Revolution, was conceived in the image of a family of nations, it gradually became self-evident that the people, and not the individual, was the image of man.

The full implication of this identification of the rights of man with the rights of peoples in the European nation-state system came to light only when a growing number of people and peoples suddenly appeared whose elementary rights were as little safeguarded by the ordinary functioning of nation-states in the middle of Europe as they would have been in the heart of Africa. The Rights of Man, after all, had been defined as "inalienable" because they were supposed to be independent of all governments; but it turned out that the moment human beings lacked their own government and had to fall back upon their minimum rights, no authority was left to protect them and no institution was willing to guarantee them. Or when, as in the case of the minorities, an international body arrogated to itself a nongovernmental authority, its failure was apparent even before its measures were fully realized; not only were the governments more or less openly opposed to this encroachment on their sovereignty, but the concerned nationalities themselves did not recognize a nonnational guarantee, mistrusted everything which was not clear-cut support of their "national" (as opposed to their mere "linguistic, religious, and ethnic") rights, and preferred either, like the Germans or Hungarians, to turn to the protection of the "national" mother country, or, like the Jews, to some kind of interterritorial solidarity.[47]

The stateless people were as convinced as the minorities that loss of national rights was identical with loss of human rights, that the former inevitably entailed the latter. The more they were excluded from right in any form, the more they tended to look for a reintegration into a national, into their own national community. The Russian refugees were only the first to insist on their nationality and to defend themselves furiously against attempts to lump them together with other stateless people. Since them, not a single group of refugees or Displaced Persons has failed to develop a fierce, violent group consciousness and to clamor for rights as—and only as—Poles or Jews or Germans, etc.

Even worse was that all societies formed for the protection of the Rights of Man, all attempts to arrive at a new bill of human rights were sponsored by marginal figures—by a few international jurists without political experience or professional philanthropists supported by the uncertain sentiments of professional idealists. The groups they formed, the declarations they issued, showed an uncanny similarity in language and composition to that of societies for the prevention of cruelty to animals. No statesman, no political figure of any importance could possibly take them seriously; and none of the liberal or radical parties in Europe thought it necessary to incorporate into their program a new declaration of human rights. Neither before nor after the second World War have the victims themselves ever invoked these fundamental rights, which were so evidently denied them, in their many attempts to find a way out of the barbed-wire labyrinth into which events had driven them. On the contrary, the victims shared the disdain

---

[47] Pathetic instances of this exclusive confidence in national rights were the consent, before the second World War, of nearly 75 per cent of the German minority in the Italian Tyrol to leave their homes and resettle in Germany, the voluntary repatriation of a German island in Slovenia which had been there since the fourteenth century or, immediately after the close of the war, the unanimous rejection by Jewish refugees in an Italian DP camp of an offer of mass naturalization by the Italian government. In the face of the experience of European peoples between the two wars, it would be a serious mistake to interpret this behavior simply as another example of fanatic nationalist sentiment; these people no longer felt sure of their elementary rights if these were not protected by a government to which they belonged by birth. See Eugene M. Kulisher, *op. cit.*

and indifference of the powers that be for any attempt of the marginal societies to enforce human rights in any elementary or general sense.

The failure of all responsible persons to meet the calamity of an evergrowing body of people forced to live outside the scope of all tangible law with the proclamation of a new bill of rights was certainly not due to ill will. Never before had the Rights of Man, solemnly proclaimed by the French and the American revolutions as the new fundament for civilized societies, been a practical political issue. During the nineteenth century, these rights had been invoked in a rather perfunctory way, to defend individuals against the increasing power of the state and to mitigate the new social insecurity caused by the industrial revolution. Then the meaning of human rights acquired a new connotation: they became the standard slogan of the protectors of the underprivileged, a kind of additional law, a right of exception necessary for those who had nothing better to fall back upon.

The reason why the concept of human rights was treated as a sort of stepchild by nineteenth-century political thought and why no liberal or radical party in the twentieth century, even when an urgent need for enforcement of human rights arose, saw fit to include them in its program seems obvious: civil rights—that is the varying rights of citizens in different countries—were supposed to embody and spell out in the form of tangible laws the eternal Rights of Man, which by themselves were supposed to be independent of citizenship and nationality. All human beings were citizens of some kind of political community; if the laws of their country did not live up to the demands of the Rights of Man, they were expected to change them, by legislation in democratic countries or through revolutionary action in despotisms.

The Rights of Man, supposedly inalienable, proved to be unenforceable—even in countries whose constitutions were based upon them—whenever people appeared who were no longer citizens of any sovereign state. To this fact, disturbing enough in itself, one must add the confusion created by the many recent attempts to frame a new bill of human rights, which have demonstrated that no one seems able to define with any assurance what these general human rights, as distinguished from the rights of citizens, really are. Although everyone seems to agree that the plight of these people consists precisely in their loss of the Rights of Man, no one seems to know which rights they lost when they lost these human rights.

The first loss which the rightless suffered was the loss of their homes, and this meant the loss of the entire social texture into which they were born and in which they established for themselves a distinct place in the world. This calamity is far from unprecedented; in the long memory of history, forced migrations of individuals or whole groups of people for political or economic reasons look like everyday occurrences. What is unprecedented is not the loss of a home but the impossibility of finding a new one. Suddenly, there was no place on earth where migrants could go without the severest restrictions, no country where they would be assimilated, no territory where they could found a new community of their own. This, moreover, had next to nothing to do with any material problem of overpopulation; it was a problem not of space but of political organization. Nobody had been aware that mankind, for so long a time considered under the image of a family of nations, had reached the stage where whoever was thrown out of one of these tightly organized closed communities found himself thrown out of the family of nations altogether.[48]

The second loss which the rightless suffered was the loss of government protection, and this did not imply just the loss of legal status in their own, but in all countries. Treaties of reciprocity and international agreements have woven a web around the earth that makes it possible for the citizen of every country to take his legal status with him no matter where he goes (so that, for instance, a German citizen under the Nazi regime might not be able to enter a mixed marriage abroad because of the Nuremberg laws). Yet, whoever is no longer caught in it finds himself out of legality altogether (thus during the last war stateless people were invariably in a worse position than enemy aliens who were still indirectly protected by their governments through international agreements).

By itself the loss of government protection is no more unprecedented than the loss of a home. Civilized countries did offer the right of asylum to those who, for political reasons, had been persecuted by their governments, and this practice, though never officially incorporated into any constitution, has functioned well enough throughout the nineteenth and even in our century. The trouble arose when it appeared that the new categories of persecuted were far too numerous to be handled by an unofficial practice destined for exceptional cases. Moreover, the majority could hardly qualify for the right of asylum, which implicitly presupposed political or religious convictions which were not outlawed in the country of refuge. The new refugees were persecuted not because of what they had done or thought, but because of what they unchangeably were—born into the wrong kind of race or the wrong kind of class or drafted by the wrong kind of government (as in the case of the Spanish Republican Army).[49]

The more the number of rightless people increased, the greater became the temptation to pay less attention to the deeds of the persecuting governments than to the status of the persecuted. And the first glaring fact was that these people, though persecuted under some political pretext, were no

[48] The few chances for reintegration open to the new migrants were mostly based on their nationality: Spanish refugees, for instance, were welcomed to a certain extent in Mexico. The United States, in the early twenties, adopted a quota system according to which each nationality already represented in the country received, so to speak, the right to receive a number of former countrymen proportionate to its numerical part in the total population.

[49] How dangerous it can be to be innocent from the point of view of the persecuting government, became very clear when, during the last war, the American government offered asylum to all those German refugees who were threatened by the extradition paragraph in the German-French Armistice. The condition was, of course, that the applicant could prove that he had done something against the Nazi regime. The proportion of refugees from Germany who were able to fulfill this condition was very small, and they, strangely enough, were not the people who were most in danger.

longer, as the persecuted had been throughout history, a liability and an image of shame for the persecutors; that they were not considered and hardly pretended to be active enemies (the few thousand Soviet citizens who voluntarily left Soviet Russia after the second World War and found asylum in democratic countries did more damage to the prestige of the Soviet Union than millions of refugees in the twenties who belonged to the wrong class), but that they were and appeared to be nothing but human beings whose very innocence—from every point of view, and especially that of the persecuting government—was their greatest misfortune. Innocence, in the sense of complete lack of responsibility, was the mark of their rightlessness as it was the seal of their loss of political status.

Only in appearance therefore do the needs for a reinforcement of human rights touch upon the fate of the authentic political refugee. Political refugees, of necessity few in number, still enjoy the right to asylum in many countries, and this right acts, in an informal way, as a genuine substitute for national law.

One of the surprising aspects of our experience with stateless people who benefit legally from committing a crime has been the fact that it seems to be easier to deprive a completely innocent person of legality than someone who has committed an offense. Anatole France's famous quip, "If I am accused of stealing the towers of Notre Dame, I can only flee the country," has assumed a horrible reality. Jurists are so used to thinking of law in terms of punishment, which indeed always deprives us of certain rights, that they may find it even more difficult than the layman to recognize that the deprivation of legality, *i.e.*, of *all* rights, no longer has a connection with specific crimes.

This situation illustrates the many perplexities inherent in the concept of human rights. No matter how they have once been defined (life, liberty, and the pursuit of happiness, according to the American formula, or as equality before the law, liberty, protection of property, and national sovereignty, according to the French); no matter how one may attempt to improve an ambiguous formulation like the pursuit of happiness, or an antiquated one like unqualified right to property; the real situation of those whom the twentieth century has driven outside the pale of the law shows that these are rights of citizens whose loss does not entail absolute rightlessness. The soldier during the war is deprived of his right to life, the criminal of his right to freedom, all citizens during an emergency of their right to the pursuit of happiness, but nobody would ever claim that in any of these instances a loss of human rights has taken place. These rights, on the other hand, can be granted (though hardly enjoyed) even under conditions of fundamental rightlessness.

The calamity of the rightless is not that they are deprived of life, liberty, and the pursuit of happiness, or of equality before the law and freedom of opinion—formulas which were designed to solve problems *within* given communities—but that they no longer belong to any community whatsoever. Their plight is not that they are not equal before the law, but that no law exists for them; not that they are oppressed but that nobody wants even to oppress them. Only in the last stage of a rather lengthy process is their right to live threatened; only if they remain perfectly "superfluous," if nobody can be found to "claim" them, may their lives be in danger. Even the Nazis started their extermination of Jews by first depriving them of all legal status (the status of second-class citizenship) and cutting them off from the world of the living by herding them into ghettos and concentration camps; and before they set the gas chambers into motion they had carefully tested the ground and found out to their satisfaction that no country would claim these people. The point is that a condition of complete rightlessness was created before the right to live was challenged.

The same is true even to an ironical extent with regard to the right of freedom which is sometimes considered to be the very essence of human rights. There is no question that those outside the pale of the law may have more freedom of movement than a lawfully imprisoned criminal or that they enjoy more freedom of opinion in the internment camps of democratic countries than they would in any ordinary despotism, not to mention in a totalitarian country.[50] But neither physical safety—being fed by some state or private welfare agency—nor freedom of opinion changes in the least their fundamental situation of rightlessness. The prolongation of their lives is due to charity and not to right, for no law exists which could force the nations to feed them; their freedom of movement, if they have it at all, gives them no right to residence which even the jailed criminal enjoys as a matter of course; and their freedom of opinion is a fool's freedom, for nothing they think matters anyhow.

These last points are crucial. The fundamental deprivation of human rights is manifested first and above all in the deprivation of a place in the world which makes opinions significant and actions effective. Something much more fundamental than freedom and justice, which are rights of citizens, is at stake when belonging to the community into which one is born is no longer a matter of course and not belonging no longer a matter of choice, or when one is placed in a situation where, unless he commits a crime, his treatment by others does not depend on what he does or does not do. This extremity, and nothing else, is the situation of people deprived of human rights. They are deprived, not of the right to freedom, but of the right to action; not of the right to think whatever they please, but of the right to opinion. Privileges in some cases, injustices in most, blessings and doom are meted out to them according to accident and without any relation whatsoever to what they do, did, or may do.

We became aware of the existence of a right to have rights (and that means to live in a framework where one is judged by one's actions and

---

[50] Even under the conditions of totalitarian terror, concentration camps sometimes have been the only place where certain remnants of freedom of thought and discussion still existed. See David Rousset, *Les Jours de Notre Mort*, Paris, 1947, *passim*, for freedom of discussion in Buchenwald, and Anton Ciliga, *The Russian Enigma*, London, 1940, p. 200, about "isles of liberty," "the freedom of mind" that reigned in some of the Soviet places of detention.

opinions) and a right to belong to some kind of organized community, only when millions of people emerged who had lost and could not regain these rights because of the new global political situation. The trouble is that this calamity arose not from any lack of civilization, backwardness, or mere tyranny, but, on the contrary, that it could not be repaired, because there was no longer any "uncivilized" spot on earth, because whether we like it or not we have really started to live in One World. Only with a completely organized humanity could the loss of home and political status become identical with expulsion from humanity altogether.

Before this, what we must call a "human right" today would have been thought of as a general characteristic of the human condition which no tyrant could take away. Its loss entails the loss of the relevance of speech (and man, since Aristotle, has been defined as a being commanding the power of speech and thought), and the loss of all human relationship (and man, again since Aristotle, has been thought of as the "political animal," that is one who by definition lives in a community), the loss, in other words, of some of the most essential characteristics of human life. This was to a certain extent the plight of slaves, whom Aristotle therefore did not count among human beings. Slavery's fundamental offense against human rights was not that it took liberty away (which can happen in many other situations), but that it excluded a certain category of people even from the possibility of fighting for freedom—a fight possible under tyranny, and even under the desperate conditions of modern terror (but not under any conditions of concentration-camp life). Slavery's crime against humanity did not begin when one people defeated and enslaved its enemies (though of course this was bad enough), but when slavery became an institution in which some men were "born" free and others slave, when it was forgotten that it was man who had deprived his fellow-men of freedom, and when the sanction for the crime was attributed to nature. Yet in the light of recent events it is possible to say that even slaves still belonged to some sort of human community; their labor was needed, used, and exploited, and this kept them within the pale of humanity. To be a slave was after all to have a distinctive character, a place in society—more than the abstract nakedness of being human and nothing but human. Not the loss of specific rights, then, but the loss of a community willing and able to guarantee any rights whatsoever, has been the calamity which has befallen ever-increasing numbers of people. Man, it turns out, can lose all so-called Rights of Man without losing his essential quality as man, his human dignity. Only the loss of a polity itself expels him from humanity.

The right that corresponds to this loss and that was never even mentioned among the human rights cannot be expressed in the categories of the eighteenth century because they presume that rights spring immediately from the "nature" of man—whereby it makes relatively little difference whether this nature is visualized in terms of the natural law or in terms of a being created in the image of God, whether it concerns "natural" rights or divine commands. The decisive factor is that these rights and the human dignity they bestow should remain valid and real even if only a single human being existed on earth; they are independent of human plurality and should remain valid even if a human being is expelled from the human community. When the Rights of Man were proclaimed for the first time, they were regarded as being independent of history and the privileges which history had accorded certain strata of society. The new independence constituted the newly discovered dignity of man. From the beginning, this new dignity was of a rather ambiguous nature. Historical rights were replaced by natural rights, "nature" took the place of history, and it was tacitly assumed that nature was less alien than history to the essence of man. The very language of the Declaration of Independence as well as of the *Déclaration des Droits de l'Homme*—"inalienable," "given with birth," "self-evident truths"—implies the belief in a kind of human "nature" which would be subject to the same laws of growth as that of the individual and from which rights and laws could be deduced. Today we are perhaps better qualified to judge exactly what this human "nature" amounts to; in any event it has shown us potentialities that were neither recognized nor even suspected by Western philosophy and religion, which for more than three thousand years have defined and redefined this "nature." But it is not only the, as it were, human aspect of nature that has become questionable to us. Ever since man learned to master it to such an extent that the destruction of all organic life on earth with man-made instruments has become conceivable and technically possible, he has been alienated from nature. Ever since a deeper knowledge of natural processes instilled serious doubts about the existence of natural laws at all, nature itself has assumed a sinister aspect. How should one be able to deduce laws and rights from a universe which apparently knows neither the one nor the other category?

Man of the twentieth century has become just as emancipated from nature as eighteenth-century man was from history. History and nature have become equally alien to us, namely, in the sense that the essence of man can no longer be comprehended in terms of either category. On the other hand, humanity, which for the eighteenth century, in Kantian terminology, was no more than a regulative idea, has today become an inescapable fact. This new situation, in which "humanity" has in effect assumed the role formerly ascribed to nature or history, would mean in this context that the right to have rights, or the right of every individual to belong to humanity, should be guaranteed by humanity itself. It is by no means certain whether this is possible. For, contrary to the best-intentioned humanitarian attempts to obtain new declarations of human rights from international organizations, it should be understood that this idea transcends the present sphere of international law which still operates in terms of reciprocal agreements and treaties between sovereign states; and, for the time being, a sphere that is above the nations does not exist. Furthermore, this dilemma would by no means be eliminated by the establishment of a "world government." Such a world government is indeed within the realm of possibility, but one may suspect that in reality it might differ considerably from the version promoted by idealistic-minded organizations. The crimes against human rights, which have become a specialty of totalitarian regimes, can always be justified by the pretext that right is equivalent to being good or useful for the whole in distinction to its parts. (Hitler's motto that "Right is what is good for the German people" is only the vulgarized form of a conception of law which can be found everywhere and which in practice will remain ineffectual only so long as older traditions that are still effective in the constitutions prevent this.) A conception of law which identifies what is right with the notion of what is good for—for the individual, or the family, or the people, or the largest number—becomes inevitable once the absolute and transcendent measurements of religion or the law of nature have lost their authority. And this predicament is by no means solved if the unit to which the "good for" applies is as large as mankind itself. For it is quite conceivable, and even within the realm of practical political possibilities, that one fine day a highly organized and mechanized humanity will conclude quite democratically—namely by majority decision—that for humanity as a whole it would be better to liquidate certain parts thereof. Here, in the problems of factual reality, we are confronted with one of the oldest perplexities of political philosophy, which could remain undetected only so long as a stable Christian theology provided the framework for all political and philosophical problems, but which long ago caused Plato to say: "Not man, but a god, must be the measure of all things."

These facts and reflections offer what seems an ironical, bitter, and belated confirmation of the famous arguments with which Edmund Burke opposed the French Revolution's Declaration of the Rights of Man. They appear to buttress his assertion that human rights were an "abstraction," that it was much wiser to rely on an "entailed inheritance" of rights which one transmits to one's children like life itself, and to claim one's rights to be the "rights of an Englishman" rather than the inalienable rights of man.[51] According to Burke, the rights which we enjoy spring "from within the nation," so that neither natural law, nor divine command, nor any concept of mankind such as Robespierre's "human race," "the sovereign of the earth," are needed as a source of law.[52]

The pragmatic soundness of Burke's concept seems to be beyond doubt in the light of our manifold experiences. Not only did loss of national rights in all instances entail the loss of human rights; the restoration of human rights, as the recent example of the State of Israel proves, has been achieved so far only through the restoration or the establishment of national rights. The conception of human rights, based upon the assumed existence of a human being as such, broke down at the very moment when those who professed to believe in it were for the first time confronted with people who had indeed lost all other qualities and specific relationships—except that they were still human. The world found nothing sacred in the abstract nakedness of being human. And in view of objective political conditions, it is hard to say how the concepts of man upon which human rights are based—that he is

[51] Edmund Burke, *Reflections on the Revolution in France*, 1790, edited by E. J. Payne, Everyman's Library.
[52] Robespierre, *Speeches*, 1927. Speech of April 24, 1793.

created in the image of God (in the American formula), or that he is the representative of mankind, or that he harbors within himself the sacred demands of natural law (in the French formula)—could have helped to find a solution to the problem.

The survivors of the extermination camps, the inmates of concentration and internment camps, and even the comparatively happy stateless people could see without Burke's arguments that the abstract nakedness of being nothing but human was their greatest danger. Because of it they were regarded as savages and, afraid that they might end by being considered beasts, they insisted on their nationality, the last sign of their former citizenship, as their only remaining and recognized tie with humanity. Their distrust of natural, their preference for national, rights comes precisely from their realization that natural rights are granted even to savages. Burke had already feared that natural "inalienable" rights would confirm only the "right of the naked savage," [53] and therefore reduce civilized nations to the status of savagery. Because only savages have nothing more to fall back upon than the minimum fact of their human origin, people cling to their nationality all the more desperately when they have lost the rights and protection that such nationality once gave them. Only their past with its "entailed inheritance" seems to attest to the fact that they still belong to the civilized world.

If a human being loses his political status, he should, according to the implications of the inborn and inalienable rights of man, come under exactly the situation for which the declarations of such general rights provided. Actually the opposite is the case. It seems that a man who is nothing but a man has lost the very qualities which make it possible for other people to treat him as a fellow-man. This is one of the reasons why it is far more difficult to destroy the legal personality of a criminal, that is of a man who has taken upon himself the responsibility for an act whose consequences now determine his fate, than of a man who has been disallowed all common human responsibilities.

Burke's arguments therefore gain an added significance if we look only at the general human condition of those who have been forced out of all political communities. Regardless of treatment, independent of liberties or oppression, justice or injustice, they have lost all those parts of the world and all those aspects of human existence which are the result of our common labor, the outcome of the human artifice. If the tragedy of savage tribes is that they inhabit an unchanged nature which they cannot master, yet upon whose abundance or frugality they depend for their livelihood, that they live and die without leaving any trace, without having contributed anything to a common world, then these rightless people are indeed thrown back into a peculiar state of nature. Certainly they are not barbarians; some of them, indeed, belong to the most educated strata of their respective countries; nevertheless, in a world that has almost liquidated savagery, they appear as the first signs of a possible regression from civilization.

The more highly developed a civilization, the more accomplished the

---

[53] Introduction by Payne to Burke, *op. cit.*

world it has produced, the more at home men feel within the human artifice —the more they will resent everything they have not produced, everything that is merely and mysteriously given them. The human being who has lost his place in a community, his political status in the struggle of his time, and the legal personality which makes his actions and part of his destiny a consistent whole, is left with those qualities which usually can become articulate only in the sphere of private life and must remain unqualified, mere existence in all matters of public concern. This mere existence, that is, all that which is mysteriously given us by birth and which includes the shape of our bodies and the talents of our minds, can be adequately dealt with only by the unpredictable hazards of friendship and sympathy, or by the great and incalculable grace of love, which says with Augustine, *"Volo ut sis* (I want you to be)," without being able to give any particular reason for such supreme and unsurpassable affirmation.

Since the Greeks, we have known that highly developed political life breeds a deep-rooted suspicion of this private sphere, a deep resentment against the disturbing miracle contained in the fact that each of us is made as he is—single, unique, unchangeable. This whole sphere of the merely given, relegated to private life in civilized society, is a permanent threat to the public sphere, because the public sphere is as consistently based on the law of equality as the private sphere is based on the law of universal difference and differentiation. Equality, in contrast to all that is involved in mere existence, is not given us, but is the result of human organization insofar as it is guided by the principle of justice. We are not born equal; we become equal as members of a group on the strength of our decision to guarantee ourselves mutually equal rights.

Our political life rests on the assumption that we can produce equality through organization, because man can act in and change and build a common world, together with his equals and only with his equals. The dark background of mere givenness, the background formed by our unchangeable and unique nature, breaks into the political scene as the alien which in its all too obvious difference reminds us of the limitations of human activity—which are identical with the limitations of human equality. The reason why highly developed political communities, such as the ancient city-states or modern nation-states, so often insist on ethnic homogeneity is that they hope to eliminate as far as possible those natural and always present differences and differentiations which by themselves arouse dumb hatred, mistrust, and discrimination because they indicate all too clearly those spheres where men cannot act and change at will, *i.e.,* the limitations of the human artifice. The "alien" is a frightening symbol of the fact of difference as such, of individuality as such, and indicates those realms in which man cannot change and cannot act and in which, therefore, he has a distinct tendency to destroy. If a Negro in a white community is considered a Negro and nothing else, he loses along with his right to equality that freedom of action which is specifically human; all his deeds are now explained as "necessary" consequences of some "Negro" qualities; he has become some specimen of an animal species, called man. Much the same thing happens to those who have lost all distinctive political qualities and have become human beings and nothing else. No doubt, wherever public life and its law of equality are completely victorious, wherever a civilization succeeds in eliminating or reducing to a minimum the dark background of difference, it will end in complete petrifaction and be punished, so to speak, for having forgotten that man is only the master, not the creator of the world.

The great danger arising from the existence of people forced to live outside the common world is that they are thrown back, in the midst of civilization, on their natural givenness, on their mere differentiation. They lack that tremendous equalizing of differences which comes from being citizens of some commonwealth and yet, since they are no longer allowed to partake in the human artifice, they begin to belong to the human race in much the same way as animals belong to a specific animal species. The paradox involved in the loss of human rights is that such loss coincides with the instant when a person becomes a human being in general—without a profession, without a citizenship, without an opinion, without a deed by which to identify and specify himself—*and* different in general, representing nothing but his own absolutely unique individuality which, deprived of expression within and action upon a common world, loses all significance.

The danger in the existence of such people is twofold: first and more obviously, their ever-increasing numbers threaten our political life, our human artifice, the world which is the result of our common and co-ordinated effort in much the same, perhaps even more terrifying, way as the wild elements of nature once threatened the existence of man-made cities and countrysides. Deadly danger to any civilization is no longer likely to come from without. Nature has been mastered and no barbarians threaten to destroy what they cannot understand, as the Mongolians threatened Europe for centuries. Even the emergence of totalitarian governments is a phenomenon within, not outside, our civilization. The danger is that a global, universally interrelated civilization may produce barbarians from its own midst by forcing millions of people into conditions which, despite all appearances, are the conditions of savages.[54]

[54] This modern expulsion from humanity has much more radical consequences than the ancient and medieval custom of outlawry. Outlawry, certainly the "most fearful fate which primitive law could inflict," placing the life of the outlawed person at the mercy of anyone he met, disappeared with the establishment of an effective system of law enforcement and was finally replaced by extradition treaties between the nations. It had been primarily a substitute for a police force, designed to compel criminals to surrender.

The early Middle Ages seem to have been quite conscious of the danger involved in "civil death." Excommunication in the late Roman Empire meant ecclesiastical death but left a person who had lost his membership in the church full freedom in all other respects. Ecclesiastical and civil death became identical only in the Merovingian era, and there excommunication "in general practice [was] limited to temporary withdrawal or suspension of the rights of membership which might be regained." See the articles "Outlawry" and "Excommunication" in the *Encyclopedia of Social Sciences.* Also the article "Friedlosigkeit" in the *Schweizer Lexikon.*

Bibliography

American Friends Service Bulletin, General Relief Bulletin, March, 1943.

Andler, Charles, *Les Origines du Pangermanisme*, 1915.

Angus, H. F., editor, "Canada and the Doctrine of Peaceful Changes," *International Studies Conference. Demographic Questions. Peaceful Changes*, 1937.

Arndt, Ernst Moritz, *Ein Blick aus der Zeit auf die Zeit*, 1814; *Phantasien zur Berichtigung der Urteile über künftige deutsche Verfassungen*, 1815; *Erinnerungen aus Schweden*, 1818.

Azcarate, Pablo de, "Minorities. League of Nations," in *Encyclopaedia Britannica*, 1929.

Bangert, Otto, *Gold oder Blut*, 1927.

Barker, Ernest, *Political Theory in England from Herbert Spencer to the Present Day*, 1915; *Ideas and Ideals of the British Empire*, Cambridge, 1941.

Barnes, Leonard, *Caliban in Africa. An Impression of Colour Madness*, Philadelphia, 1931.

Barrès, Maurice, *Scènes et doctrines du nationalisme*, Paris, 1899.

Barzun, Jacques, *Race. A Study in Modern Superstition*, New York, 1937.

Bassermann, Ernst, "Nationalliberale," in *Handbuch der Politik*, vol. 2, 1914.

Bauer, Otto, *Die Nationalitätenfrage und die österreichische Sozialdemokratie*, Vienna, 1907.

Beamish, Henry Hamilton, *South Africa's Kosher Press*, London, 1937.

Becker, Paul, *Carl Peters, die Wirkung der deutschen Kolonialpolitik*, 1934.

Bell, Sir Hesketh, *Foreign Colonial Administration in the Far East*, 1928.

Benedict, Ruth, *Race, Science and Politics*, 1940.

Benians, E. A., "The European Colonies," *Cambridge Modern History. The Latest Age*, vol. 12, 1934.

Benjamin, Walter, *Über den Begriff der Geschichte*, in *Werke*, Frankfurt, 1955.

Bentwich, Norman, "South Africa. Dominion of Racial Problems," *The Political Quarterly*, vol. 10, no. 3, 1939.

Bérard, Victor, *L'Empire russe et le tsarisme*, 1905.

Bergstraesser, Ludwig, *Geschichte der politischen Parteien*, 1921.

Bibl, Viktor, *Der Zerfall Oesterreichs*, 1924.

Bluntschli, Johann Caspar, *Charakter und Geist der Politischen Parteien*, 1869.

Bodelsen, C. A., *Studies in Mid-Victorian Imperialism*, 1924.

Bodin, Jean, *Six Livres de la République*, 1576.

Bonhard, Otto, *Geschichte des alldeutschen Verbandes*, 1920.

Boulainvilliers, Comte Henri de, *Histoire de l'Ancien Gouvernement de la France*, 1727.

Braun, Robert, "Political Parties. Succession States," in *Encyclopedia of Social Sciences*.

Brie, Friedrich, *Imperialistische Strömungen in der englischen Literatur*, Halle, 1928; *Der Einfluss der Lehren Darwins auf den britischen Imperialismus*, 1927.

Bronner, Fritz, "Georg, Ritter v. Schoenerer," *Volk im Werden*, vol. 7, no. 3, 1939.

Bruecher, Heinz, "Ernst Haeckel. Ein Wegbereiter biologischen Staatsdenkens," *Nationalsozialistische Monatshefte.* no. 69, 1935.
Brunschwig, Henri, *Mythes et Réalités de l'Impérialisme Colonial Français, 1871-1914*, Paris, 1960.
Bruun, Geoffrey, *Europe and the French Empire*, 1938.
Bryce, Viscount James, *Studies in History and Jurisprudence*, 1901.
Bubnoff, Nicolai, *Kultur und Geschichte im russischen Denken der Gegenwart* (Osteuropa: Quellen und Studien, no. 2), 1927.
Buffon, Georges-Louis Leclerc, Comte de, *Histoire Naturelle*, 1769-1789.
Burke, Edmund, *Reflections on the Revolution in France* (1790), Everyman's Library; *Upon Party*, 1850, 2nd ed.
Burns, Elinor, *British Imperialism in Ireland*, 1931.

Cambridge History of the British Empire, vol. 5, *The Indian Empire 1858-1918*, 1932; vol. 8, *South Africa*, 1936.
Carlyle, Thomas, "Occasional Discourse on the Nigger Question," in *Critical and Miscellaneous Essays.*
Carr-Saunders, A. M., *World Population*, Oxford, 1936.
Carthill, Al. (pseudonym), *The Lost Dominion*, 1924.
Chamberlin, W. H., *The Russian Revolution, 1917-1927*, New York, 1935.
Cherikover, E. "New Materials on the Pogroms in Russia at the Beginning of the Eighties," *Historishe Shriftn*, vol. 2, Vilna, 1937.
Chesterton, Cecil, and Belloc, Hilaire, *The Party System*, London, 1911.
Chesterton, Gilbert K., *The Crimes of England*, 1915.
Childs, Stephen Lawford, "Refugees—a Permanent Problem in International Organization," in *War is not Inevitable, Problems of Peace*, 13th series, published by the International Labor Office, London, 1938.
Clapham, J. H., *The Abbé Siéyès*, London, 1912.
Class, Heinrich (pseudonym Einhart), *Deutsche Geschichte*, Leipzig, 1910; *Zwanzig Jahre alldeutscher Arbeit und Kämpfe*, Leipzig, 1910; (pseudonym Daniel Fryman), *Wenn ich der Kaiser wär. Politische Wahrheiten und Notwendigkeiten*, 1912.
Cleinow, Georg, *Die Zukunft Polens*, Leipzig, 1914.
Comte, Auguste, *Discours sur l'Ensemble du Positivisme*, 1848.
Conditions of India (no author, preface by Bertrand Russell), London, 1934.
Conrad, Joseph, "The Heart of Darkness," in his *The Youth and Other Tales*, 1902; *Victory*, 1915.
Cooke, George W., *The History of Party*, London, 1836.
Coquart, A., *Pisarev et l'idéologie du nihilisme russe*, Paris, 1946.
Cromer, Lord, Evelyn Baring, "The Government of Subject Races," *Edinburgh Review*, January, 1908; "Disraeli," *Spectator*, November, 1912.
Crozier, John B., *History of Intellectual Development on the Lines of Modern Evolution*, 1897-1901.
Crozier, W. P., "France and her 'Black Empire,' " *New Republic*, January 23, 1924.
Curzon, Lord George N., *Problems of the Far East*, 1894.

Damce, E. H., *The Victorian Illusion*, London, 1928.
Danilewski, Nikolai Yakovlevich, *Russia and Europe*, 1871.
Darcy, Jean, *France et Angleterre, Cent années de rivalité coloniale*, 1904.
(Davidson, John), *Testament of John Davidson*, 1908.
Deckert, Emil, *Panlatinismus, Panslawismus und Panteutonismus in ihrer Bedeutung für die Weltlage*, Frankfurt, 1914.
Delbrück, Hans, "Die Alldeutschen," *Preussische Jahrbücher*, vol. 154, December, 1913; *Ludendorffs Selbstportrait*, Berlin, 1922.
Delos, J.-T., *La Nation*, Montreal, 1944.
Detweiler, E. G., "The rise of modern race antagonism," *American Journal of Sociology*, 1932.
Dilke, Charles W., *Problems of Greater Britain*, 4th ed., London, 1890.

Dornath, J. v., "Die Herrschaft des Panslawismus," *Preussische Jahrbücher,* vol. 95, Berlin, 1898.

Dreyfus, Robert, "La Vie et les prophéties du Comte de Gobineau," *Cahiers de la Quinzaine,* ser. 6, cahier 16, 1905.

Dubuat-Nançay, Comte Louis Gabriel, *Les Origines; ou, l'Ancien Gouvernement de la France, de l'Allemagne et de l'Italie,* 1789.

Duesberg, Jacques, "Le Comte de Gobineau," *Revue Générale,* 1939.

Dulles, Allan W., *The Craft of Intelligence,* New York, 1963.

Duverger, Maurice, *Political Parties. Their Organization and Activity in the Modern State,* New York, 1959.

Ehrenberg, Hans, and Bubnoff, Nicolai, editors. *Östliches Christentum. Dokumente,* 1925.

Emden, Paul H., *Jews of Britain. A Series of Biographies,* London, 1944.

Erdstein, David, *Le Statut juridique des minorités en Europe,* Paris, 1932.

Estève, Louis, *Une nouvelle Psychologie de l'Impérialisme. Ernest Seillière,* 1913.

Faure, Elie, "Gobineau et le Problème des races," *Europe,* 1923.

Fiala, Vaclav, "Les Partis politiques polonais," *Monde Slave,* February, 1935.

Fischel, A., *Der Panslawismus bis zum Weltkriege,* 1919.

Freeman, Orville L., "Malthus, Marx and the North American Breadbasket," *Foreign Affairs,* July, 1967.

The French Colonial Empire (Information Department Papers, no. 25), published by the Royal Institute of International Affairs, London, 1941.

"Friedlosikeit," in *Schweizer Lexikon,* 1945.

Froude, J. A., *Short Studies on Great Subjects,* 1867-1882.

Gagarin, Ivan S., *La Russie sera-t-elle catholique?,* 1856.

Galton, Sir Francis, *Hereditary Genius,* 1869.

Gehrke, Achim, *Die Rasse im Schrifttum,* 1933.

Gelber, N. M., "The Russian Pogroms in the Early Eighties in the Light of the Austrian Diplomatic Correspondence," *Historishe Shriftn,* vol. 2, Vilna, 1937.

George, David Lloyd, *Memoirs of the Peace Conference,* Yale, 1939.

Gobineau, Clément Serpeille de, "Le Gobinisme et la Pensée moderne," *Europe,* 1923.

Gobineau, Comte Joseph-Arthur de, *Essai sur l'inégalité des races humaines,* 1853; *The Inequality of Human Races,* English ed., translated by Adrien Collins, 1915; "Ce qui est arrivé à la France en 1870," *Europe,* 1923.

Goerres, Josef, *Politische Schriften,* Munich, 1854-1874.

Gohier, Urbain, *La Race a parlé,* 1916.

Grégoire, Abbé Henri, *De la Littérature des Nègres, ou recherches sur leurs qualités morales,* Paris, 1808; *De la Noblesse de la peau ou du préjugé des blancs contre la couleur des Africains,* Paris, 1826.

Gregory, Theodore, *Ernst Oppenheimer and the Economic Development of Southern Africa,* New York, 1962.

Grell, Hugo, *Der alldeutsche Verband, seine Geschichte, seine Bestrebungen, seine Erfolge* (Flugschriften des alldeutschen Verbandes, no. 8), Munich, 1898.

Gunenin, E., *L'Épopée coloniale de la France,* 1932.

Hadsel, Winifred N., "Can Europe's refugees find new Homes?", *Foreign Policy Reports,* vol. 10, no. 10, 1943.

Halévy, Elie, *L'Ere des Tyrannies,* Paris, 1938.

Hallgarten, W., *Vorkriegsimperialismus,* 1935.

Hancock, William K., *Survey of British Commonwealth Affairs,* London, 1937-1942; *Smuts: The Sanguine Years, 1870-1919,* New York, 1962.

Hanotaux, Gabriel, "Le Général Mangin," *Revue des Deux Mondes,* vol. 27, 1925.

Hargreaves, J., "Towards a History of the Partition of Africa," *Journal of African History,* London, 1960.

Harlow, Vincent, *The Character of British Imperialism,* 1939.

Harvey, Charles H., *The Biology of British Politics,* 1904.

Hasse, Ernst, *Deutsche Weltpolitik* (Flugschriften des Alldeutschen Verbandes, no. 5), 1897; *Deutsche Politik*, 1905-1906.

Hazeltine, H. D., "Excommunication," in *Encyclopedia of Social Sciences*.

Heinberg, John Gilbert, *Comparative Major European Governments, an Introductory Study*, New York, 1937.

Herrmann, Louis, *History of the Jews in South Africa*, 1935.

Hilferding, Rudolf, *Das Finanzkapital*, Vienna, 1910.

Hobbes, Thomas, *Leviathan* (1651), Cambridge Edition, 1935.

Hobson, J. H., "Capitalism and Imperialism in South Africa," *Contemporary Review*, 1900; *Imperialism* (1905), unrevised edition, 1938.

Hoetzsch, Otto, *Russland; eine Einführung auf Grund seiner Geschichte von 1904-1912*, Berlin, 1913.

Hoffmann, Karl, *Ölpolitik und angelsächsisches Imperium*, 1927.

Holborn, Louise W., "The Legal Status of Political Refugees, 1920-1938," *American Journal of International Law*, 1938.

Holcombe, Arthur N., "Political Parties," in *Encyclopedia of Social Sciences*.

Hotman, François, *Franco-Gallia*, 1573.

Huebbe-Schleiden, *Deutsche Kolonisation*, 1881.

Huxley, Thomas, *The Struggle for Existence in Human Society*, 1888.

Ipseri, H. P., "Vom Begriff der Partei," *Zeitschrift für die gesamte Staatswissenschaft*, 1940.

James, Selwyn, *South of the Congo*, New York, 1943.

Janeff, Janko, "Der Untergang des Panslawismus," *Nationalsozialistische Monatshefte*, no. 91, 1937.

Janowsky, Oscar J., *The Jews and Minority Rights*, New York, 1933; *Nationalities and National Minorities*, New York, 1945.

Jermings, R. Yewdall, "Some International Aspects of the Refugee Question," *British Yearbook of International Law*, 1939.

Kabermann, Heinz, "Das internationale Flüchtlingsproblem," *Zeitschrift für Politik*, vol. 29, no. 3, 1939.

Kaehler, Siegfried, editor, *Deutscher Staat und deutsche Parteien*, Munich, 1922.

Karbach, Oscar, "The Founder of Modern Political Antisemitism: Georg von Schoenerer," *Jewish Social Studies*, vol. 7, no. 1, January, 1945.

Kat Angelino, A. D. A. de, *Colonial Policy*, Chicago, 1931.

Kauffman, Kenneth M., and Stalson, Helena, "U.S. Assistance to less developed Countries," *Foreign Affairs*, July, 1967.

Kehr, Eckart, *Schlachtflottenbau und Parteipolitik*, 1930.

Kidd, Benjamin, *Social Evolution*, 1894.

Kiewiet, C. W. de, *A History of South Africa. Social and Economic*, Oxford, 1941.

Kipling, Rudyard, "The First Sailor," in his *Humorous Tales*, 1891; "The Tomb of His Ancestor," in his *The Day's Work*, 1898; *Stalky and Company*, 1899; *Kim*, 1900.

Klemm, Gustav, *Allgemeine Kulturgeschichte der Menschheit*, 1843-1852.

Klyuchevsky, V. O., *A History of Russia*, London, 1911-1931.

Koebner, Richard, and Schmidt, Helmut Dan, *Imperialism: The Story and Significance of a Political Word, 1840-1860*, New York, 1964.

Koestler, Arthur, *Scum of the Earth*, 1941.

Kohn, Hans, *Nationalism*, 1938; *Panslavism: History and Ideology*, Notre Dame, 1953.

Koyré, Alexandre, *Etudes sur l'histoire de la pensée philosophique en Russie*, Paris, 1950.

Kruck, Alfred, *Geschichte des alldeutschen Verbandes 1890-1939*, Wiesbaden, 1954.

Kuhlenbeck, L., *Rasse und Volkstum* (Flugschriften des alldeutschen Verbandes, no. 23).

Kulischer, Eugene M., *The Displacement of Population in Europe* (International Labor Office), Montreal, 1943.

Kulischer, J., *Allgemeine Wirtschaftsgeschichte*, 1928-1929.

Landsberg, P. L., "Rassenideologie," *Zeitschrift für Sozialforschung*, 1933.

Langer, William, *The Diplomacy of Imperialism*, 1890-1902.

Larcher, M., *Traité Elémentaire de Législation Algérienne*, 1903.

Lawrence, T. E., "France, Britain and the Arabs," *The Observer*, 1920; *Seven Pillars of Wisdom*, 1926; *Letters*, edited by David Garnett, New York, 1939.

Lehr, *Zwecke und Ziele des alldeutschen Verbandes* (Flugschriften des alldeutschen Verbandes, no. 14).

Lemonon, Ernest, *L'Europe et la politique britannique. 1882-1911*, 1912.

Lenin, V. I., *Imperialism, the Last Stage of Capitalism*, 1917.

Levine, Louis, *Pan-Slavism and European Politics*, New York, 1914.

Lewis, Sir George Cornewall, *An Essay on the Government of Dependencies*, Oxford, 1844.

Lippincott, Benjamin E., *Victorian Critics of Democracy*, University of Minnesota, 1938.

Lossky, N. O., *Three Chapters from the History of Polish Messianism* (International Philosophical Library, vol. 2, no. 9), Prague, 1936.

Lovell, Reginald Ivan, *The Struggle for South Africa, 1875-1899*, New York, 1934.

Low, Sidney, "Personal Recollections of Cecil Rhodes," *Nineteenth Century*, vol. 51, May, 1902.

Ludendorff, Erich, *Die überstaatlichen Mächte im letzten Jahre des Weltkrieges*, Leipzig, 1927; *Die Judenmacht, ihr Wesen und Ende*, Munich, 1938; *Feldherrnworte*, 1938.

Luxemburg, Rosa, *Die Akkumulation des Kapitals* (1913), Berlin, 1923.

Macartney, C. A., *The Social Revolution in Austria*, Cambridge, 1926; *National States and National Minorities*, London, 1934.

Mahan, Alfred T., *The Problem of Asia and its Effect upon International Policies*, Boston, 1900.

Maine, Sir Henry, *Popular Government*, 1886.

Mangin, Charles Marie Emmanuel, *La Force noire*, 1910; *Des Hommes et des Faits*, Paris, 1923.

Mangold, Ewald K. B., *Frankreich und der Rassegedanke; eine politische Kernfrage Europas*, 1937.

Mansergh, Nicholas, *Britain and Ireland* (Longman's Pamphlets on the British Commonwealth), London, 1942; *South Africa 1960-1961*, New York 1962.

Marcks, Erich, editor, *Lebensfragen des britischen Weltreichs*, 1921.

Marx, Karl, *The Eighteenth Brumaire of Louis Bonaparte* (1852), 1898.

Masaryk, Th. G., *Zur russischen Geschichts- und Religionsphilosophie*, 1913.

Mauco, Georges, "L'Emigration, problème révolutionnaire," *Esprit*, 7th year, no. 82, July, 1939.

Maunier, René, *Sociologie coloniale*, 1932-1936.

Metzer, E., *Imperialismus und Romantik*, Berlin, 1908.

Michaelis, Alfred, editor, *Die Rechtsverhältnisse der Juden in Preussen seit dem Beginn des 19. Jahrhunderts*, Berlin, 1910.

Michel, P. Charles, "A Biological View of Our Foreign Policy," *Saturday Review*, London, February, 1896.

Michell, Lewis, *Rhodes*, London, 1910.

Michels, Robert, "Prolegomena zur Analyse des nationalen Leitgedankens," *Jahrbuch für Soziologie*, vol. 2, 1927; *Political Parties; a sociological study of the oligarchical tendencies of modern democracy*, Glencoe, 1949.

Millin, S. Gertrude. *Rhodes*, London, 1933.

Model, Leo, "The Politics of private foreign Investment," *Foreign Affairs*, July, 1967.

Molisch, Paul, *Geschichte der deutschnationalen Bewegung in Österreich*, Jena, 1926.

Montesquieu, C. L. de Secondat de, *Esprit des Lois*, 1748.
Morrison, T., *Imperial Rule in India*, 1899.
Multatuli (pseudonym for Eduard Douwes Dekker), *Max Havelaar*, 1868.

Nadolny, R., *Germanisierung oder Slavisierung?*, 1928.
Naumann, Friedrich, *Central Europe*, London, 1916.
Neame, L. E., *The History of Apartheid*, London, 1962.
Nettlau, Max, *Der Anarchismus von Proudhon zu Kropotkin*, 1927.
Neumann, Sigmund, *Die Stufen des preussischen Konservativismus* (Historische Studien, no. 190), 1930; *Die deutschen Parteien*, 1932.
Neuschäfer, Fritz Albrecht, *Georg, Ritter von Schoenerer*, Hamburg, 1935.
Nicolson, Harold, *Curzon: The Last Phase 1919-1925*, Boston, New York, 1934.
Nippold, Gottfried, *Der deutsche Chauvinismus*, 1913.
Novalis (pseudonym for Friedrich Hardenberg), *Neue Fragmentensammlung*, 1798.

Oakesmith, John, *Race and Nationality, an Inquiry into the Origin and Growth of Patriotism*, 1919.
Oertzen, A. F. von, *Nationalsozialismus und Kolonialfrage*, Berlin, 1935.
Oesterley, W. O. E., *The Evolution of the Messianic Idea*, London, 1908.

Le Panlatinism, Confédération Gallo-Latine et Kelto-Gauloise . . . ou projet d'union fédérative . . ., Paris, 1860.
Pearson, Karl, *National Life*, 1901.
Peters, Carl, "Das Deutschtum als Rasse," *Deutsche Monatsschrift*, April, 1905; *Die Gründung von Deutsch-Ostafrika. Kolonialpolitische Erinnerungen*, 1906.
Pichl, Eduard (pseudonym Herwig), *George Schoenerer*, 1938.
Pinon, René, *France et Allemagne*, 1912.
Pirenne, Henri, *A History of Europe from the Invasions to XVI Century*, London, 1939.
Plucknett, Theodore F. T., "Outlawry," in *Encyclopedia of Social Sciences*.
Pobyedonostzev, Constantin, *L'Autocratie russe. Mémoires politiques, correspondance officielle et documents inédits . . . 1881-1894*, Paris, 1927; *Reflections of a Russian Statesman*, London, 1898.
Preuss, Lawrence, "La Dénationalisation imposée pour des motifs politiques," *Revue Internationale Française du Droit des Gens*, vol. 4, nos. 1, 2, 5, 1937.
Priestley, H. J., *France Overseas: a study of modern imperialism*, New York, 1938.
Propyläen Weltgeschichte, vol. 10, *Das Zeitalter des Imperialismus*, 1933.
Pundt, Alfred, *Arndt and the National Awakening in Germany*, New York, 1935.

Reimer, E., *Pangermanisches Deutschland*, 1905.
Reismann-Grone, Th., *Überseepolitik oder Festlandspolitik?* (Flugschriften des alldeutschen Verbandes, no. 22), 1905.
Renan, Ernest, *Histoire générale et système comparé des langues*, 1863; *Qu'est-ce qu'une nation?*, Paris, 1882. English translation in *The Poetry of the Celtic Races, and Other Studies*, translated by William G. Hutchison, London, 1896.
Renner, Karl, *Der Kampf der österreichischen Nationen unter dem Staat*, 1902; *Österreichs Erneuerung. Politisch-programmatische Aufsätze*, Vienna, 1916; *Das Selbstbestimmungsrecht der Nationen*, Leipzig, 1918.
Richard, Gaston, *Le Conflit de l'autonomie nationale et de l'impérialisme*, 1916.
Ritter, Paul, *Kolonien im deutschen Schrifttum*, 1936.
Robert, Cyprienne, *Les deux Panslavismes*, 1847; *Le Monde slave*, 1852.
Robespierre, Maximilien de, *Oeuvres*, 1840; *Speeches*, 1927.
Robinson, Jacob, "Staatsbürgerliche und wirtschaftliche Gleichberechtigung," *Süddeutsche Monatshefte*, July, 1929.
Robinson, Ronald, and Gallagher, John, *Africa and the Victorians*, London, 1961; "The Imperialism of Free Trade," *Economic History Review*, London, 1953.

Roepke, Wilhelm, "Kapitalismus und Imperialismus," *Zeitschrift für Schweizerische Statistik und Volkswirtschaft*, vol. 70, 1934.

Rohan, Henri, Duc de, *De l'Intérêt des princes et Etats de la Chrétienté*, 1638.

Rohden, Peter R., editor, *Demokratie und Partei*, Vienna, 1932.

Rohrbach, Paul, *Der deutsche Gedanke in der Welt*, 1912; *Die alldeutsche Gefahr*, 1918.

Roscher, Wilhelm, *Die Grundlagen der Nationalökonomie*, 1900.

Rosenkranz, Karl, *Über den Begriff der politischen Partei*, 1843.

Roucek, Joseph, *The Minority Principle as a Problem of Political Science*, Prague, 1928.

Rozanov, Vassilij, *Fallen Leaves*, 1929.

Rudlin, W. A., "Political Parties. Great Britain," in *Encyclopedia of the Social Sciences*.

Russell, Lord John, *On Party*, 1850.

Samuel, Horace B., *Modernities*, London, 1914.

Schnee, Heinrich, *Nationalismus und Imperialismus*, 1928.

Schultze, Ernest, "Die Judenfrage in Südafrika," *Der Weltkampf*, vol. 15, no. 178, 1938.

Schumpeter, Joseph, "Zur Sociologie der Imperialismen," *Archiv für Sozialwissenschaften und Sozialpolitik*, vol. 46, 1918-1919; *Capitalism, Socialism, and Democracy*, New York, 1942; *Imperialism; Social Classes*, New York, 1951.

Schuyler, Robert L., *The Fall of the Old Colonial System. A Study in British Free Trade, 1770-1870*, New York, 1945.

Seeley, John Robert, *The Expansion of England*, 1883.

Seillière, Ernest, *La Philosophie de l'impérialisme*, 1903-1906; *Mysticisme et domination. Essais de critique impérialiste*, 1913.

Semmel, Bernard, *Imperialism and Social Reform. English Social-Imperial Thought, 1895-1914*, London, 1960.

Shepperson, G., "Africa, the Victorians and Imperialism," *Revue Belge de Philologie et d'Histoire*, 1962.

Sieveking, H. J., "Wirtschaftsgeschichte," in *Enzyklopädie der Rechts- und Staatswissenschaften*, vol. 47, 1935.

Siéyès, Abbé E. J., *Qu'est-ce que le Tiers Etat?*, 1789.

Simar, Théophile, *Etude Critique sur la formation de la doctrine des races au 18e et son expansion au 19e siècle*, Bruxelles, 1922.

Simpson, John Hope, *The Refugee Problem* (Institute of International Affairs), Oxford, 1939.

Sitzungsbericht des Kongresses der organisierten nationalen Gruppen in den Staaten Europas, 1933.

Solovyov, Vladimir, *Judaism and the Christian Question*, 1884.

Sommerland, Theo, *Der deutsche Kolonialgedanke und sein Werden im 19. Jahrhundert*, Halle, 1918

Spiess, Camille, *Impérialismes. Gobinisme en France*, Paris, 1917.

Sprietsma, Cargill, *We Imperialists. Notes on Ernest Seillière's Philosophy of Imperialism*, New York, 1931.

Staehlin, Karl, *Geschichte Russlands von den Anfängen bis zur Gegenwart*, 1923-1939; "Die Entstehung des Panslawismus," *Germano-Slavica*, no. 4, 1936.

Stephen, Sir James F., *Liberty, Equality, Fraternity*, 1873; "Foundations of the Government of India," *Nineteenth Century*, vol. 80, 1883.

Stoddard, Th. L., *Rising Tide of Color*, 1920.

Stokes, Eric, "Great Britain and Africa: The Myth of Imperialism," *History To-day*, London, 1960; *The Political Ideas of English Imperialism*, London, 1960.

Strieder, Jakob, "Staatliche Finanznot und Genesis des modernen Grossunternehmertums," *Schmollers Jahrbücher*, vol. 49, 1920.

Strzygowski, Josef, *Altai, Iran und Völkerwanderung*, Leipzig, 1917.

Suarès, André, *La Nation contre la race*, Paris, 1916.
Sumner, B. H., *Russia and the Balkans*, Oxford, 1937; *A Short History of Russia*, New York, 1949.
Sydacoff, Bresnitz von, *Die panslawistische Agitation und die südslawiche Bewegung in Österreich-Ungarn*, Berlin, 1899.
Szpotański, Stanislaw, "Les Messies au 19e siècle," *Revue Mondiale*, 1920.

Talleyrand, C. M. de, "Essai sur les avantages à retirer des colonies nouvelles dans les circonstances présentes" (1799), *Académie des Sciences Coloniales, Annales*, vol. 3, 1929.
Thierry, A., *Lettres sur l'histoire de la France*, 1840.
Thompson, L. M., "Afrikaner Nationalist Historiography and the Policy of Apartheid,[ii] *The Journal of African History*, vol., III, no. 1, 1962.
Thring, Lord Henry, *Suggestions for Colonial Reform*, 1865.
Tirpitz, Alfred von, *Erinnerungen*, 1919.
Tocqueville, Alexis de, "Lettres de Alexis de Tocqueville et de Arthur Gobineau," *Revue des Deux Mondes*, vol. 199, 1907; *L'Ancien Régime et la Révolution*, 1856.
Tonsill, Ch. C., "Racial Theories from Herder to Hitler," *Thought*, vol. 15, 1940.
Townsend, Mary E., *Origin of Modern German Colonialism, 1871-1885*, New York, 1921; *Rise and Fall of Germany's Colonial Empire*, New York, 1930; *European Colonial Experience since 1871*, New York, 1941.
Tramples, Kurt, "Völkerbund und Völkerfreiheit," *Süddeutsche Monatshefte*, July, 1929.
Tyler, J. E., *The Struggle for Imperial Unity*, London, Toronto, New York, 1938.

Unwin, George, *Studies in Economic History*, ed. by R. H. Tawney, 1927.

Vichniac, Marc, "Le Statut international des apatrides," *Recueil des Cours de l'Académie de Droit International*, vol. 33, 1933.
Voegelin, Erich, *Rasse und Staat*, 1933; *Die Rassenidee in der Geistesgeschichte*, Berlin, 1933; "The Origins of Scientism," *Social Research*, December, 1948.
Voelker, K., *Die religiöse Wurzel des englischen Imperialismus*, Tübingen, 1924.
Vrba, Rudolf, *Russland und der Panslawismus; statistische und sozialpolitische Studien*, 1913.

Wagner, Adolf, *Vom Territorialstaat zur Weltmacht*, 1900.
Weber, Ernst, *Volk und Rasse. Gibt es einen deutschen Nationalstaat?*, 1933.
Webster, Charles Kingsley, "Minorities. History," in *Encyclopaedia Britannica*, 1929.
Wenck, Martin, *Alldeutsche Taktik*, 1917.
Werner, Bartholomäus von, *Die deutsche Kolonialfrage*, 1897.
Werner, Lothar, *Der alldeutsche Verband, 1890-1918* (Historische Studien, no. 278), Berlin, 1935.
Wertheimer, Mildred S., *The Pan-German League, 1890-1914*, 1924.
Westarp, Graf Kuno F. V. von, *Konservative Politik im letzten Jahrzehnt des Kaiserreiches*, 1935.
White, John S., "Taine on Race and Genius," *Social Research*, February, 1943.
Whiteside, Andrew G., "Nationaler Sozialismus in Österreich vor 1918," *Vierteljahrshefte für Zeitgeschichte*, 9. Jg. (1961).
Williams, Basil, *Cecil Rhodes*, London, 1921.
Williams, Sir John Fischer, "Denationalisation," *British Year Book of International Law*, vol. 7, 1927.
Winkler, Wilhelm, *Statistisches Handbuch der europäischen Nationalitäten*, Vienna, 1931.
Wirth, Max, *Geschichte der Handelskrisen*, 1873.
Wise, David, and Ross, Thomas B., *The Invisible Government*, New York, 1964.
Wolmar, Wolfram von, "Vom Panslawismus zum tschechisch-sowjetischen Bündnis," *Nationalsozialistische Monatshefte*, no. 104, 1938.

Zetland, Lawrence J., *Lord Cromer*, 1932.
Ziegler, H. O., *Die moderne Nation*, Tübingen, 1931.
Zimmermann, Alfred, *Geschichte der deutschen Kolonialpolitik*, 1914.
Zoepfl, G., "Kolonien und Kolonialpolitik," in *Handwörterbuch der Staatswissenschaften*, 3rd edition.

Index

Authors are listed only in case of special discussion or reference. Subjects of footnotes are listed. Chapter headings and bibliographical references are not included.